# Administering Special Education Programs

# Administering Special Education Programs

*A Practical Guide for School Leaders*

EDITED BY H. ROBERTA WEAVER,
MARY F. LANDERS, THOMAS M. STEPHENS,
AND ELLIS A. JOSEPH

Westport, Connecticut
London

**Library of Congress Cataloging-in-Publication Data**

Administering special education programs / edited by H. Roberta Weaver, Mary F.
  Landers, Thomas M. Stephens and Ellis A. Joseph.
       p.  cm.
  Includes bibliographical references and index.
  ISBN 0–89789–870–2 (alk. paper)
  1. Special education—United States—Administration. 2. Students with
disabilities—Education—United States. 3. School administrators—United States.
I. Weaver, H. Roberta. II. Landers, Mary F. III. Stephens, Thomas M. IV. Joseph,
Ellis A.
LC3969.A36 2003
371.9'042—dc21          2003048237

British Library Cataloguing in Publication Data is available.

Library of Congress Catalog Card Number: 2003048237
ISBN: 0–89789–870–2

First published in 2003

Praeger Publishers, 88 Post Road West, Westport, CT 06881
An imprint of Greenwood Publishing Group, Inc.
www.praeger.com

Printed in the United States of America

The paper used in this book complies with the
Permanent Paper Standard issued by the National
Information Standards Organization (Z39.48–1984).

10 9 8 7 6 5 4 3 2

# Contents

# Tables

# Preface

This book is an outgrowth of the strategic planning process of the State of Ohio Superintendent's Task Force for Preparing Special Education Personnel. That process identified the crucial role of school administrators in properly implementing special education programs.

Following the lead of the Task Force, the editors examined the materials (books) used by the institutions of higher education that have the highest enrollments in their administration preparation programs. This examination revealed that scant attention is devoted to administering programs for special needs populations. Thus, the purpose of this book is to provide administrator preparation programs with practical knowledge related to administering programs for special needs populations.

In deciding on the contents of this book, the editors conducted half-day focus groups with school administrators, professors of educational administration, teachers, and professors of special education. These focus groups indicated a preference for the following emphases: state and federal role, the nature of the special education population, curriculum, administration of program and services, resource utilization, collaboration and communication, and understanding the role of parents.

# Acknowledgments

The editors are grateful for the support of Susan Tave Zelman, State of Ohio Superintendent of Public Instruction. John Herner, former director of the Office for Exceptional Children, was a great advocate of this project. The work of the Task Force staff has been invaluable. We wish to thank Marie Weller, Christopher Kania, Kathy Richards, and Andrea Phillips. Helen Sutherland, former assistant director of the Task Force, was a great help to the editors in scheduling focus groups. Much appreciation is expressed to the following members of the Task Force who helped to conceptualize this project: Bernard Badiali, Chair, Department of Educational Leadership, Miami University of Ohio; Lisa Barnhouse, Director, Hopewell Special Education Regional Resource Center; Thomas Frew, Associate Dean, Cleveland State University; Colleen Finegan, Wright State University; Marge Goldstein, secondary special education teacher, Toledo Public Schools; Larry Johnson, Dean, College of Education, University of Cincinnati; Patricia Renick, Wright State University; Judy Howard Rhode, retired Deputy Superintendent, Mid-Ohio Educational Service Center; Beth Stroble, Dean, College of Education, University of Akron; Dave Todt, Chair, Department of Teacher Education, Shawnee State University; and Ellen Williams, Interim Dean, College of Education and Human Development, Bowling Green State University. Cynthia Puckett of the Ohio Department of Education has been a valued advisor.

The editors wish especially to thank Ms. Colleen Wildenhaus and Ms. Carole Warrick of the University of Dayton for editing and administrative assistance. Dean Thomas Lasley II of the University of Dayton School of Education and Allied Professions has supported the editors throughout the period this book was being developed. He is a dean who places great value upon scholarship; therefore, the editors felt constantly reinforced in their work.

The editors are grateful for the support of the staff of the Greenwood Publishing Group.

*Ellis A. Joseph*
*Chair, State Superintendent's Task Force for Preparing*
*Special Education Personnel*

# Chapter 1

# What Do Building Administrators Need to Know about Special Education?

*Thomas M. Stephens and Jon J. Nieberding*

"We are all ignorant, but about different things." Will Rogers, a humorist and philosopher, is said to have uttered these words as a way of explaining human frailties. The truth of Rogers' words is demonstrated daily throughout our lives. But, when lack of knowledge is harmful to others, or when it results in a failure to perform one's expected duties, it is more than just a human weakness; it can do real harm to people. Schools are one setting where harm can be the unintended result of not knowing.

Most often, misinformed or ill-prepared teachers come to mind—teachers who are not well versed in the current "best practices" or who are otherwise "behind the times." Improving teacher knowledge is often addressed through district or school-sponsored professional development sessions and graduate and continuing education, for which there is oftentimes ample opportunity. While building principals' inservice needs are not neglected totally, these needs tend to be served mainly by their professional organizations. Sometimes, statewide professional organizations that provide conferences for building principals offer special education content through workshops or conferences. Even then, the instruction is rarely provided in a systematic way through a needs assessment against a well-established, current, and comprehensive curriculum. Too often, the supplemental training that is offered is sporadic and lacking in continuity. The Ohio Association of Secondary School Administrators (Ohio Association of Secondary School Administrators, 2002), for example, offers a one-day workshop about special education law and practice, in addition to other one-to two-day workshops and conferences where special education is one of many issues on the proposed agenda. In a survey of state directors of special education, Valesky and Hirth (1992) found that while a majority (39) of states reported conducting inservice programs on the topic of special education law, most often these inservices were two- to three-day annual workshops.

Moreover, special education is treated inadequately, if at all, in the majority of administrator preparation programs (Sirotnik & Kimball, 1994). While opportunities like those offered by professional organizations are certainly valuable, much more content and time are needed if principals are to provide effective school leadership for both the general and special education populations.

## BUILDING PRINCIPALS' IMPACT ON PROGRAMS FOR STUDENTS WITH DISABILITIES

Numerous special education authorities (Algozzine, Ysseldyke, & Campbell, 1994; Goor, Schwenn, & Boyer, 1997; Kirner, Vatour, & Vatour, 1993; Lowe & Brigham, 2000) have cited the importance of the building principal's ability to be the school's instructional leader. In special education, the principal's role as the instructional leader will often determine the efficacy and the quality of special education services (Burrello, Schrup, & Barnett, 1992; Sirotnik & Kimball, 1994; Valesky & Hirth, 1992). But research and authoritative opinion generally reveal that building principals are not sufficiently knowledgeable about important aspects of the education of students with disabilities. A major explanation as to why building principals are typically uninformed about special education is that their professional preparation may be inadequate. Many school administrators report that they received little or no training for supervising special educators and they feel inadequate for such assignments (Aspen, 1992; Lowe & Brigham, 2000). This finding is also supported by research conducted by Stephens and Joseph (1995). In that study, a review of 11 textbooks used in the preparation programs of major universities for general education administrators indicated that little, if any, content of the texts addressed special education policy, procedures, or student programming.

In a related study, the same authors (Stephens & Joseph, 1996) surveyed all state directors of special education or their designees. Respondents were asked to rate the degree of knowledge they believed that the "typical" education administrator possesses about special education and what impact an increased amount of knowledge would have on the typical administrator's performance. Their findings indicated that general education administrators are perceived as possessing insufficient knowledge in 17 areas. Respondents generally stated that an increase in knowledge would significantly ($p < .05$) improve their performance.

In considering the content for this chapter, we asked the question: What should school principals know about special education in order to fulfill their duties? Our strategy for answering this question included a review of the extant literature on the subject. We also revisited smaller studies that we had completed in the last few years and conducted telephone interviews of building principals and experienced special education practitioners, teachers, and program supervisors.

Our study, an informal phone survey conducted by the School Study Council of Ohio (SSCO) in October 2001, was designed to assess the knowledge of randomly selected Central Ohio principals, special education administrators, and teachers about special education issues. Each of those surveyed was asked to rate his or her assessment of what level of knowledge principals needed in order to do their jobs effectively. We used a three-level scale: (1) *no knowledge required;* (2) *a basic, working knowledge required;* and (3) *intimate knowledge required.* Those surveyed were asked questions in four basic categories: Instruction and Programming, Placement Procedures, Federal and State Laws and Regulations, and Procedural Safeguards. The results provided some preliminary data on how the perceived roles of building principals differed when viewed by district level special education personnel and practitioners as contrasted to building principals. Results also showed that building principals recognize the need for a high level of knowledge about many areas of special education. On some topics, principals indicated that knowledge at an awareness level was needed. For others, the administrators reported that they saw no need for knowledge. For this preliminary study, we validated the survey's contents through a review of the literature and expert opinion. These results will form the basis of a more comprehensive study with a much larger sample.

Twenty-six items across four categories were identified as relevant to the administration of special education. The same areas were assessed for special education program managers, special education teachers, and intervention specialists. Results from this preliminary survey of program managers and special education teachers differed from the results of the building principal survey. The two groups were in agreement on the idea that principals should have a basic knowledge of most special education programs, particularly as they relate to the issues surrounding instruction and programming. However, special education practitioners and managers felt, without exception, that every survey item deserved either a basic, working knowledge or an intimate knowledge. Conversely, many principals felt they needed no knowledge of many of the same items, most notably inclusion in large scale assessment and accountability programs, allowable accommodations and modifications to standardized tests, the uses and availability of assistive technology, all aspects of the Individualized Education Program (IEP) process, child find, the concept of the surrogate parent, and the concept of free and appropriate public education.

It is not surprising that special educators feel that building principals need to have a basic or intimate knowledge of most, if not all, concepts and issues in special education. Indeed, most educators would expect the "instructional leader" to be broadly aware of all instructional programs under his or her purview. Yet, principals' perceptions and expectations of the same issues were different. In fact, the data are most revealing when viewed across the two groups:

- 100% of special education managers (e.g., district level special education supervisors) felt that principals should have *intimate knowledge* of inclusion models for students with disabilities, as compared to 60% of principals;
- 20% of principals felt they needed *no knowledge* of strategies for access to and participation in large-scale assessment programs, compared to 67% of special education managers who felt principals needed *intimate knowledge* of such strategies;
- 100% of special education managers felt principals needed *intimate knowledge* of child find, as opposed to 0% of principals.

Analysis of the qualitative data yielded by the survey reveals that special education managers agree that principals too often take a reactive rather than a proactive stance in addressing special education law and practice and how it affects students in their schools. Moreover, special education managers expressed concern with principals' over-reliance on special consultants, teachers, or district level administrators to deal with the issues that arise among special education populations.

Survey responses to the item "manifestation determination" are of considerable interest. Manifestation determination refers to the consideration that must be given to a student with disabilities before he or she is suspended or expelled from school because of misbehavior. If the misbehavior is a manifestation of the disability, federal law (Individuals with Disabilities Education Act [IDEA], 1997) requires the school district to retain the student in school. Clearly, a full understanding of this and other legal concepts should be very important to principals in order to meet legal requirements, especially when considering that special education issues are typically the main cause for principals being taken to court (Johnson & Bauer, 1992).

Twenty percent of principals were unfamiliar with the concept of manifestation determination, and 75% who answered believed principals need only be knowledgeable about the concept at the basic awareness level. Clearly, for a building administrator to make an informed decision about school suspension, an action that may be taken by the principal in Ohio, he or she needs to have a thorough knowledge of the concept. Conversely, 80% of special education respondents indicated that building principals must have an intimate understanding of manifestation determination.

Similarly, a concern should be raised about the building administrators' responses to the survey items about the concept of "free and appropriate public education"(FAPE). Only 20% of the principals believed that they needed an intimate knowledge of FAPE, which is at the core of special education—both legally and programmatically. Without this basic understanding, it is hard to imagine how a principal could be fully qualified for his or her leadership position.

## THE IMPORTANCE OF BUILDING ADMINISTRATORS' SUPPORT

A second, more extensive mail survey that addressed issues related to teacher retention in Ohio was conducted by the School Study Council of Ohio (Stephens & Phillips, 2001). A total of 378 special education teachers, with teaching experience ranging from one year to more than 31 years, responded to a series of questions about a number of factors that contribute to teachers staying in special education.

From a focus group, 17 factors were identified for the survey. One factor, "the responsiveness of their building administrators to special education issues," is of particular interest. Nearly one-third (32.1%) ranked the responsiveness of their building administrators in the top 5 of the 17 factors that were included in the survey. The general tenor of the comments was uniformly positive about the level of knowledge and commitment to special education of the administrators to whom they reported. It is of interest to note the perceptions of these special education teachers regarding the importance of support from their building administrators. This same study found that general education teachers view the support of building administrators as equally important. One may infer from these results that, regardless of teaching assignment, teachers expect and need support from their building principals. In an early study, Fimian (1986) concluded that inferior supervision of special educators is directly related to the attrition of special education specialists in schools. The issue for this chapter, however, is that while building principals typically come to their positions from a general education perspective, few come with special education preparation.

## RELATED FINDINGS

Other studies, over many years, have shown that building principals' knowledge of special education law is lacking (Cline, 1981; Hirth & Valesky, 1990; Johnson & Bauer, 1992; Sirotnik & Kimball, 1994; Valesky & Hirth, 1992; Weinstein, 1989).

In an early study, Weinstein (1989) found that building principals were unaware of guidelines for student placement and exit from special education programs. He concluded that his sample of building principals failed to take responsibility for their special education programs. Consider the converse situation for typical students if the building principal were uncertain about placement—age, grade, and achievement. And, if he or she were unsure of the students' requirements for progressing to other program levels—middle, junior high, and high school. At a minimum, the principal would be considered incompetent!

A more recent study (Wigle & Wilcox, 1999) investigated the competencies of general education administrators on 35 skills identified by the Council for Exceptional Children (CEC) as important for professionals who work in special education. General education administrators were asked to self-report their competencies from the CEC list. Their reports were then compared with the competencies on the same set of skills as reported by two other groups: education directors and special educators. Of the three groups, the special education directors rated themselves the highest, followed by special educators and general education administrators.

What is surprising about these results is that 20% of the special educators and 18% of the general education administrators rated themselves as *inadequate*. Moreover, only 26% of the general education administrators considered themselves *skilled* in the area of special education.

Asperdon (1992) found that over 85% of all principals believe that formal preparation in special education is needed to be a successful principal, but over 40% of all principals had none. Yet, over 75% of the principals had responsibility for supervising and evaluating special education teachers. Valesky and Hirth (1992) found that of the states that require general knowledge of special education (65%), the most common method (38%) of ensuring this knowledge was taking a general or introductory course.

## SUGGESTIONS FOR A KNOWLEDGE BASE

In order for building principals to be instructional leaders for all students, we believe they should be aware of all of their students' educational needs. Increasingly diverse and ever-expanding populations of students receiving special education services, coupled with an expanding knowledge base, makes this awareness crucial to effective leadership. Awareness allows principals to make judgments about instructional programs, teacher competencies, and directions for improvement. Further, they should have an intimate understanding of certain aspects of programs for students with disabilities.

The categories that we identified in preparation for our telephone survey of October 2001 were repeatedly found in professional writings. (These references have been cited earlier in this chapter.) These items are:

1. Instruction and Programming

    *Awareness Level*

    _____Allowable accommodations and modifications to standardized tests
    _____Access and participation in district and state tests and assessments

_____Policy and procedures for alternative assessments for students with disabilities

_____The uses and availability of assistive technology

*Intimate Level*

_____Concept of differentiated instruction

_____How students with disabilities gain access to the general education curriculum

_____Inclusion models for students with disabilities

2. Placement Procedures

*Awareness Level*

_____The IEP Process

_____The multifactor education process

_____The differentiated referral process

*Intimate Level*

_____The least restrictive environment

_____Availability of extended school year services

_____Transition services

3. Procedural Safeguards

*Awareness Level*

_____The functional behavior assessment and behavior intervention plan

_____Child find

*Intimate Level*

_____Manifestation determination regarding the disability's relationship to the behavior

_____Concept of free and appropriate public education

_____The need for and significance of confidentiality (FERPA)

_____Due process procedures

_____Concept of the surrogate parent

4. Federal and State Laws and Regulations

*Awareness Level*

_____Individuals with Disabilities Education Act, 1997

_____Related services

_____Section 504 of the Rehabilitation Act

_____Strategies for early identification and assessment of disabling conditions in children

_____Federal and state case laws and their impact on educating students who are disabled

Readers are invited to review this suggested list and add those that they believe are important for building principals.

## CONCLUSIONS

The review of the extant literature conducted for the development of this chapter revealed three fundamental findings. First, the problem of principals not knowing what they must know about the education of the handicapped is longstanding and has serious implications for the leadership role principals must take. Second, the knowledge base of this topic continues to expand. Thus, current principals may be less knowledgeable than their counterparts were just a decade ago. Moreover, student populations, including those students with disabilities, are becoming more and more diverse, in terms of language, culture, and learning style. This diversity, coupled with the mandates put forth in IDEA '97 concerning mainstreaming strategies, and inclusion models for the classroom and for participation in large-scale assessment and accountability programs, has put the need for knowledgeable building principals at a premium. Third, information concerning what principals should know in order to be knowledgeable and effective leaders of general and special education programs is available.

However, the question of how to reach this level of understanding remains. The major barrier seems to be lack of opportunity. Simply put, there is a scarcity of systematic, sustained programs of professional development in special education tailored to the needs of the building principal. The information is "out there"; the problem is access to it. Research findings suggest that administrator preparation programs should place more emphasis and time on core special education competencies, such as those discussed earlier. Further, school principals must have the opportunity and the incentive to participate in sustained and systematic special education programs. Developers of such programs, though, must consider strategies for increasing accessibility: flexible course schedules, stipends or scholarships to cover costs of tuition, materials, child care, transportation and the like, and distance learning and video-conferencing technologies. Only then will we move closer toward alleviating the acute need that exists for principals who can effectively lead special education programs in schools.

## REFERENCES

Algozzine, B., Ysseldyke, J., & Campbell, P. (1994). Strategies and tactics for effective instruction. *Teaching Exceptional Children, 26*(3), 34–35.

Aspen, M. (1992). *Principals' attitudes toward education: Results and implications of a comprehensive study.* A paper presented at the 70th Annual Convention of the Council for Exceptional Children, Baltimore, MD.

Asperdon, M. (1992). *Principals' attitudes toward special education.* Paper presented at the 70th Annual Convention of the Council for Exceptional Children, Baltimore, MD.

Burrello, L., Schrup, M., & Barnett, B. (1992). *The principal as the special education leader.* Bloomington: University of Indiana.

Cline, R. (1981). Principals' attitudes and knowledge about handicapped children. *Exceptional Children, 48*(2), 172–176.

Fimian, M. (1986). Social support and occupational stress in special education. *Exceptional Children, 52*(4), 436–442.

Goor, M., Schwenn, J., & Boyer, L. (1997). Preparing principals for leadership in special education. *Intervention in School and Clinic, 32*(3), 133–141.

Hirth, M., & Valesky, T. (1990). Survey of universities: Education knowledge requirements in school administration preparation programs. *Planning and Changing, 21*(3), 165–172.

Individuals with Disabilities Education Act (IDEA). (1997).

Johnson, L. J., & Bauer, A. M. (1992). Meeting the needs of special students: Legal, ethical, and practical ramifications. Newbury Park, CA: Corwin Press.

Kirner, M., Vatour, J., & Vatour, M. B. (1993). *Enhancing instructional programs within schools: Training school principals in special education administration.* Paper presented at the International Conference of the Learning Disabilities Association, San Francisco.

Lowe, M. A., & Brigham, F. J. (2000). Supervising education instruction: Does it deserve a special place in administrative preparatory programs? Eric Document. ED 448530, 22 pages.

Ohio Association of Secondary School Administrators. (2002). OASSA's 2001–2002 conference schedule. Retrieved February 15, 2002 from www.oassa.org/Conference.html.

Sirotnik, T. J., & Kimball, K. (1994). The unspecial place of special education in programs that prepare school administrators. *Journal of School Leadership, 4*(6), 598–630.

Stephens, T. M., & Joseph, E. A. (1995). *Survey of textbooks used for introductory educational administration courses.* Columbus, OH: School Study Council of Ohio.

Stephens, T. M., & Joseph, E. A. (1996). *Report of a survey of state departments of education.* Columbus, OH: School Study Council of Ohio.

Stephens, T. M., & Phillips, A. (2001). *Ohio teacher retention: Survey results.* Columbus, OH: School Study Council of Ohio.

Valesky, T. C., & Hirth, M. A. (1992). Survey of the states: Special education knowledge requirements for school administrators. *Exceptional Children, 59*(5), 399–405.

Weinstein, D. F. (1989). The school administrator and special education programs: Quality control of placement and instruction. *ERS Spectrum, 1*(3), 35–41.

Wigle, S. E., & Wilcox, D. J. (1999). The special education competencies of general education administrators. *Reading Improvement, 36*(1), 4–14.

# Chapter 2

# What Attitudes Do Building Administrators Need to Have toward Special Education?

*H. Roberta Weaver and Mary F. Landers*

Picture two secondary school principals. One promotes selective scheduling for students on sport teams, in the band, or in special education; the other, however, promotes selective scheduling for band and sports members, but not for special education students.

Now picture two elementary school principals. One works with parents and teachers to include alternate grading plans in IEPs to ensure a grade reflective of the student's developmental level. The other principal works against including alternate grading plans in IEPs in an effort to maintain a single grading scale so as to be fair.

The positions taken here are clearly based on attitude. These principals hold beliefs that influence their decision making. Effective leaders, according to Haberman (1999), possess an ideology that "derives from a set of beliefs that predispose the principal to act in a certain way" (p. 75). Goldberg (2001) talks about great leaders as holding bedrock beliefs, being willing to swim upstream, exercising a social conscience, maintaining a seriousness of purpose, and fitting personal skills to the task at hand. Neither Haberman nor Goldberg denies the need for knowledge. They simply point out the influence of personal values on decision making and leadership. Hasazi, Johnson, Liggett, and Schattman (1994) conclude from their study of multi-state and multi-district implementation of the least restrictive environment (LRE) provision of IDEA that "values represented a commitment; knowledge provided the fundamental capacity to carry out the commitment" (p. 505).

## HOW IMPORTANT IS THE PRINCIPAL'S ATTITUDE TOWARD SPECIAL EDUCATION?

A number of researchers (Bailey & du Plessis, 1997; Bain & Dolbel, 1991; Barnett & Monda-Amaya, 1998; Cook, Semmel, & Gerber, 1999; Gameros, 1995; Hasazi, et al., 1994; Idol & Griffith, 1998; Morgan & Demchak, 1996; Salisbury & McGregor, 2002; Villa, Thousand, Meyers, & Nevin, 1996; West, 2001) have found a strong relationship between administrator or principal attitude and special education service delivery. Idol and Griffith's (1998) study of special education service delivery in four Texas elementary schools found that teachers viewed their principals as being supportive of them and as facilitators of inclusive practices. Morgan and Demchak (1996) point out that staff and students often mirror the administrator's attitude toward inclusion. Gameros (1995) found the leadership of the principal to be a critical factor in "the extent to which students with disabilities and special education programs are incorporated within the school's vision, climate, and culture" (p. 2).

In their LRE study, Hasazi et al. (1994) found that movement toward increasing options in the general education setting was not made without explicit leadership from either the special education administrator or the superintendent. It was also found that if the administrator did not believe in integration, the existing service delivery model remained intact. On the other hand, if the administrator believed in integration, options to the existing system were promoted. A similar picture was seen at the school level among the principals. Those convinced of integration created program options; those opposed did not and in some instances even sabotaged efforts. Studies done in Australia (Bailey & du Plessis, 1997; Bain & Dolbel, 1991) report similar findings. A survey (Bailey & du Plessis, 1997) of 200 school principals in Australia representing preschool, primary, special, and high schools indicated that almost 75% of them supported inclusion. The authors, however, concluded that these principals supported qualified inclusion. Factors such as "attitudes and commitment of their staff, their training, the adequacy of the human and physical resources to cope with the student, and the likelihood of success of the enrollment" (p. 438) influenced their commitment to enrolling a student with special needs. Bain and Dolbel (1991) reported on the survey data collected from principals of Australian elementary and secondary schools and special education support centers. They found that program cooperation and success were directly related to teacher and principal attitudes.

## WHAT ADMINISTRATOR OR PRINCIPAL COMPETENCIES ARE ASSOCIATED WITH AN ATTITUDE SUPPORTIVE OF SPECIAL EDUCATION?

A study done by Ingram (1997) examined the relationship of two leadership styles, transactional leadership and transformational leadership, with the leadership behaviors of principals in inclusive educational settings. Transactional leadership was defined as a leader-follower relationship based on extrinsic reward systems. Transformational leadership, on the other hand, was based on the leader gaining follower commitment to the organization's mission, objectives, and strategies. Forty-four of 72 teachers returned ratings of their principal's behaviors. The ratings indicated "principals in schools which educated students with moderate and severe disabilities in regular classrooms [were] perceived by teachers to exhibit a greater degree of transformational than transactional leadership behaviors" (p. 420). The study also suggested that the transformational leader had "a greater impact on teacher motivation to perform beyond expectations" (p. 425). Behaviors associated with transformational leaders are charisma, inspiration, and consideration of individual teacher needs. The transformational leader strives to develop shared values and beliefs, meanings, and commitment to common goals. Salisbury and McGregor's study (2002) of five elementary schools engaged in inclusive practices also showed personal attributes similar to those found in the transformational leaders. The principals "tended to be leaders who shared decision-making power with their staff, led by example, extended the core values of inclusiveness and quality to initiatives throughout their buildings, and actively promoted learning communities" (p. 269). They promoted change through collaborative, intentional, and supportive practices.

A number of authors have identified lists (see Table 2.1) of tips (Potter & Hulsey, 2001), factors (Guzman, 1997), competencies (Heizman, 2001), and strategies (Lipsky & Gartner, 1997) important for principals who support special education services and student needs.

Perusal of the lists provides a variety of perspectives based on their origin. The Guzman (1997) list resulted from the study of six elementary school principals from Colorado schools who were successfully including students with disabilities in general education classroom programs. The eight factors found were common among all principals (Guzman, 1997). All of the factors exemplify commitment on the part of the principals. Factor four, in particular, addressed the values needed to provide the vision and establish the culture of the school for inclusion. In all cases included in the building philosophy was "a belief in the right of all students to learn, a belief that inclusive classrooms are beneficial for all students to learn, and a commitment to ensuring optimal academic success for all students" (p. 446). The Potter and Hulsey (2001) list and the Heizman (2001) list come from newsletters—the former, a special education administrator newsletter and the latter, a special education parent newsletter. Potter and Hulsey's purpose was to give direction to principals who did not feel well prepared to operate successful special education programs. It is interesting to note that 3 of the 10 tips address attitude: lead by example, advocate for all students; build bridges with parents, establish personal and professional relationships; and project a calm, positive attitude toward the spe-

**Table 2.1**
**Lists of Principal Behaviors Supportive of Special Education**

| Guzman, 1997, pp. 445-447 | 1. Uses a system of communication that allows staff members to disagree with policies and practices and to make recommendations for change.<br><br>2. Is actively involved in the IEP development process.<br><br>3. Is personally involved in dialogue with the parents of the student with disabilities.<br><br>4. Works with staff to agree collaboratively on a building philosophy of inclusion.<br><br>5. Establishes policies for addressing specific discipline issues arising from students with disabilities.<br><br>6. Follows a personal plan of professional development that incorporates issues associated with inclusion.<br><br>7. Demonstrates skills in data gathering: listening, observing, and interpretation.<br><br>8. Demonstrates skills in problem solving: assessing needs, planning action collaboratively, timely implementation, gathering feedback, and evaluating results. |
|---|---|
| Potter & Hulsey, 2001, pp. 2, 7 | 1. Makes a commitment to an annual meeting for special education and updates.<br><br>2. Has competent and knowledgeable staff members, both teachers and paraprofessionals.<br><br>3. Makes full use of mentors for all new teachers and/or paraprofessionals who work with special needs students.<br><br>4. Visits all of the special education classrooms and special programs.<br><br>5. Leads by example.<br><br>6. Builds bridges with parents.<br><br>7. Provides opportunities for students with disabilities to feel that they are a part of the school.<br><br>8. Is certain that counselors are ready, willing, and able to assist students with disabilities.<br><br>9. Maintains confidentiality of records. |

**Table 2.1** (*continued*)
**Lists of Principal Behaviors Supportive of Special Education**

| | |
|---|---|
| | 10. Projects a calm, positive attitude toward the special education program. |
| Heizman, 2001, pp. 3-5 | 1. Demonstrates collaboration skills and consistent use of the problem-solving sequence. |
| | 2. Uses skills and knowledge to develop a continuous array of assessment and educational services for all children |
| | 3. Plans for the education of students with developmental disabilities through the IEP process. |
| | 4. Responds to challenging or negative behaviors: Understanding requirements of the law and utilizing positive behavioral supports. |
| | 5. Utilizes knowledge of internal resources. |
| | 6. Evidences the ability to evaluate program |
| | 7. Fosters student progress and assessment. |
| | 8. Creates a budget that provides for the education of students with disabilities. |
| | 9. Provides services to preschool students. |
| | 10. Supports school to work transitions. |
| Lipsky & Gartner, 1997, pp. 135-136 | 1. Organizes a team of parents and staff members, including the administrator, to help plan inclusive school strategies and practices |
| | 2. Makes sure teachers, paraprofessionals, substitute teachers, related service personnel, other building support staff, and parents get the ongoing training and support they need. |
| | 3. Makes sure teachers and staff get the planning time they need. |
| | 4. Arranges visits for teachers and staff to inclusive schools. |
| | 5. Explores co-teaching with the staff. |
| | 6. Knows the rights of students with disabilities and their families and the responsibilities of school personnel. |
| | 7. Uses the same report card for all students. |
| | 8. Makes sure all parents are full partners in the school. |
| | 9. Has a clear understandable policy on discipline so every child and every adult |

**Table 2.1** (*continued*)
**Lists of Principal Behaviors Supportive of Special Education**

| | knows what is expected. |
|---|---|
| | 10. Establishes a school-wide behavior management plan so that the staff can be assured that support will be provided at critical times. |
| | 11. Makes sure that the focus is always on what each child needs. |
| | 12. Provides teachers with a list of resources. |
| | 13. Monitors and assesses constantly. |
| | 14. Engages the outside community in the work of the school. |
| | 15. Remembers that [not everything] will work. Is willing to fail, regroup and try a different approach. Lets the staff know that failure is something to be learned from, not something to be punished for. |
| | 16. Empowers and supports the staff. |

cial education program. Heizman's 10 competencies were generated by a Cincinnati Public Schools Special Education workgroup. However, in another part of the same newsletter, Heizman's response to, "What makes a good principal?" was "good principals must know and appreciate their community...understand the diversity, the culture, the values of the people who live there. They need to like the people who live there" (p. 1). The 16 strategies cited by Lipsky and Gartner (1997) were identified by a group of 12 schools involved in the Working Group on Inclusive Education.

Perhaps the most useful list of guidelines for principals is the one published by the Council for Exceptional Children (CEC) (2001) and the National Association of Elementary School Principals (NAESP) in collaboration with the IDEA Local Implementation by Local Administrators Partnership (ILIAD). The publication, *Implementing IDEA: A Guide for Principals,* is based on IDEA '75 regulations and organized around the categories identified in the general standards for quality elementary and middle schools: school organization, curriculum and instruction, staff development, school climate, and assessment. Each of the five categories is further defined by the NAESP-developed standards and guidelines. The quality indicator, "the principal's values, beliefs, and personal characteristics inspire people to accomplish the school's mission" (p. 51) suggests that the principal's values and beliefs (dispositions) are important in the implementation of IDEA '97. The quality indicator, "the school's environment encourages the capabilities and emphasizes the worth of all individuals" (p. 59), suggests the significant role of the principal in establishing school climate.

Krajewski and Krajewski (2000) are parents who are pleased that guidelines for principals are provided but feel that, more importantly, they want principals who "value equalizing opportunities for special needs students" (p. 53). They define equalizing opportunities as making available to students with disabilities those school opportunities (e.g., honor societies, band, cheerleading, etc.) that are afforded students without disabilities.

## WHAT ADMINISTRATOR OR PRINCIPAL ATTITUDES OR VALUES FACILITATE EFFECTIVE SPECIAL EDUCATION SERVICES?

Principal attitude is measured by how closely "the walk matches the talk." Support of special education is measured by how closely the resources allocated for special education and general education are equitable to the needs of the respective students. The following suggest behaviors that "match the talk."

### Build a Team

Cook, Semmel, and Gerber (1999) found the principal's attitude to be important in facilitating inclusion but not the only attitude to consider when implementing inclusion. They found significant attitudinal discrepancies between the principal and the special education teachers. The authors "conjecture that...discrepancies may pose a possible explanation for inclusion policies being increasingly implemented and not generally producing improved outcomes" (p. 206). Villa et al. (1996) collected data from school sites in Canada and in five states in the U.S. They found "that administrators must: foster a collaborative climate, model shared decision-making, arrange supports and incentives for collaboration, establish collaboration as expected behavior through job descriptions and program evaluations, and communicate that collaboration is not a voluntary act" (p. 40).

### Get Involved

Powell and Hyle (1997) studied the implementation of inclusion at three high schools. Although all three schools espoused inclusion, the benchmarks used to assess the quality of the programs indicated inclusion was not being implemented. The major finding was that the principals in these sites delegated special education to others. They did not get directly involved. In successful settings, Petersen and Swan (1996) found that a majority of the middle school principals were actively involved in inclusion efforts. They also found that leadership efforts to facilitate inclusion were not related to age, sex, degrees, or years of experience. McLeskey and Waldron (2000) advocate the principal taking a systematic approach to designing, implementing, and monitoring inclusive schools. They provide nine steps to follow:

1. Begin with a discussion of schooling for all students.
2. Form a team.
3. Examine your school.
4. Develop a plan for the inclusive school.
5. Review and discuss the plan with the entire school community.
6. Incorporate feedback from the school community regarding the plan for inclusion.
7. Get ready.
8. Implement the plan.
9. Monitor, evaluate, and change the inclusive program, as needed. (p. 121)

### Embrace Change

McLaughlin and Hyle (2001) found that "creating a context for change is a critical factor in successfully navigating the change process…creat[ing] a context by using the underlying cultural beliefs, attitudes and norms of the school" (p. 34). Barnett and Monda-Amaya (1998) surveyed elementary, junior high, and high school principals regarding elements necessary for successful inclusion. They found no relationship between the number of years in education and attitude toward inclusion. Principals identified heterogeneous or multi-age grouping, collaboration, and cooperative learning as the top three strategies to facilitate inclusion. They felt inclusion could work, but not for all children. The authors point out that principals need to understand that inclusion necessitates change. Putting students with disabilities into programs as they exist will not work. Villa et al. (1996) advise that administrators "give heterogeneous education initiatives at least 4–6 years of support"(p. 42). Haberman (1999) echoes the need for sustaining effort by opining "schools fail to offer the project for a long enough period to realize or assess its value or impact" (p. 81). Fullan (1999) points out that with more and more emphasis placed on high stakes testing for accountability "the greater the gap [becomes] between the advantaged and disadvantaged student" (p. 19). Schools will continue to change. Principals who stay the course "will see that breakthroughs occur when we begin to think of conflict, diversity and resistance as positive, absolutely essential forces for success" (Fullan, 1999, p. ix).

It is evident that supporting students with special learning needs is more successful when the principal's attitude is positive and supportive. At the same time it must be recognized that a great deal of effort and time go into building a successful service delivery model.

It takes a strong instructional leader to ensure that all children achieve. It takes a strong instructional leader to ensure that all children and their teachers receive the supports and services they need to learn and develop. And, it takes a strong instructional leader to create a positive learning climate that embodies a unifying philosophy of respect for all children and stakeholders in the total school community. (CEC, 2001, p. 6)

## REFERENCES

Bailey, J., & du Plessis, D. (1997). Understanding principals' attitudes towards inclusive schooling. *Journal of Educational Administration, 35*(5), 428–438.

Bain, A., & Dolbel, S. (1991). Regular and special education principals' perceptions of an integration program for students who are intellectually handicapped. *Education and Training in Mental Retardation, 26*(1), 33–42.

Barnett, C., & Monda-Amaya, L. E. (1998). Principals' knowledge of and attitudes toward inclusion. *Remedial and Special Education, 19*(3), 181–192.

Cook, B. G., Semmel, M. I., & Gerber, M. M. (1999). Attitudes of principals and special education teachers toward the inclusion of students with mild disabilities. *Remedial and Special Education, 20*(4), 199–207.

Council for Exceptional Children. (2001). *Implementing IDEA: A guide for principals.* Arlington, VA: Author.

Fullan, M. (1999). *Change forces: The sequel.* New York: Falmer Press.

Gameros, P. (1995). The visionary principal and the inclusion of students with disabilities. *NASSP Bulletin, 79*(568), 15–17.

Goldberg, M. F. (2001). Leadership in education: Five commonalities. *Phi Delta Kappan, 82*(10), 757–761.

Goor, M. B., Schwenn, J. O., & Boyer, L. (1997). Preparing principals for leadership in special education. *Intervention in School and Clinic, 32*(3), 133–141.

Guzman, N. (1997) Leadership for successful inclusive schools. *Journal of Educational Administration, 35*(5), 439–450.

Haberman, M. (1999). *Star principals: Serving children in poverty.* Indianapolis, IN: Kappa Delta Pi.

Hasazi, S. B., Johnson, A. P., Liggett, A.M., & Schattman, R. A. (1994). A qualitative policy study of the least restrictive environment provision of the Individuals with Disabilities Education Act. *Exceptional Children, 60*(6), 491–507.

Heizman, C. (2001). Ten principal competencies related to the education of students with special needs. *Parent to Parent, XIV*(III), 3–5.

Idol, L., & Griffith, J. (1998). A study of four schools: Moving toward inclusion of special education students in general education. (ERIC Document Reproduction Service No. ED432083)

Ingram, P.D. (1997). Leadership behaviours of principals in inclusive educational settings. *Journal of Educational Administration, 35*(5), 411–427.

Krajewski, B., & Krajewski, L. (2000). Inclusion strategies: Equalizing opportunities for cognitively disabled students. *NASSP Bulletin, 84*(613), 48–53.

Lipsky, D.K., & Gartner, A. (1997). *Inclusion and school reform.* Baltimore: Paul H. Brookes Publishing Co.

McLaughlin, L., & Hyle, A.E. (2001, April). *The school principal as change agent: An explanatory case study.* Paper presented at the American Educational Research Association Annual Meeting, Seattle, WA. (ERIC Document Reproduction Service No. ED456516)

McLeskey, J., & Waldron, N.L. (2000). *Inclusive schooling in action: Making differences ordinary.* Alexandria, VA: ASCD.

Morgan, C.R., & Demchak, M. (1996). Addressing administrative needs for successful inclusion of students with disabilities. *Rural goals 2000: Building programs that work.* (ERIC Document Reproduction Service No. ED394767)

Petersen, M.D., & Swan, W.W. (1996, Fall). Middle school principals' tasks and strategies to facilitate inclusion of students with disabilities in general education classes. *Research in Middle Level Education Quarterly, 20*(1) 65–89.

Potter, L., & Hulsey, D.E. (2001). Tips for principals to improve their special education programs. *CASE, 42*(5), 2, 7.

Powell, D., & Hyle, A.E. (1997). Principals and school reform. *Journal of School Leadership, 7,* 301–326.

Salisbury, C.L., & McGregor, G. (2002). The administrative climate and context of inclusive elementary schools. *Exceptional Children, 68*(2), 259–274.

Villa, R.A., Thousand, J.S., Meyers, H., & Nevin, A. (1996). Teacher and administrator perceptions of heterogeneous education. *Exceptional Children, 63*(1), 29–45.

West, L.S. (2001, April). *The influence of principals on the institutionalization of developmentally appropriate practices: A multiple case study.* Paper presented at the annual meeting of the American Research Association, Seattle, WA. (ERIC Service Document Reproduction No. ED456543)

## Sources for Support

http://iris.peabody.vanderbilt.edu—IDEA and Research for Inclusive Settings (IRIS). The IRIS Center for Faculty Enhancement was designed in response to a request from the U.S. Department of Education's Office of Special Education Programs. The national effort, serving college faculty working in preservice preparation programs, aims to ensure that general education teachers, school administrators, school nurses, and school counselors are well prepared to work with students who have disabilities and with their families.

http://www.aasa.org—American Association of School Administrators. The AASA is a professional organization for educational leaders, which is dedicated to the support and development of effective school leaders. Information on IDEA is found under the "Government Relations" section. Resources on current issues can be found under "Issues and Insight" which also includes information for professors under "Professional Development."

http://www.cec.sped.org—Council for Exceptional Children (CEC). *The* website for special education. The Council for Exceptional Children is the most prominent special education organization in the field. This site is filled with information and resources for children with disabilities.

http://www.ed/gov/offices/OSERS/Policy/IDEA/geninfo.html—IDEA '97.

## Attitude Clarification Activity

Goor, Schwenn, and Boyer (1997) emphasize the need, in any principal preparation program, to first address beliefs because "effective principals believe they are responsible for the education of all children and that teachers can teach a wide variety of students" (p. 140). Following is such an activity. The activity is designed for pre-service administrators to explore attitudes and concepts towards serving students with special learning needs. The term "heterogeneous schools" is another term for "inclusionary schools," meaning all children are educated with the necessary supports in general education environments in their neighborhood schools (Villa et al., 1996).

# ATTITUDE CLARIFICATION ACTIVITY

## Steps

1. Individuals—Respond to the *Assumptions of Heterogeneous Schooling* form, adapted from Villa, Thousand, Meyers, and Nevin (1996).

2. Small Groups—Discuss range of responses and share perspectives.

3. Group Reporting—Share group's "most agreed upon" and "most divergent" responses.

4. Large Group—What conclusions can be drawn about group's perspectives?

5. Individuals—Write a self-reflection on your perspective related to group and class discussions. What experiences or lack thereof affect your beliefs? What do you need to address to ensure continued growth on your part?

6. Suggested Reading: Chapter 15, *An Inclusion Talkback: Critics' Concerns and Advocates' Responses,* in Lipsky and Gartner (1997).

**Table 2.2**
**Assumptions of Heterogeneous Schooling**

| Assumptions of Heterogeneous Schooling | | | | |
|---|---|---|---|---|
| **Indicate your agreement with each of the following statements:** | **Strongly Agree** | **Agree** | **Disagree** | **Strongly Disagree** |
| 1. All children belong (zero reject) in general education classrooms in their neighborhood schools. | | | | |
| 2. The needs of all students can be met in general education through technical assistance, team teaching, administrative support, and collaboration with parents, students, related service personnel, educators, and community members. | | | | |
| 3. General and special educators are coequal partners who share responsibility for the education of all children in their school. | | | | |
| 4. General educators and special educators acquire new skills through collaboration, training, and experience with children who present challenges. | | | | |
| 5. Everyone benefits from heterogeneous educational practices. | | | | |
| 6. Schools must be restructured to facilitate role redefinition and make it all right for students to have individual academic and social goals. | | | | |

**Table 2.2** (*continued*)
**Assumptions of Heterogeneous Schooling**

| | | | | |
|---|---|---|---|---|
| 7. The body of decision makers in schools must be expanded to include teachers, students, and community members. | | | | |
| 8. Attitudes change over time due to successful experiences. | | | | |

# Chapter 3

# Legal Issues in Special Education

*Charles J. Russo and Allan G. Osborne, Jr.*

American children with disabilities benefit from broad-based statutory protections, most notably under the Individuals with Disabilities Education Act[1] (IDEA) and Section 504 of the Rehabilitation Act of 1973.[2] In light of the far-reaching impact that these two statutes have on schooling in Ohio[3] and throughout the nation, this chapter primarily focuses on federal law, because the IDEA and Section 504, much more than state law, truly are the engines that drive special education.

## EARLY HISTORY OF SPECIAL EDUCATION

The impetus for ensuring equal educational opportunities for all American children can be traced to *Brown v. Board of Education, Topeka*.[4] Although resolved in the context of school desegregation, in *Brown* the Supreme Court set the tone for later developments in its declaration that "education is perhaps the most important function of state and local governments."[5]

Following *Brown*, an attitude of neglect remained in effect with regard to the disabled. In fact, throughout the 1950s, 28 states had laws requiring the sterilization of individuals with disabilities while others limited such basic rights as voting, marrying, and obtaining a driver's license.[6] By the 1960s, the percentages of children who were served in public schools began to rise; the 12% of children in schools in 1948 increased to 21% in 1963 and 38% in 1968.[7] As of July 1, 1974, the Bureau for the Education of the Handicapped reported that about 78.5% of the nation's 8,150,000 eligible children with disabilities received some form of public education. Of these children, 47.8% received special education and related services, 30.7% did not receive related services, and the remaining 21.5% did not receive educational services at all.[8]

These data aside, the major push for the development of special education came in two federal cases. In *Pennsylvania Association for Retarded Children v. Pennsylvania (PARC)*,[9] a federal trial court, in a consent decree, established the bases for what developed into the IDEA. In *PARC* the parties agreed that children with disabilities could neither be denied admission to a public school nor be subjected to a change in educational placement unless their parents received procedural due process and that a placement in a regular school classroom was preferable to one in a more restrictive setting. Similarly, in *Mills v. Board of Education of the District of Columbia*,[10] another federal trial court ruled that despite the school system's claims that it lacked the resources for all of its students, it could not deny services to children with disabilities and that they could not be excluded from public schools without receiving due process. Insofar as *Mills* originated in Washington, D.C., it was probably among the more significant influences moving federal lawmakers to act to ensure adequate protection for children with disabilities by adopting Section 504 and the IDEA.

In light of legal developments following *PARC* and *Mills*, this section of the chapter reviews major statutory developments, under Section 504 of the Rehabilitation Act and the IDEA, in safeguarding the educational rights of American children with disabilities. In the wake of the literally thousands of lawsuits that have been filed in federal and state courts, rather than cases being addressed in separate sections, they are generally incorporated in the Notes at the end of the chapter.

## Section 504 of the Rehabilitation Act of 1973

The Rehabilitation Act of 1973 was the first federal civil rights law protecting the rights of the disabled. Among its provisions, Section 504 declares that "no otherwise qualified individual with a disability in the United States ... shall, solely by reason of her or his disability, be excluded from the participation in, be denied the benefits of, or be subjected to discrimination under any program or activity receiving federal financial assistance. "[11]

According to Section 504, recipients of federal financial aid must file an assurance of compliance; engage in remedial actions where violations are proven; take voluntary steps to overcome the effects of conditions that resulted in limiting the participation of students with disabilities in their programs; conduct a self-evaluation; designate a staff member, typically at the central office level, as compliance coordinator; adopt grievance procedures; and provide notice to students and their parents that their programs are nondiscriminatory.[12]

Section 504 offers broad-based protection to individuals with disabilities. It is important to note that while Section 504 covers both students and employees, this chapter focuses on the rights of children. The Act defines an individual with a disability as one "who (i) has a physical or mental impairment which substantially limits one or more of such person's major life activities, (ii) has a record of such an impairment, or (iii) is regarded as having such an impairment."[13]

In order to have a record of impairment, an individual must have a history of, or been identified as having, a mental or physical impairment that substantially limits one or more major life activities,[14] including schooling. Once a student is identified as having a disability, the next step is to determine whether he or she is "otherwise qualified." In order to be qualified, as the term is applied to preschool, elementary, and secondary school students, a child must be "(i) of an age during which nonhandicapped persons are provided such services, (ii) of any age during which it is mandatory under state law to provide such services to handicapped persons, or (iii) [a student] to whom a state is required to provide a free appropriate public education [under the IDEA]."[15] An individual who is "otherwise qualified," meaning that he or she is eligible to participate in a program or activity despite the existence of an impairment, must be permitted to participate in the program or activity as long as it is possible to do so by means of a "reasonable accommodation."

Reasonable accommodations may involve modest adjustments such as permitting a child to be accompanied by a service dog[16] or providing basic health services to allow a student with a physical impairment to be present in a classroom.[17] Further, in making a modification, officials do not have to make every classroom or area of a building available; it may be enough to bring services to a child such as offering a keyboard for musical instruction rather than revamping an entire music room for a student who wishes to take piano classes.[18]

Even if a child appears to be otherwise qualified, schools can rely on one of three defenses to avoid being charged with noncompliance. First, school officials can be excused from making accommodations that would result in "a fundamental alteration in the nature of [a] program."[19] This defense illustrates a major difference between Section 504 and the IDEA.

The second defense permits school officials to avoid compliance if a modification imposes "undue financial burdens."[20] This is a second major difference between Section 504 and the IDEA since the latter requires school systems to provide programs regardless of their cost.

The third defense available under Section 504 is that an otherwise qualified student with a disability can be excluded from a program if his or her presence creates a substantial risk of injury to himself or to others. For example, a child with a spastic condition who has difficulty controlling his movements may be excluded from a chemistry laboratory due to fear of exposure to the flames of a Bunsen burner. In order to comply with Section

504, a school may have to offer the reasonable accommodation of providing a computer-assisted program to simulate the laboratory class environment.

Section 504 also prohibits discrimination by requiring educators to make individualized modifications for otherwise qualified students with disabilities. This means that school officials must provide aid, benefits, and/or services that are comparable to those available to students who are not disabled. As such, children with disabilities must receive comparable materials, teacher quality, length of school term, and daily hours of instruction. These programs should not be separate from those available to those who are not disabled, unless such segregation is necessary for the program to be effective. If programs are separate, facilities must be comparable.

After being identified, each qualified student with a disability is entitled to an appropriate public education, regardless of the nature or severity of his or her disability. In order to guarantee that an appropriate education is made available, Section 504's regulations include due process requirements for evaluation and placement similar to those under the IDEA.[21]

## INDIVIDUALS WITH DISABILITIES EDUCATION ACT

Unlike Section 504, which has fairly broad standards, in order to qualify under the IDEA, a child with a disability must meet three statutory requirements. First, the child must be between the ages of 3 and 21.[22] Second, the child must have a specifically identified disability.[23] Third, the child must be in need of special education,[24] meaning that he or she must receive a free appropriate education (FAPE)[25] in the least restrictive environment that conforms to an individualized education program (IEP).[26] Further, if necessary, each child with a disability is entitled to needed related services to assist him or her in benefiting from the IEP.[27]

### Appropriate Placement

Although the IDEA requires school boards to provide each student with a disability with a FAPE, the Act offers little guidance in defining what may be considered appropriate. The IDEA's regulations indicate that an appropriate education consists of special education and related services that are provided in conformance with an IEP.[28] Even so, a precise definition of the term *appropriate* cannot be found in either the statute or its regulations. As such, it is necessary to turn to judicial interpretation for further guidance on the meaning of FAPE.

In *Board of Education of the Hendrick Hudson Central School District v. Rowley*,[29] the Supreme Court offered a minimal definition of FAPE. *Rowley* arose when the parents of a kindergarten student who was hearing impaired protested their school board's refusal to provide their daughter with a sign-language interpreter. Lower courts ordered the board to provide the interpreter on the basis that an appropriate education was one that would have allowed the child to achieve at a level commensurate with that of her peers who were not disabled. The Court, in noting that the child was achieving passing marks and advancing from grade to grade without the sign-language interpreter, reversed. The Court held that an appropriate education was one that was formulated in accordance with all of the IDEA's procedures and is "sufficient to confer some educational benefit"[30] upon a child with a disability. Since the student in *Rowley* received some educational benefit without the sign-language interpreter, the Court ruled that educators were not required to provide one even though she might have achieved at a higher level with the services.

*Rowley* establishes a minimum standard of what constitutes a FAPE under federal law. Yet, individual states, such as North Carolina,[31] New Jersey,[32] Massachusetts,[33] Michigan,[34] and California[35] have upheld higher standards of appropriateness. In some of these instances, courts have specifically noted that the higher state standards replaced the federal requirements since one of the essential elements of the IDEA is that special education programs must meet "the standards of the state educational agency."[36]

The *Rowley* standard has been further refined as courts have indicated that the "some educational benefit" criteria requires more than just minimal or trivial benefits.[37] Other courts have expanded the criteria by declaring that the educational benefit must be meaningful[38] or appreciable.[39] One court went so far as to maintain that the gains made by a student must be measurable to meet the *Rowley* criteria.[40]

## Least Restrictive Environment

According to the IDEA, each student with a disability must be educated in the least restrictive environment[41] (LRE). In two cases, federal appellate courts in New Jersey and California ordered school boards to place students with disabilities in regular settings as opposed to segregated special education classrooms.[42] In these cases, the courts held that educators must consider a variety of factors when determining the LRE for a student. As summarized by the Ninth Circuit, the four factors that must be addressed in making a placement are the educational benefits of placing a child with a disability in a regular classroom; the nonacademic benefits of such a placement; the effect that the student's presence would have on the teacher and other children in the class; and the costs of an inclusionary placement.[43] Inherent in these decisions is the principle that educators must make reasonable efforts to place students with disabilities in mainstream settings by providing them with supplementary aids and services to ensure success.

Even with the focus on inclusion, not all students with disabilities must be placed in regular education classes. Courts have approved segregated settings where educators showed that students could not function in regular classrooms or would not benefit in such settings, even with supplementary aids and services.[44] The bottom line is that an inclusionary placement should be the setting of choice, and a segregated setting should be contemplated only if an inclusionary placement has failed despite the best efforts of educators or if there is overwhelming evidence that it is not feasible.

### Private and Residential School Placements

Insofar as the IDEA's preference for placing students in the mainstream is not feasible for all students, the law requires school officials to offer a continuum of placement alternatives to meet the educational needs of children with disabilities.[45] In this regard, a private school setting may be required when a board lacks an appropriate placement, such as when a student has a low incidence disability and there are not enough children with the same type of disability within the system to warrant the development of a program.[46] Courts have recognized that since smaller boards cannot afford to develop specialized programs for small numbers of students, they must look elsewhere for placements.

A court may order a residential placement for a student with severe, profound, or multiple disabilities[47] if the child needs 24-hour programming or consistency between the school and home environments. Residential placements may also be necessary for a student with significant behavioral disorders[48] or who requires total immersion in an educational environment in order to progress.[49]

If a residential placement is required for purely educational reasons, its cost must be fully borne by a school board, which cannot require parents to contribute toward the cost of a residential placement.[50] However, if a placement is made for other than educational purposes, for example, for medical or social purposes, then a school system is only required to pay for the educational component of the residential setting[51] and may enter into a cost-share agreement with other agencies.

### Extended School Year Programs

If a student with a disability requires an educational program that extends beyond the regular school year, it must be provided.[52] An extended school year program is generally required when a student regresses, and the time it takes to recoup lost skills interferes with overall progress toward the attainment of the goals and objectives of the child's

IEP.[53] Any regression that a student suffers must be greater than the regression that normally occurs during a school vacation. If a regression is minimal, an extended school year program is not required.[54]

### Related Services

School boards must provide related, or supportive, services to a child with a disability if they are necessary to help the student benefit from special education.[55] The only limit on a related service is that medical services are exempted unless they are specifically for diagnostic or evaluative purposes.

One of the most controversial topics under the rubric of related services involves the distinction between medical and school health services. In 1984 the Supreme Court held that a service such as catheterization that can be performed by a school nurse or trained layperson is a required related service under the IDEA.[56] Procedures that must, by law, be performed by a licensed physician would be exempted medical services. Thus, psychiatric therapy would not be a related service since a psychiatrist is a licensed physician. Many students with significant medical needs require round-the-clock nursing services. This type of service falls somewhere on the continuum between school health services and medical services. Most recently, in *Cedar Rapids Community School District v. Garret F.*,[57] the Supreme Court ruled that a school board was required to provide, and pay for, a full-time nurse while a student was in school since his medical condition required constant nursing services.

Another potentially costly related service, discussed next, covers assistive technology devices[58] or services.[59] An assistive technology device is an item or piece of equipment that is used to increase, maintain, or improve the functional capabilities of individuals with disabilities. These devices may include commercially available, modified, or customized equipment. An assistive technology service is designed to assist an individual in the selection, acquisition, or use of an assistive technology device.[60] These services are required when it is necessary for a child to receive an appropriate education under the *Rowley* standard and may also allow a student with a disabilitiy to benefit from education in a less restrictive setting.

### Assistive Technology

In 1990 Congress amended the IDEA to include definitions of assistive technology devices and services. These definitions were expanded and carried over into the 1997 IDEA amendments. Comprehensive guidelines for implementing the assistive technology provisions of the IDEA were included in the final regulations for implementation of the 1997 IDEA amendments, which were released by the United States Department of

Education in 1999.[61] Interestingly, assistive technology is not specifically included in either the definition of special education or related services. It does fit within the definition of special education as specially designed instruction and within the definition of related services as a developmental, corrective, or supportive service. However, instead of including assistive technology within either of these two definitions, Congress chose to create assistive technology as a category separate from both special education and related services. Thus, assistive technology can be considered a special education service, a related service, or simply a supplementary aid or service. School boards are required to provide students with disabilities with supplementary aids and services to allow them to be educated in the least restrictive environment.[62]

The IDEA and its implementing regulations define an assistive technology device as any item, piece of equipment, or product system that is used to increase, maintain, or improve the functional capabilities of individuals with disabilities.[63] These devices may include commercially available, modified, or customized equipment. An assistive technology service is designed to provide direct assistance to an individual with a disability in the selection, acquisition, or use of an assistive technology device.[64] It includes (A) an evaluation of the student's needs, including a functional evaluation of the individual in the student's customary environment, (B) purchasing, leasing, or otherwise providing for the acquisition of the assistive technology device, (C) selecting, designing, fitting, customizing, adapting, applying, maintaining, repairing, or replacing the assistive technology device, (D) coordinating and using other therapies, interventions, or services with assistive technology devices, such as those associated with existing education and rehabilitation programs, (E) training or technical assistance for the student or his or her family, and (F) training and technical assistance for professionals who will provide education or rehabilitation services, employers, or other individuals who will provide services to the student with disabilities.

As indicated, assistive technology may be provided as a special education service, a related service, or as supplementary aids and services. Assistive technology is required when it is necessary for a student to receive an appropriate education under the standard established by the Supreme Court in *Rowley*. Further, assistive technology may allow many students with disabilities to benefit from education in less restrictive settings and thus may also be required under the IDEA's least restrictive environment provision.[65]

The team that is charged with the responsibility of developing a student's IEP must consider whether a child requires assistive technology devices and services in order to receive an appropriate education.[66] However, there are no provisions requiring the team to document that it considered a student's assistive technology needs and determined that assistive technology was not required. If the team determines that assistive technology is required, this must be written into the IEP.

School boards are specifically required to ensure that assistive technology devices and services are made available to a student if either or both are required as part of a student's special education, related services, or supplementary aids and services.[67] Further, the use of school-provided assistive technology devices is required in the student's home if the IEP team determines that a student needs access to assistive technology in order to receive a FAPE.[68]

In explanatory material accompanying the 1999 regulations, the Department of Education made it clear that school boards are not required to provide personal devices that a student would require regardless of whether the child attended school.[69] This includes items such as eyeglasses, hearing aids, or braces. The Department also clarified that students with disabilities are entitled to have access to any general technology that is available to students who are not disabled. Yet, if a student with a disability requires accommodations in order to use general technology, those accommodations must be provided.

### Minimum Competency Tests

Ohio has recently joined the thrust of educational reform movements by adopting high-stakes testing in the call for greater accountability in the nation's classrooms. It is important to focus on legal issues surrounding minimum competency tests (MCTs), or basic skills tests, as these have been developed and are being administered in many states to address the need for greater accountability. These tests may be used either as a graduation requirement to ensure that students receiving a diploma have a specified knowledge base or to identify students who have not achieved competency in basic skills and thus may require remedial instruction.

States clearly have the authority to develop and administer MCTs, more commonly referred to as proficiency tests in Ohio,[70] and to establish graduation requirements. While Ohio law permits IEP teams to justify a student with a disability being excused from taking a proficiency test,[71] the same provision forbids school officials from prohibiting such a child from taking a proficiency test. Further, the IDEA requires the participation of students with disabilities in some form of state assessment.[72]

It is now well settled that states may require students to pass MCT-type tests to receive standard high school diplomas as long as they satisfy three primary guidelines. First, when these tests are used as a graduation requirement, they must be a valid and reliable measure of what has been taught, and students must be given sufficient notice that they must pass a minimum competency test to receive a standard diploma.[73] Second, minimum competency tests may not be racially, linguistically, or ethnically discriminatory.[74] Third, in order to have students with disabilities take, and pass, a minimum competency test before receiving a standard high school diploma,[75] they must be given sufficient notice, and their IEPs should include instruction in the areas to be tested.[76]

Students with disabilities taking minimum competency tests may require some modifications. School boards may be required to modify how a test is administered but are not likely to be required to modify the actual content of the test or to offer an alternate examination. For example, a blind student should be given a Braille version of the test, or a student with physical disabilities may need assistance writing or filling in the circles on a machine-scored answer sheet. However, it is unlikely that school boards will be required to develop and administer a test with fewer items or easier items for a student with intellectual impairments.[77] Basically, school officials are required to provide modifications that will allow the student to take the test but are not required to modify the item content or compromise the validity of the test. Most recently, the federal Office of Civil Rights (OCR) ruled in favor of a school board when educational officials rejected a parent's request in Florida that a proctor be permitted to read an MCT to her child. In finding that since the communications section of the test was designed to test the student's reading and comprehension skills, OCR decided that school officials had the authority to reject the mother's request since granting it would have compromised the validity of the test.[78]

Parents of children with disabilities are responsible for working with other members of an IEP team in determining the components of their child's IEP. School officials should make parents aware of the general content of the tests, where and how they are to be administered, and the purposes for which the results are to be used. Following the evaluation period, and prior to placement, a decision should be made regarding the appropriateness of including MCT material in a child's IEP. If an IEP team in Ohio decides that such content is not appropriate, the parents may always appeal to an impartial hearing officer. Consequently, to the extent that educators routinely follow these practices, there is not likely to be much litigation involving proficiency testing of students with disabilities in Ohio.

### Remedies

When a school board fails to provide a student with disabilities with a FAPE, the IDEA authorizes the courts to grant appropriate relief.[79] Frequently, the relief orders educational officials to provide specified special education and related services. However, if parents have unilaterally obtained the necessary services at their own expense, the courts may order educators to reimburse them for all legitimate expenses.

## Damages

Courts generally have not imposed punitive damages on school authorities for failing to provide a FAPE to a child with a disability.[80] Similarly, general damages awards for "pain and suffering" have not been prevalent.[81] Yet, recent litigation indicates that this may be changing.[82] Courts have indicated that monetary damages may be available under other statutes, such as Section 504, if the parents can show that school officials intentionally discriminated against the student or egregiously disregarded the student's rights.[83] The operative word here is intentional. If school officials act in good faith but their efforts fall short of meeting statutory requirements, they should be immune from damages.

## Tuition Reimbursement

Sometimes parents who are dissatisfied with their child's placement unilaterally enroll the child in a private school and seek to recover tuition expenses. The Supreme Court has held that parents are entitled to tuition reimbursement if they can show that a school official failed to offer a FAPE and that their chosen placement is appropriate.[84] The Court reasoned that awarding reimbursement simply requires a school board to pay retroactively the costs it should have been paying all along. The Court later held that parents are also entitled to reimbursement even if their chosen placement is not in a state approved facility as long as it provided an otherwise appropriate education.[85] Even so, when parents unilaterally place their children, they do so at their own financial risk, because they are not entitled to reimbursement if school officials can show that they offered, and could provide, an appropriate educational placement. Parents are also entitled to reimbursement for unilaterally obtained related services if they can demonstrate that a school board failed to provide the needed services.[86]

## Compensatory Services

Tuition reimbursement is likely to be of little use to parents who are unable to make a unilateral placement in a private school because they cannot afford to pay the tuition. When parents cannot afford to make a unilateral placement, their child may remain in an inappropriate setting while the dispute winds its way through due process hearings and judicial proceedings. In such a situation, a court may award additional educational services and prospective relief to compensate the parents and child for the loss of appropriate educational services.

The courts have ruled that compensatory services, like reimbursement, compensate a student for a school board's failure to provide a FAPE. The reasoning behind a compensatory services award is that an appropriate remedy should not be available only to students whose parents can afford to provide them with an alternate educational placement while litigation is pending.[87] Generally, compensatory services are provided for a period of time equal to that for which the child was denied services[88] and may be granted even after a student has passed the ceiling age for eligibility under the IDEA.[89] As with tuition reimbursement, awards of compensatory educational services are granted only when a hearing officer or court has determined that a board failed to provide an appropriate placement.

### Attorney Fees

Litigation can cost a great deal. Many parents, after prevailing in court against a school board, believe that they should be reimbursed for their expenses. These parents typically argue that they achieved hollow victories when they prevailed but were left with burdensome legal bills.

In 1984, the Supreme Court held that recovery of legal expenses was not available under the IDEA.[90] However, two years later Congress responded by amending the IDEA with the passage of the Handicapped Children's Protection Act (HCPA).[91] The HCPA gave courts the power to award reasonable attorney fees to parents who prevailed against school boards in actions or proceedings brought pursuant to the IDEA. An award must be based on the prevailing rates in the community in which the case arose. Under the HCPA, a court may determine what is a reasonable amount of time spent preparing and arguing a case. An award may be limited if a school system made a settlement offer more than 10 days before the proceedings began that was equal to or more favorable than the final relief obtained.[92] Further, a court may reduce an award if it finds that parents unreasonably protracted a dispute,[93] an attorney's hourly rate was excessive,[94] or the time spent and legal services furnished were excessive in light of the issues.[95] The HCPA was made retroactive to July 4, 1984, the day before the Supreme Court declared that attorney fees were unavailable under the IDEA.

### Discipline

Perhaps the most controversial legal issue in special education concerns disciplinary sanctions and students with disabilities.[96] In fact, until its 1997 amendments were adopted, the IDEA did not make a direct reference to discipline. Discipline of students with disabilities is a sensitive issue because it pits the duty of administrators to maintain order, discipline, and a safe environment against the rights of each child to receive a FAPE in the LRE. Even though most will agree that the power of school officials to maintain discipline should not be frustrated, it must be understood that a student should not be denied the rights accorded by the IDEA if misconduct is caused by the child's disability.

School officials may impose disciplinary sanctions on a special education child as long as they follow procedures that do not deprive the student of his or her rights. As such, educators may use normal disciplinary sanctions, including suspensions, with special education students by following usual procedures and providing customary due process.[97] Administrators face some restrictions when they intend to impose more drastic punishments such as an expulsion or wish to change a student's placement for disciplinary reasons. Basically, in these situations, the due process procedures in the IDEA replace the normal due process protections.

A long line of case law holds that although students with disabilities cannot be expelled for misconduct that is related to their disabilities, they can be excluded if there was no relationship between their misconduct and disability.[98] While the Supreme Court's landmark decision in *Honig v. Doe*[99] supported the prohibition of expelling students for disability-related misconduct, this ruling did permit special education students to be suspended for up to 10 days. During that cooling-off period, school personnel may attempt to negotiate an alternative placement with a student's parents. If they are unsuccessful and can show that the student is truly dangerous, educators may obtain an injunction or order allowing them to exclude the student from school.

The 1997 amendments, which codified case law since *Honig*, while clarifying many of the gaps in the statute, implemented the most far-reaching changes to the IDEA since it was enacted. The IDEA now contains specific requirements and provisions for disciplining students with disabilities. Further, regulations promulgated by the United States Department of Education explicitly state that the removal of a student with a disability from the child's current educational placement for more than 10 consecutive school days constitutes a change of placement.[100] The regulations add that a series of shorter removals accumulating to more than 10 days may be considered a change in placement depending on the length of each exclusion, the cumulative days that the child is out of school, and the proximity of the removals to one another.[101] Earlier, the 10-day rule was interpreted strictly; now, if a student receives a series of short-term, two- or three-day suspensions spread out over the school year that exceed the 10-day rule by a few days, and it is late in the school year, it is less certain that this will be interpreted as an impermissible change of placement.

In another major change, the IDEA increases the authority of educators to deal with students with disabilities who possess weapons or drugs.[102] Under these provisions, educators may transfer a student with a disability to an interim alternative placement for up to 45 days for possession of a weapon or possession, use, sale, or solicitation of drugs on school property or at a school function.[103] School officials may also order a change in placement to an interim alternative setting if this sanction is used for students who are not disabled under similar circumstances.[104]

When a student with a disability is moved to an alternative placement, educators must conduct a functional behavioral assessment and implement a behavioral intervention plan for the child if one is not already in place.[105] If a behavioral intervention plan was in place when the child misbehaved, the IEP team must review the plan and its implementation in order to make any necessary modifications.[106] Should a parent disagree with the alternative placement and request a hearing, consistent with the so-called stay-put provision, the student must remain in the alternative setting.[107] Once the 45-day period expires, educators must return the student to his or her prior educational placement[108] unless they can demonstrate that it is dangerous to do so.[109]

The amended IDEA has expanded the authority of hearing officers to order interim alternative placements of up to 45 days after an expedited due process hearing.[110] Previously, under *Honig*, educators could not impose such a change unless they had a court order. Even with this change, educators bear the burden of proving that keeping a student in the then-current placement is substantially likely to result in injury to the child or others.[111] Still, school officials must show that they took reasonable measures to minimize that risk in the student's current placement.[112]

The IDEA also requires an interim alternative placement to permit a student to continue to progress in the general education curriculum where he or she will still receive necessary services as outlined in his or her IEP.[113] Additionally, educators must include services and modifications designed to prevent the misbehavior from recurring in the student's program.[114]

For the first time, the amended IDEA establishes procedures required to evaluate whether misconduct is related to a student's disability.[115] The IDEA calls for this judgment to be made by the team that developed the student's IEP[116] within 10 school days of when it chose to take disciplinary action.[117] At the so-called manifestation determination, the team must consider evaluative and diagnostic information, observations of the student, and the child's IEP and placement.[118] In evaluating whether misconduct is a manifestation of a disability, a team should examine whether a child's disability impaired his or her ability to understand the impact and consequences of the misbehavior along with whether the disability impaired the student's ability to control the behavior.[119] If, in making the determination, an IEP team is convinced that there were deficiencies in the student's IEP, its implementation, or the child's placement, it must order immediate steps to be taken to remedy those shortcomings.[120]

If an IEP team is convinced that a student's misbehavior is not a manifestation of the disability, then the child may be disciplined in the same manner as any child who is not disabled.[121] The disciplinary options available to educators include expulsion if it is the usual sanction for the misbehavior in question. A parent may challenge the result of a manifestation determination by requesting an expedited due process hearing.[122]

Another important change clarifies whether school officials can discontinue educational services for a student who is properly expelled for misconduct that is not disability-related. This provision codified existing policy from the United States Department of Education, which ordered the delivery of educational services in this situation and effectively reversed a controversial decision of the Fourth Circuit which held that no such requirement existed under the IDEA.[123] The revised IDEA makes it clear that a FAPE must be made available to all students with disabilities including those who have been expelled from school.[124] In other words, even if a student with a disability has been expelled in accord with the IDEA's provisions, the child must be provided with services that will allow him or her to progress in the general education curriculum and achieve the goals of the student's IEP.[125] The regulations do not require officials to provide services to a child who has been suspended for 10 days or less.[126]

It is important to note that a student with a disability can still be suspended for up to 10 school days as long as this penalty can be imposed on a child who is not disabled.[127] Even so, under such a circumstance, school officials must conduct a functional behavioral assessment, if they have not already done so, and must address the student's misbehavior.[128]

The courts have disagreed over the treatment of a student who has yet to be determined to be disabled but claims to be covered by the IDEA. School officials must now provide the IDEA's protections to a student if they knew that the child was disabled before the misbehavior occurred.[129] School officials are considered to have this knowledge if a parent expresses concern that his or her child may need special education or makes a request for an evaluation. Educators may also be considered to be on notice of a child's disability based on a student's prior behavioral and academic history or concerns expressed by teachers.[130] An exception exists if educators already conducted an evaluation and determined that the student was not disabled.[131] If a parent requests an evaluation during the time when a student is subject to disciplinary sanctions, it must be conducted in an expedited manner.[132] Consistent with the IDEA's stay-put provision, until an expedited evaluation is completed, the student remains in the placement deemed appropriate by educators.[133] If the evaluation team decides that the child is disabled, school officials must provide the student with special education services.[134]

A final change in the law and regulations indicates that the IDEA cannot be interpreted as prohibiting school officials from reporting a crime committed by a student with a disability to the proper authorities or impeding law enforcement and judicial authorities from carrying out their responsibilities.[135] When school officials do report a crime, they must furnish a student's special education and disciplinary records to the appropriate authorities[136] to the extent that this is permitted under the Family Educational Rights and Privacy Act.[137]

## PRACTICAL GUIDELINES

As educators seek to digest the many nuances in Section 504 and the IDEA, the following guidelines should provide some direction as how to better deal with parents.

1. *Take affirmative action.* While the IDEA clarifies the extent to which parents must be informed about the extent of the IEPs of their children, educators must avoid a de facto "don't ask, don't tell" policy. Oftentimes educators do not want to tell parents that their child is eligible to receive costly related services; however, when parents discover this on their own, school officials may face even more costly due process hearings and litigation. Thus, educators should explain everything that parents need to know about the education of their children. Educators are also responsible for making specific recommendations to parents regarding placement. School officials, rather than parents, are responsible to determine which of several placements might be appropriate for a child.

2. *Listen with patience and understanding.* Educators will benefit from listening to parents as they develop IEPs for special education students. Listening to parents with patience and understanding will have a dual effect: It will enable educators to develop appropriate IEPs while sending the unspoken message that parental input is welcomed. The ensuing rapport that develops may come in handy if parents and educators later disagree over special education matters.

3. *Provide parents with the information that they need.* Research shows that when parents find out that their child has a disability, they are interested in obtaining information to learn about the disability. Educators would be wise to direct parents to local support groups to further their understanding of their child's disability and the special education process and provide the parents with understandable information about the disability and the special education process.

4. *Provide support.* In addition to directing parents to outside sources of information, educators should provide support through such mechanisms as resource centers, parent advocates, and community liaisons. These efforts will generate good will while enabling educators to help ensure the accuracy of the information that parents receive.

5. *Maintain accurate and up-to-date records.* Parents of special education students have a right to copies of the educational records of their children to refer to when a disagreement arises. Hence, educators must maintain up-to-date and accurate student records. Such records may prove invaluable if the disagreement results in a due process hearing or judicial action. Proper documentation is essential to proving that all proper procedures were followed.

6. *Pay careful attention to details.* Many IEPs contain extensive lists of accommodations and modifications for regular education settings that may be overlooked. If parents realize that something has been overlooked, a confrontation might arise. By paying careful attention to detail, conflicts can be eliminated before they can arise.

7. *Provide parents with honest and realistic expectations.* Too often parents may perceive special education as a tutorial service that will permit children to catch up quickly with their peers. Since the data indicate otherwise, from the outset educators need to discuss the possible outcomes of a special education placement with parents, such as the fact that a child may develop many functional life-skills but not earn a high school diploma. It is best to provide parents with information that will allow them to make a realistic assessment of the situation from the start. Parents who set too high expectations may later be disappointed and could blame school officials for the child's failure to meet those expectations. On the other hand, setting too low expectations may result in the child not achieving to his or her potential. Expectations must be realistic.

8. *Provide hope.* By the time most children are placed in special education, they have already experienced school failure. Consequently, parents are inundated with statements about what the child is unable to do. Once a child is placed in special education, educators should spend time explaining what the student is capable of and how these skills can serve as a foundation for the future.

9. *Involve parents as equal partners in the special education process.* Remember that parents are part of the solution, not part of the problem. Parents of special education students are sometimes unfortunately viewed as potential troublemakers who seek due process hearings and file lawsuits rather than as colleagues who can help address the needs of their children. Yet, educators should keep in mind that, relative to parents, they are transient in a child's life. With this in mind, school personnel should view parents as partners in the process of designing IEPs best suited to the needs of children with disabilities.

10. *Provide staff with in-service training to make sure they know and follow the rules.* Classroom teachers and principals interact with parents more than other educators. Thus, building-level personnel must comply with guidelines of the type presented here. However, they must be provided with training to ensure that they know and understand the myriad rules and regulations governing special education service delivery. Frequent in-service training should be provided to ensure that all staff know the rules, and adequate supervision must be provided to make sure that the rules are followed.

## CONCLUSION

Special education is governed primarily by two major statutes: Section 504 of the Rehabilitation Act and the IDEA. Section 504 is an antidiscrimination law rather than an affirmative action statute. Put another way, pursuant to Section 504, an individual must be otherwise qualified despite his or her disability before being afforded statutory protection. On the other hand, the IDEA requires school systems to take affirmative steps to provide each student with a disability with a FAPE. In addition to providing students with disabilities with a basic floor of opportunity, the IDEA contains an elaborate due process mechanism spelling out how children are to be identified, evaluated, and provided services.

# QUESTIONS TO PONDER

1. What reasonable accommodations has your school board provided for qualified students, staff, parents, and/or visitors pursuant to Section 504?

2. Does your school board rely on formal Section 504 plans in serving qualified students?

3. What proactive steps does your board have in place to meet the needs of children with disabilities and their parents, whether under Section 504 or the IDEA?

4. Does your school provide in-service education for all faculty and staff to better familiarize them with their legal obligations in meeting the needs of children under both Section 504 and the IDEA?

5. Do IEP teams in your district regularly complete functional behavioral assessments for all students with disabilities?

# QUESTIONS FOR DISCUSSION

1. Would a star athlete on a high school team who is also President of the National Honor Society and who lost sight in one eye as a result of an injury sustained in competition likely be entitled to special education under IDEA because of this injury?

2. Can special education students in Ohio be totally excluded from taking the state proficiency exams?

3. Under Section 504, is a public school likely to be required to make whatever accommodations are necessary for a student, regardless of their cost?

4. Between Section 504 and the IDEA, which protects the legal rights of a larger group of people?

5. Would the mother of a child with a disability who also had a physical disability have any recourse if she were unable to attend a meeting with her child's teacher because the meeting was in a classroom that was on the fourth floor of an old school building that did not have an elevator?

# ANSWERS TO QUESTIONS FOR DISCUSSION

1. Probably not. The injury in question is one that would probably require a Section 504 accommodation since the student is unlikely to need an IEP.

2. Whether a child can take a proficiency test depends on the contents of the child's IEP.

3. Because cost can be a defense under Section 504, it depends on the nature of the accommodation. Cost is not supposed to be a defense under the IDEA.

4. Since Section 504 has no age restrictions, it covers more people, including adults, than does the IDEA.

5. Such a parent could request, and school officials would have to provide, a reasonable accommodation under Section 504. Such an accommodation might simply require the teacher to conduct the meeting in a room that the parent could enter.

## NOTES

    1.    20 U.S.C. § 1400 *et seq.*

    2.    29 U.S.C. § 794. A third statute, the Americans with Disabilities Act (ADA), although similar to Section 504, is beyond the scope of this chapter. The ADA, 42 U.S.C. § 12101 et seq., was passed in 1990 to provide "a comprehensive national mandate for the elimination of discrimination against individuals with disabilities." 42 U.S.C. § 12101(b)(2). The ADA effectively extends the protections of Section 504 to the private sector but has implications for public entities such as schools.

    3.    Ohio's statutes on special education are located in Chapter 3323 of the Ohio Revised Code (O.R.C.).

    4.    347 U.S. 483 (1954).

    5.    *Id.* at 493.

    6.    S.B. Thomas & C.J. Russo, Special Education: Issues & Implications for the '90s (NOLPE 1995) at 4–5.

    7.    J. Ballard, B.A. Ramirez, & F.J. Weintraub. (1982). Special education in America: Its legal and governmental foundations. Reston, VA: Council for Exceptional Children at 2.

    8.    House Report No. 332, 94th Congress (1975) at 11.

    9.    334 F. Supp. 1257 (E.D. Pa. 1971) and 343 F. Supp. 279 (E.D. Pa. 1972).

    10.    348 F. Supp. 866 (D.D.C. 1972).

    11.    29 U.S.C. § 794(a).

    12.    34 C.F.R. § 104.

    13.    29 U.S.C. § 706(7)(B). The regulations further define physical or mental impairments as including:

(A) any physiological disorder or condition, cosmetic disfigurement, or anatomical loss affecting one or more of the following body systems: neurological; musculoskeletal; special sense organs; respiratory, including speech organs; cardiovascular; reproductive, digestive, genito-urinary; hemic and lymphatic; skin; and endocrine; or

(B) any mental or psychological disorder, such as mental retardation, organic brain syndrome, emotional or mental illness, and specific learning disorders. 45 C.F.R. § 84.3(j)(2)(i), 34 C.F.R. § 104(j)(2)(i).

Further, a note accompanying this list indicates that it merely provides examples of the types of impairments that are covered; it is not meant to be exhaustive.

    14.    An individual who is regarded as having an impairment has:

(A) a physical or mental impairment that does not substantially limit major life activities but that is treated by a recipient as constituting such a limitation; (B) a physical or mental impairment that substantially limits major life activities only as a result of the attitudes of others toward such impairment; or (C) none of the impairments…but is treated by a recipient as having such an impairment. 45 C.F.R. § 84.3(j)(2)(iv), 34 C.F.R. § 104.3(j)(2)(iv).

15.    45 C.F.R. § 84.3(k)(2).
16.    Sullivan v. Vallejo City Unified Sch. Dist., 731 F. Supp. 947 (E.D. Cal 1990).
17.    *Cf.* Irving Indep. Sch. Dist. v. Tatro, 468 U.S. 883 (1984); Cedar Rapids Community Sch. Dist. v. Garrett F., 526 U.S. 66 (1999). *See* notes 56–57 *infra* and accompanying text for a discussion of these cases.
18.    At the same time, at least one court has held that Section 504 does not require affirmative efforts to overcome a student's disability but only prohibits discrimination on the basis of the disability. *See* Lyons v. Smith, 829 F. Supp. 414 D.D.C. (1993).
19.    Southeastern Community College v. Davis, 442 U.S. 397, 410 (1979).
20.    *Id.* at 412.
21.    34 C.F.R. § 104.36.
22.    20 U.S.C. § 1400.
23.    20 U.S.C. § 1401(3) offers the following definition:

(3) Child with a disability—
  (A) In general
     The term "child with a disability" means a child—
        (i) with mental retardation, hearing impairments (including deafness), speech or language impairments, visual impairments (including blindness), serious emotional disturbance (hereinafter referred to as "emotional disturbance"), orthopedic impairments, autism, traumatic brain injury, other health impairments, or specific learning disabilities; and
        (ii) who, by reason thereof, needs special education and related services.
  (B) Child aged 3 through 9
   The term "child with a disability" for a child aged 3 through 9 may, at the discretion of the State and the local educational agency, include a child—
        (i) experiencing developmental delays, as defined by the State and as measured by appropriate diagnostic instruments and procedures, in one or more of the following areas: physical development, cognitive development, communication development, social or emotional development, or adaptive development; and
        (ii) who, by reason thereof, needs special education and related services.

24.    *Id.* § 1401(3)(A)(ii).
25.    20 U.S.C. § 1401(8). Free appropriate public education [reads]:

The term "free appropriate public education" means special education and related services that—
     (A) have been provided at public expense, under public supervision and direction, and without charge;
     (B) meet the standards of the State educational agency;
     (C) include an appropriate preschool, elementary, or secondary school education in the State involved; and
     (D) are provided in conformity with the individualized education program required under section 1414(d) of this title.

26.    20 U.S.C. §§ 1401(11), 1414(d), cf. O.R.C. § 3323.011.
27.    *Id.* § 1401(3)(A)(ii).

28.    34 C.F.R. § 300.8.

29.    458 U.S. 176 (1982).

30.    *Id.* at 200.

31.    Harrell v. Wilson County Sch., 293 S.E.2d 687 (N.C. Ct. App. 1982); Burke County Bd. of Educ. v. Denton, 895 F.2d 973 (4th Cir. 1990).

32.    Geis v. Bd. of Educ. of Parsippany-Troy Hills, 774 F.2d 575 (3d Cir. 1985).

33.    David D. v. Dartmouth Sch. Comm., 775 F.2d 411 (1st Cir. 1985); Roland M. v. Concord Sch. Comm., 910 F.2d 983 (1st Cir. 1990).

34.    Nelson v. Southfield Pub. Sch., 384 N.W.2d 423 (Mich. Ct. App. 1986); Barwacz v. Michigan Dep't of Educ., 681 F. Supp. 427 (W.D. Mich. 1988).

35.    Pink v. Mt. Diablo Unified Sch. Dist., 738 F. Supp. 345 (N.D. Cal. 1990).

36.    20 U.S.C. § 1401(a)(18)(B).

37.    Hall v. Vance County Bd. of Educ., 774 F.2d 629 (4th Cir. 1985); Carter v. Florence County Sch. Dist. Four, 950 F.2d 156 (4th Cir. 1991), *aff'd on other grounds sub nom.* Florence County Sch. Dist. Four v. Carter, 510 U.S. 7 (1993).

38.    Board of Educ. of East Windsor Reg'l Sch. Dist. v. Diamond, 808 F.2d 987 (3d Cir. 1986); Polk v. Susquehanna Intermediate Unit 16, 853 F.2d 171 (3d Cir. 1988).

39.    Chris C. v. Gwinnett County Sch. Dist., 780 F. Supp. 804 (N.D. Ga. 1991).

40.    J.S.K. v. Hendry County Sch. Bd., 941 F.2d 1563 (11th Cir. 1991).

41.    20 U.S.C. § 1412(5)(A).

42.    Oberti v. Board of Educ. of the Borough of Clementon Sch. Dist., 995 F.2d 1204 (3d Cir. 1993); Sacramento City Unified Sch. Dist. Bd. of Educ. v. Rachel H., 14 F.3d 1398 (9th Cir. 1994).

43.    *Id.* Rachel H.

44.    *See, e.g.,* Clyde K. v. Puyallup Sch. Dist. No. 3, 35 F.3d 1396 (9th Cir. 1994); Capistrano Unified Sch. Dist. v. Wartenberg, 59 F.3d 884 (9th Cir. 1995).

45.    34 C.F.R. § 300.551(a).

46.    *See, e.g.,* Colin K. v. Schmidt, 715 F.2d 1 (1st Cir. 1983).

47.    Gladys J. v. Pearland Indep. Sch. Dist., 520 F. Supp. 869 (S.D. Tex. 1981).

48.    Chris D. v. Montgomery County Bd. of Educ., 743 F. Supp. 1524 (M.D. Ala. 1990).

49.    Abrahamson v. Hershman, 701 F.2d F.2d F.2d 223 (1st Cir. 1983).

50.    Parks v. Pavkovic, 753 F.2d 1397 (7th Cir. 1985).

51.    McKenzie v. Jefferson, EHLR 554:338 (D.D.C. 1983).

52.    It is worth noting that Ohio law requires school boards to provide all children, including those with disabilities, with an academic year of not less than 182 days. O.R.C. § 3313.48.

53.    Armstrong v. Kline, 476 F. Supp. 583 (E.D. Pa. 1979), *rem'd sub nom.* Battle v. Commonwealth of Pa., 629 F.2d 269 (3d Cir. 1980), *on rem'd* 513 F. Supp. 425 (E.D. Pa. 1981).

54.    Anderson v. Thompson, 658 F.2d 1205 (7th Cir. 1981).

55.    20 U.S.C. § 1401(a)(22). The IDEA specifically lists developmental, supportive, or corrective services such as transportation, speech pathology, audiology, psychological services, physical therapy, occupational therapy, recreation (including therapeutic recreation), social work services, counseling services (including rehabilitation counseling), medical services (for diagnostic or evaluative purposes only), and early identification and assessment as related services.

56.    Irving Indep. Sch. Dist. v. Tatro, 468 U.S. 883 (1984).

57.    526 U.S. 66 (1999). For a full discussion of this case, *see* C.J. Russo (1999). "*Cedar Rapids Community School District v. Garret F.:* School Districts Must Pay for Nursing Services Under the IDEA." *School Business Affairs, Vol. 65, No. 6,* 35–38.

58.    20 U.S.C. § 1401(a)(1).

59.    20 U.S.C. § 1401(a)(2).

60.    20 U.S.C. § 1401(a)(2).

61.    34 C.F.R. § 300 *et seq.*

62.    Oberti v. Board of Educ. of the Borough of Clementon Sch. Dist., 995 F.2d 1204 (3d Cir. 1993).

63.    20 U.S.C. § 1401(1) and 34 C.F.R. § 300.5.

64.    20 U.S.C. § 1401(2) and 34 C.F.R. § 300.6.

65.    R. Julnes & S. Brown, The legal mandate to provide assistive technology in special education programming. 82 Educ. L. Rep. 737 (1993).

66.    34 C.F.R. § 300.346.

67.    34 C.F.R. § 300.308.

68.    34 C.F.R. § 300.308.

69.    *Supra* n. 67 at 12540.

70.    O.R.C. §§ 33.0710–331.0711.

71.    O.R.C. § 33.0711(C)(1).

72.    20 U.S.C. § 1412(a)(17) and 34 C.F.R. § 300.138.

73.    Debra P. v. Turlington, 730 F.2d 1405 (11th Cir. 1984). *See also Anderson v. Banks,* 520 F. Supp. 472 (S.D. Ga. 1981), *modified,* 540 F. Supp. 761 (S.D. Ga. 1982), *appeal dismissed sub. nom.,* Johnson v. Sikes, 730 F.2d 644 (11th Cir. 1984) (upholding the use of the California Achievement Test [CAT] where school officials were able to provide empirical data to support a claim of instructional validity in a district that had operated under de jure segregation); Board of Educ. of Northport-East Northport Union Free Sch. Dist. v. Ambach, 458 N.Y.S.2d 680 (N.Y. App. Div. 1982) (upholding minimum competency testing without having to prove instructional validity because, unlike *Debra P.* and *Anderson,* no prior de jure race discrimination occurred).

74.    Debra P. v. Turlington, 730 F.2d 1405 (11th Cir. 1984).

75.    Debra P. (striking down testing on the basis that thirteen-month notice was insufficient) *Id.;* but see Brookhart v. Illinois State Bd. of Educ., 697 F.2d 179 (7th Cir. 1983) (although unwilling to define adequate notice in terms of a specific number of years, the court ruled that by changing a diploma requirement and by providing only one and one-half years notice for students to prepare for a minimum competency test, school officials deprived failing students of both property and liberty rights; further, the court stipulated that the school board must ensure that students with disabilities be exposed to most of the test material or show that a well-informed decision was made not to pursue an MCT-based program); Anderson v. Banks, 520 F. Supp. 472 (S.D. Ga. 1981), *modified* 540 F. Supp. 761 (S.D. Ga. 1982) (wherein a twenty-four month notice was found to be sufficient due to the presumed general applicability of the CAT, the availability of remedial alternatives, and the ease of coordinating activities in a single district).

76.    According to Ohio law, a child with a disability who has completed his or her IEP is entitled to a high school diploma. O.R.C. § 3313.61(A)(1).

77.    Brookhart v. Illinois State Bd. of Educ., 697 F.2d 179 (7th Cir. 1983).

78. 28 I.D.E.L.R. 1002, O.C.R. 1998.

79. 20 U.S.C. § 1415(e)(2).

80. *See, e.g.,* Marvin H. v. Austin Indep. Sch. Dist., 714 F.2d 1348 (5th Cir. 1983).

81. *See, e.g.,* Ft. Zumwalt Sch. Dist. v. Missouri State Bd. of Educ., 865 F. Supp. 604 (E.D. Mo. 1994).

82. For a discussion of this topic, *see* C.J. Russo & A.G. Osborne (2000). "Recent Developments in the USA: Damages in Special Education." *Education and the Law, Vol. 12, No. 4,* 297–302.

83. *See, e.g.,* W.B. v. Matula, 67 F.3d 484 (3d Cir. 1995); Whitehead v. School Dist. for Hillsborough County, 918 F. Supp. 1515 (M.D. Fla. 1996).

84. Burlington Sch. Comm. v. Department of Educ., Commonwealth of Mass., 471 U.S. 359 (1985).

85. Florence County Sch. Dist. Four v. Carter, 510 U.S. 7 (1993).

86. Courts have ordered boards to reimburse parents for the costs of counseling or psychotherapy where they succeeded in proving that the services were necessary for their children to benefit from special education. *See, e.g.,* Gary A. v. New Trier High Sch. Dist. No. 203, 796 F.2d 940 (7th Cir. 1986); Straube v. Florida Union Free Sch. Dist., 801 F. Supp. 1164 (S.D.N.Y. 1992).

87. *See, e.g.,* Lester H. v. Gilhool, 916 F.2d 865 (3d Cir. 1990); Todd D. v. Andrews, 933 F.2d 1576 (11th Cir. 1991); Manchester Sch. Dist. v. Christopher B., 807 F. Supp. 860 (D.N.H. 1992).

88. *See, e.g.,* Valerie J. v. Derry Cooperative Sch. Dist., 771 F. Supp. 483 (D.N.H. 1991); Big Beaver Falls Area Sch. Dist. v. Jackson, 624 A.2d 806 [861] (Pa. Commw. Ct. 1993).

89. *See, e.g.,* Pihl v. Massachusetts Dep't of Educ., 9 F.3d 184 (1st Cir. 1993); Jones v. Schneider, 896 F. Supp. 488 (D.V.I. 1995).

90. Smith v. Robinson, 468 U.S. 992 (1984).

91. 20 U.S.C. § 1415(e)(4)(B).

92. *See, e.g.,* Verginia M.C. v. Corrigan-Camden Indep. Sch. Dist., 909 F. Supp. 1023 (E.D. Tex. 1995).

93. Howie v. Tippecanoe Sch. Corp., 734 F. Supp. 1485 (N.D. Ind. 1990).

94. Beard v. Teska, 31 F.3d 942 (10th Cir. 1994).

95. Mr. D. v. Glocester Sch. Comm., 711 F. Supp. 66 (D.R.I. 1989); Hall v. Detroit Pub. Sch., 823 F. Supp. 1377 (E.D. Mich. 1993).

96. For a lengthier discussion of discipline, *see* C.J. Russo & A.G. Osborne (2000). "An American Dilemma: Disciplining Students with Disabilities." *Education Law Journal, Vol. 1, No. 1,* 13–20.

97. Those procedures were spelled out in Goss v. Lopez, 419 U.S. 565 (1975).

98. *See, e.g.,* S-1 v. Turlington, 635 F.2d 342 (5th Cir. 1981).

99. 484 U.S. 305 (1988).

100. 34 C.F.R. § 300.519(a).

101. 34 C.F.R. § 300.519(b).

102. 34 C.F.R. § 300.520(a)(2).

103. 20 U.S.C. § 1415(k)(1) and 34 C.F.R. § 300.520.

104. 34 C.F.R. § 300.520(a)(2).

105. 34 C.F.R. § 300.520(b)(1)(I).

106. 34 C.F.R. § 300.520(b)(1)(ii).

107.   34 C.F.R. § 300.526(a).
108.   34 C.F.R. § 300.526(b).
109.   34 C.F.R. § 300.526(c).
110.   20 U.S.C. § 1415(k)(2), 34 C.F.R. § 300.521, and 34 C.F.R. § 300.528.
111.   34 C.F.R. § 300.521(a).
112.   34 C.F.R. § 300.521(c).
113.   34 C.F.R. § 300.522(b)(1).
114.   34 C.F.R. § 300.522(b)(2).
115.   20 U.S.C. § 1415(k)(4).
116.   34 C.F.R. § 300.523(b).
117.   34 C.F.R. § 300.523(a)(2).
118.   34 C.F.R. § 300.523(c)(1).
119.   34 C.F.R. § 300.523(c)(2).
120.   34 C.F.R. § 300.523(f).
121.   20 U.S.C. § 1415(k)(5) and 34 C.F.R. § 300.524.
122.   34 C.F.R. § 300.525.
123.   Commonwealth of Virginia Dep't of Educ. v. Riley, 106 F.3d 559 (4th Cir. 1997).
124.   20 U.S.C. § 1412(a)(1)(A).
125.   34 C.F.R. § 300.121(d)(2)(i).
126.   34 C.F.R. § 300.121(d).
127.   34 C.F.R. § 300.121(d)(1).
128.   20 U.S.C. § 1415(k)(1)(B).
129.   20 U.S.C. § 1415(k)(8).
130.   34 C.F.R. § 300.527(b).
131.   34 C.F.R. § 300.527(d).
132.   34 C.F.R. § 300.527(d)(2)(i).
133.   34 C.F.R. § 300.527(d)(2)(ii).
134.   34 C.F.R. § 300.527(d)(2)(iii).
135.   20 U.S.C. § 1415(k)(9) and 34 C.F.R. § 300.529.
136.   34 C.F.R. § 300.529(b)(1).
137.   20 U.S.C. § 1232(g).

# Chapter 4

# The Nature of
# Diverse Populations

*Beverly A. Tillman and Carolyn Talbert Johnson*

## INTRODUCTION

In developing this chapter on the nature of diverse special education populations, we considered the following standards for educational administrators as reflected in the *Interstate School Leaders Licensure Consortium (ISLLC): Standards for School Leaders* (Council of Chief State School Officers, 1996):

Standard 1: A school administrator is an educational leader who promotes the success of all students by facilitating the development, articulation, implementation, and stewardship of a vision of learning that is shared and supported by the school community. (p. 10)

Standard 2: A school administrator is an educational leader who promotes the success of all students by advocating, nurturing, and sustaining a school culture and instructional program conducive to student learning and staff professional growth. (p. 12)

Standard 3: A school administrator is an educational leader who promotes the success of all students by ensuring management of the organization, operations, and resources for a safe, efficient, and effective learning environment. (p. 14)

Standard 4: A school administrator is an educational leader who promotes the success of all students by collaborating with families and community members, responding to diverse community interests and needs, and mobilizing community resources. (p. 16)

Standard 5: A school administrator is an educational leader who promotes the success of all students by acting with integrity, fairness, and in an ethical manner. (p. 18)

Standard 6: A school administrator is an educational leader who promotes the success of all students by understanding, responding to, and influencing the larger political, social, economic, legal, and cultural context. (p. 20)

As we present information on the nature of special needs populations, we do so with these administrative standards in mind because they have a direct bearing upon the development and implementation of equitable educational environments for students with disabilities and other exceptionalities. We will address some particular administrator standards and related dispositions where appropriate throughout this chapter to highlight aspects of the administrator's role in special education programming. Readers who desire a fuller description of the standards for school leaders, including specific knowledge, dispositions, and performance criteria, are advised to review the ISLLC standards in depth.

## SPECIAL NEEDS: CHARACTERISTICS AND CONCERNS

In this section, we will provide a brief overview of the identifying characteristics, eligibility criteria, and incidence for each of the major special needs conditions. We will also discuss some of the key issues that educational administrators and classroom educators should keep in mind for each area of exceptionality. It is important to note that any condition of disability may occur on a continuum ranging from mild, to moderate, severe, or profound. Once an individual is believed to have a special need, and if prereferral intervention strategies have been unsuccessful, the student is usually referred for a formal multifactored evaluation (MFE). This multifactored, or diagnostic, assessment must be conducted under the guidelines outlined in the Individuals with Disabilities Education Act and may only be implemented with the consent of the student's parents or guardians (IDEA, 1997). The MFE typically addresses three broad areas of functioning: intellectual assessment; assessment of academic achievement; and specialized, in-depth assessment of the area of special concern. An individualized education plan (IEP) is then developed for all identified special needs students.

Students who do not qualify for special education services under IDEA may receive services under Section 504 if it is determined that they need special support in order to learn successfully. In those instances a 504 plan may be developed (Lewis & Doorlag, 1999; Smith, Polloway, Patton, & Dowdy, 2001). Section 504 is a civil rights law that prohibits discrimination against individuals with disabilities in programs that receive federal funds, such as public schools (Friend & Bursuck, 2002). (See Chapter 3 for greater detail.)

Although services for special needs students may take place in a variety of environments, from general education classrooms to specialized classrooms or programs, the emphasis in recent years has been on education in the least restrictive environment (LRE) as outlined in IDEA. The term LRE has typically denoted the setting that best meets the student's learning needs while providing opportunities to learn with typically developing peers to the extent possible. However, the setting alone does not ensure that appropriate interventions and services will be provided. It is more important to focus on the nature of the instructional practices utilized with special needs students and the resulting outcomes of those strategies (Kavale & Forness, 1996).

## Disabilities Covered under IDEA

According to IDEA '97,

The term "child with a disability" means a child (i) with mental retardation, hearing impairments (including deafness), speech or language impairments, visual impairments (including blindness), serious emotional disturbance (hereinafter referred to as "emotional disturbance"), orthopedic impairments, autism, traumatic brain injury, other health impairments, or specific learning disabilities; and (ii) who, by reason thereof, needs special education and related services. (p. 5)

## SPECIFIC LEARNING DISABILITIES (SLD)

### Introduction

Learning disabilities are complex phenomena (Bender, 2001). Children with specific learning disabilities form a very heterogeneous group. One must consider that these students represent a highly variable and complex set of characteristics and needs, and as such they represent a substantial challenge to educators and administrators. Therefore, any discussion regarding the general characteristics of children and youth with learning disabilities and their demonstration of such characteristics should be viewed as tentative. Today, addressing specific learning disabilities represents the largest single program for persons with disabilities in the U.S. Individuals with learning disabilities usually have normal or near normal intelligence, although learning disabilities can occur at all intelligence levels. Individuals with specific learning disabilities, however, achieve at unexpectedly low levels in some basic skills areas such as reading and mathematics. They may also experience social difficulties as well.

A report from the U.S. Department of Education (1997) shows that in the 1995–1996 school year, 2,597,231 (51.2%) of the students with disabilities between the ages of 6 and 22 were learning disabled. The report also shows that approximately four boys are identified to every girl.

## Identification and Eligibility

Physicians interested in brain injury in children did the initial studies of children later described as having specific learning disabilities. Terms such as minimal brain dysfunction (MBD), brain damage, central process dysfunction, and language delay have been utilized to describe these children. Unfortunately, separate definitions were also offered to explain each term (Smith et. al., 2001). The term specific learning disabilities was first adopted publicly in 1963 at a meeting of parents and professionals. Kirk (1962) developed the generic term learning disabilities in an effort to unite the field, which was torn between individuals promoting different theories regarding underachievement. The definition of learning disabilities (LD) retained in IDEA (1997), states:

"Specific learning disability" means a disorder in one or more of the basic psychological processes involved in understanding or in using language, spoken or written, spelling or doing mathematical calculations. The term includes such conditions as perceptual handicaps, brain injury, minimal brain dysfunction, dyslexia, and developmental aphasia. The term does not include children who have learning problems which are primarily the results of visual, hearing, or motor handicaps, of mental retardation, or emotional disturbance, or of environmental, cultural, or economic disadvantage. (USOE, 1977, p. 65083)

When the U.S. Office of Education (1977) published the criteria for identifying students with LD, the processing component was not included in the requirements, and the language and academic problems were described within the context of a discrepancy factor. The literature suggests several causes, primarily hereditary factors and trauma experienced prior to birth (e.g., mother's use of alcohol, cigarettes, or other drugs), during birth (e.g., prolonged labor, anoxia, prematurity), and after birth (e.g., high fever, encephalitis, meningitis) (Smith et al., 2001).

Children with learning disabilities are primarily described as having deficits in academic achievement (reading, writing, and mathematics) or language (listening or speaking). Additionally, Lerner (2000) reports that students with learning and behavior disabilities may have trouble organizing and interpreting oral and visual information despite adequate hearing and visual skills. Some of these children may experience problems with dyslexia, a severe form of reading difficulty. Or they may exhibit dyscalculia—the most widely used term for disabilities in learning and using mathematics. In general, dyscalculia means inability to calculate

(Hallahan, Kauffman, & Lloyd, 1996). It is not surprising that students who have difficulties with oral language and reading may also have difficulties with writing, such as dysgraphia, which refers to partial ability (or inability) to remember how to make certain alphabet or arithmetic symbols in handwriting and is usually associated with dyslexia. Children with learning disabilities may have difficulties in other areas, such as social interaction and emotional maturity; attention and hyperactivity; memory, cognition, and metacognition; motor skills; and perceptual abilities.

### Key Issues

*a. Educational Intervention*   Educators must be cognizant of developing appropriate classroom accommodations as they address the individualized needs of students with learning disabilities. Accommodations relevant to the student's cognitive, academic, and language deficits should be adopted, as well as a strategy to develop the student's positive self-esteem. Assistive technology is an excellent resource for improving the confidence level and strengthening the academic skills of these students. The ultimate goal is to ensure that these individuals can successfully transition into inclusive settings.

In terms of administrative standards, ISLLC Standard 1 is relevant here, as it addresses the identification and clarification of barriers to student learning, and use of a variety of instructional methodologies and resources, including technology in supporting student learning.

*b. Use of Medications*   A variety of stimulants and other medications, such as Ritalin, Cylert, and Dexedrine, are routinely prescribed to students with learning disabilities to increase attention span and ability to focus. (See the section on attention deficit hyperactivity disorder for a more extensive discussion of the use of medications with special needs students.)

ISLLC Standard 5 is of particular significance here, as it addresses the importance of bringing ethical principles to the decision making process. The administrator is in a key position to address the ethical concerns raised by the use of medications with students and to promote the use of alternative interventions whenever possible to enhance student learning and address student behaviors.

## EMOTIONAL AND BEHAVIORAL DISORDERS (E/BD)

### Introduction

Emotional and behavioral problems may result in serious and life-threatening actions (e.g., aggressiveness, violence, attempted suicide), and they have long been associated with acting-out and disruptive behaviors in classrooms (i.e., discipline problems) (Smith et al., 2001). Therefore, educators typically spend exorbitant amounts of time on student behavior and not enough time on instruction. Students who experience emotional and behavioral disorders receive a variety of labels, including severe behavior handicaps (SBH) and seriously emotionally disturbed (SED), which is the title utilized by the Individuals with Disabilities Education Act. The Council for Children with Behavior Disorders (CCBD) of the Council for Exceptional Children refers to the group as emotionally and behaviorally disordered (E/BD) because it believes the term better describes the students served in special education programs. Causes of emotional and behavioral disorders range from biological (genetic inheritance, biochemical abnormalities), to behavioral (environmental events), to sociological-ecological (role assignment or labeling, cultural transmission).

### Identification and Eligibility

Compared to children classified as having learning disabilities and mental retardation, the category of emotional and behavioral disorders represents a much smaller number of children. The 20th Report to Congress on the Implementation of the Individuals with Disabilities Education Act noted that 0.92% of the school population were served as EB/D during the 1996–1997 school year (U.S. Department of Education, 1998). Although there is no single definition that is universally accepted, the one currently utilized by the federal government for this category and adopted in most state departments of education includes: a condition exhibiting one or more of the following characteristics over a sustained period of time and to a marked extent, which adversely affects educational performance:

a. An inability to learn which cannot be explained by intellectual, sensory, or health factors;

b. An inability to build or maintain satisfactory relationships with peers and teachers;

c. Inappropriate types of behavior or feelings under normal circumstances;

d. A general pervasive mood of unhappiness or depression; or

e. A tendency to develop physical symptoms or fears associated with personal or school problems.

The EB/D category also includes children who are schizophrenic. Children who are socially maladjusted are not included unless it is determined that they are seriously emotionally disturbed (*Federal Register, 42,* p. 42478).

Children with emotional and behavioral disabilities may also fall into various classification systems or subgroups, including conduct disorder, socialized aggression, attention problems and immaturity, anxiety or withdrawal, psychotic behavior, and motor excess. Due to the aberrant behavioral repertoires of these individuals, educators and administrators have difficulty retaining these individuals within school settings. Problems typically associated with children with emotional and behavioral disorders include aggressive and acting-out behaviors (Grosenick, George, George, & Lewis, 1991); social deficits (Smith & Luckasson, 1995); irresponsibility (Smith, Finn, & Dowdy, 1993); hyperactivity and distractibility; lying, cheating, and stealing (Rosenberg, Wilson, Maheady, & Sindelar, 1992); academic deficits (Bullock, 1992); and anxiety (Kauffman, Lloyd, Baker, & Riedel, 1995). It is not uncommon for these children to experience a history of failure and frustration within school settings due to their unique behavioral concerns, which ultimately may lead to suspensions, expulsions, and programming into punishment facilities such as juvenile court rather than treatment.

Once students are identified as possibly having emotional and behavioral problems, they are referred for formal assessments to determine their eligibility for special education programs and to ascertain appropriate intervention strategies. Kaplan (1996) identifies clinical interviews, observations, rating scales, personality tests, and neurological examinations as methods for obtaining information for assessment and determining eligibility. Epstein (1999) has identified a new approach to the assessment of students with emotional and behavioral disabilities that uses strength-based assessment, which focuses on the student and his or her family

as individuals with unique talents, skills, and life events as well as with specific unmet needs. Strength-based assessment recognizes that even the most challenged children in stressed families have strengths, competencies, and resources that can be built on in developing a treatment approach. (p. x)

Functional behavioral assessment (FBA) provides a consideration of specific behaviors and behavioral patterns set within an environmental context. It has been defined as "an analysis of the contingencies responsible for behavioral problems" (Malott, Whaley, & Malott, 1997, p. 433). Functional behavioral assessment assists teachers in obtaining extensive information regarding the psychological factors (e.g., sickness or allergies, fatigue), classroom environment (e.g., high noise level, frequent disruptions), and curriculum and instructional concerns (e.g., few opportunities for making choices, activities that are too difficult). After discerning the appropriate variables, educators can then devise interventions that target a specific variable to alter a particular behavior (Foster-Johnson & Dunlap, 1993).

*Key Issues*

*a. Manifestation Determination*    A key issue in the field of emotional and behavioral disorders is the relationship between the disability itself and the behaviors that are exhibited in school (Smith et al., 2001). Under the IDEA guidelines, educators must determine whether the behavior in question functions as a manifestation of the student's disability. The key question is whether the student's disability impairs his or her ability to control the behavior or interferes with his or her awareness of the possible disciplinary action that may follow. The function of the guidelines is neither to exclude students with disabilities from normal disciplinary routines, nor to prevent educators from taking action to redirect troublesome behavior. However, the purpose is to prevent the misapplication of disciplinary actions that, considering the student's particular disability, may fail to achieve the desired objective and further exacerbate the problem (Buck, Polloway, Kirkpatrick, Patton, & Fad, 1999). To complete a manifestation determination for students with emotional and behavioral disabilities (as well as for other disabilities), school personnel should carefully consider the disability and the nature of the behavior to determine a possible relationship. Educators must remember that each student is different and that every strategy may not work with every student.

Teaching students with emotional and behavioral disabilities is clearly a challenging task for educators. These students require interventions that focus on social skills instruction, classroom management accommodations, preventive discipline, and positive behavioral support. These strategies are vital in the maintenance of socially appropriate behaviors for students with emotional and behavioral disabilities.

Standard 2 of ISLLC incorporates strategies for promoting and assessing student growth and development in all areas, not just academic. Additionally, preparing students to be contributing members of society is listed among the dispositions for Standard 2. Certainly, developing self-control over one's behavior and operating within the boundaries of good citizenship are central to the education of students with emotional and behavioral disabilities.

*b. Overrepresentation of Minorities in Emotional and Behavioral Disability Programs*    The literature supports that African American males are placed in emotional and behavioral disability classes three and one-half times more often than African American females (CEC, 2001), and children of lower socioeconomic backgrounds are also overrepresented in SED classes. The disproportionate placement of African Americans and other minority groups has also been attributed to the assessment process. Special education placement is at least partially predicated on test scores (Gollnick & Chinn, 1998). The problem of overrepresentation of minority students in special education may be due to cultural bias in testing and placing procedures. (See the cultural diversity section in this chapter for more information.)

Standard 5 of ISLLC, with its emphasis on professional codes of ethics, speaks to the need for administrators to use their influence to ensure that all students are treated fairly and in an ethical manner. If administrators are knowledgeable about the historical context that has contributed to disproportionate numbers of minority students being relegated to special education classrooms and programs, they will be better able to identify how similar factors might be operating within their particular school setting and take steps to address these inequities.

*c. Use of Medications*   A variety of stimulants and other medications, such as Ritalin, Cylert, and Dexedrine, are routinely prescribed to students with emotional and behavioral disabilities to intervene upon their aberrant behavioral repertoires. (See the section on attention deficit hyperactivity disorder for a more extensive discussion of the use of medications with special needs students.)

As noted in the previous section, Standard 5 on the ethical behavior of educational leaders is most relevant here. Medications should not be viewed as the first or only step in the treatment of behavioral challenges, but as a possible intervention to be used if other interventions prove to be ineffective. They may also be used in conjunction with other strategies, if a qualified medical professional advises that course of treatment.

## MENTAL RETARDATION (MR) AND SEVERE OR MULTIPLE DISABILITIES (MH)

### Introduction

The term mental retardation (MR) is typically used to describe below-average functioning that not only affects an individual's intellectual, or cognitive, abilities, but also impacts the individual's ability to function in nearly every aspect of everyday life. Persons with mental retardation learn at slower rates than the general population and typically manifest skills and behaviors of a younger age-level. A number of other terms are used to describe mental retardation, including intellectually impaired and educationally handicapped (Smith, Polloway, Patton, & Dowdy, 2001).

The incidence of mental retardation is believed to occur in approximately 2–3% of the population, although there is variation from one state to another, largely due to differing interpretations of the condition. Prevalence figures indicate that approximately 12% of identified special education students have diagnoses of MR, with mild retardation accounting for 85% to 90% of these students (Lewis & Doorlag, 1999).

Causes of mental retardation include genetic disorders such as Down syndrome, various pre- and postnatal biological factors, exposure to toxic substances (e.g., lead), and environmental disadvantages that limit appropriate stimulation and experiences.

## Identification and Eligibility

Grossman (1983), on behalf of the American Association on Mental Deficiency, provided the following definition for the condition known as mental retardation: "Mental retardation refers to significantly subaverage general intellectual functioning resulting in or associated with concurrent impairments in adaptive behavior and manifested during the developmental period" (p. 11).

All three of these indicators must be present in order for a formal diagnosis of mental retardation to be made. The average score on a test of intellectual ability is 100. The IQ score for persons with mental retardation is 70–75 or below. Mental retardation ranges in severity from mild, to moderate, severe, or profound, and the condition must occur during the developmental period between conception and the age of 18.

As the level of severity of cognitive impairment increases, so too does the likelihood that severe, multiple disabilities will be manifested in other areas (Lewis & Doorlag, 1999). Students with multiple disabilities typically have a primary diagnosis of mental retardation, coupled with diagnoses of communication disorders, sensory impairments, or physical and health challenges including medically fragile conditions. (See other sections of this chapter for a discussion of these conditions.)

Historically, professionals in the field have focused primarily on measured IQ scores when referring to individuals with mental retardation. This perspective provides a limited, and not altogether useful, frame of reference for educators and family members who desire to facilitate learning. In an effort to view mental retardation more functionally, the American Association on Mental Retardation (1992) defined impairment in adaptive skills as difficulty in two or more of the following areas: communication, self-care, home living, social skills, community use, self-direction, health and safety, functional academics, leisure, and work. As the level of severity of mental retardation increases, the concurrent impairments in adaptive behavior, or life skills, increase as well. Thus, persons in the mild range of mental retardation may struggle academically in school settings but may adapt reasonably well to the demands of the real world, both during their school years and into adulthood. These individuals may require only intermittent or limited supports. Those with more significant levels of impairment typically require substantial assistance with many of the tasks of everyday living, delineated by the AAMR as extensive or pervasive levels of support (Luckasson et al., 1992).

*Key Issues*

*a. Overrepresentation of Students from Minority Cultures*   As noted previously, the vast majority of students with mental retardation have a mild form of the condition. Of those students diagnosed with mild retardation, the majority tend to be persons of minority cultures and those of lower socioeconomic levels. According to Oswald, Coutinho, Best, and Singh (1999), African American students are 2.4 times more likely to be identified as having mild mental retardation than their non-African American peers. Administrators should ensure that information regarding the potential for cultural bias be shared with their faculty. A climate of high expectations for all students should be encouraged.

While ISLLC Standard 5 is crucial here in terms of ethical decision making on behalf of students, all six of the ISLLC standards address the educability of all students and sensitivity to cultural concerns. Standard 1 also stresses a willingness among effective school leaders to continuously examine their own assumptions, beliefs, and practices.

*b. Adaptive Behavior and Life Skills Instruction*   One of the key indicators of mental retardation is difficulty with functional areas of life skills, known as adaptive behavior. Thus, a major focus of the curriculum for these students is habilitation; that is, helping them acquire competence in skills necessary for successful adulthood. This includes skills for daily living, for responsible citizenship, and for career education. Educators, parents, and community members must work closely together in order to reinforce learning across environments.

ISLLC Standard 6 may be of particular relevance here, since public perceptions of the value and contributions of persons with mental retardation are often low. Educational leaders can influence community perceptions and public policies regarding persons with mental retardation by modeling equitable treatment and ensuring that effective instructional programs are provided to these students.

*c. Transition Issues*   Because persons with mental retardation have difficulty transferring or generalizing knowledge and skills learned in one setting to other settings, it is important to provide relevant experiences for the application of life skills. Transition assumes a greater portion of the curriculum as students' age and grade levels increase, and it should be carefully planned. The 1997 reauthorization of IDEA specifies that, beginning at age 14, the IEP should include a statement of the transition service needs of the student, including curricular considerations (e.g., career and vocational education) and appropriate interagency responsibilities or linkages.

Again, Standard 6 of ISLLC is addressed as educators prepare students with mental retardation and developmental disabilities to become contributing members of society.

*d. Severe and Multiple Disabilities*    In addition to the concerns and strategies already noted, it is important to attend to the needs of students with severe and multiple disabilities in terms of accessibility, augmentative devices, and the need for additional team members and support personnel (e.g., speech-language, physical, and occupational therapists; paraprofessionals; nurse attendants) in the learning environment. Respect for the human dignity of all learners is paramount, regardless of the extent of disability.

Here, ISLLC Standard 4 is significant because of its emphasis on collaborating with families and community members and mobilizing appropriate community resources to support students who need an extensive array of specialized services. In many cases, the families of students with severe and multiple disabilities are involved with a number of agencies in addition to the school. Administrators can play an important role in supporting the coordination of efforts across agencies on behalf of students with these low-incidence conditions.

## COMMUNICATION DISORDERS

### Introduction

Human interaction and socialization rely heavily upon the ability to communicate. When communication is impaired, it can affect one's overall quality of life. For school-age students, the two areas most often affected are academics and socialization. Adults with communication disabilities may not only experience difficulties in social situations, but these conditions can affect their career options as well. Communication disorders are among the most common disabilities. Speech and language impairments are found in approximately 2% of the total school-age population according to the most recent statistics from the U.S. Department of Education (1998). The number is even higher, approximately 5%, when students with some other primary disability are included. In these cases, the communication disability is a secondary condition, but the students still receive services from a speech-language pathologist. Overall, about 20% of students with identified disabilities have impairments in speech or language skills. Students whose primary disability is in the area of communication are typically served in general education classrooms. In fact, the general educator is often the person who observes difficulties students may be experiencing in speech and language development and who initiates subsequent referrals for diagnostic evaluation.

### Identification and Eligibility

There are two types of communication disorders—those affecting language and those affecting speech. According to the American Speech-

Language-Hearing Association (ASHA, 1982), there are clear distinctions between the two conditions:

A language disorder is characterized by an inability to use the symbols of language through (a) proper use of words and their meanings, (b) appropriate grammatical patterns, and (c) proper use of speech sounds. A speech disorder is characterized by difficulty in (a) producing speech sounds (articulation), (b) maintaining speech rhythm (fluent speech), and (c) controlling voice production (voice). (p. 1)

Speech disorders result from both organic and functional factors. Organic factors account for only about 1% of communication disorders. Cleft palate, dental abnormalities, injuries or trauma to the larynx, hearing loss, brain damage, and neurological impairments fall under this category of causes. The remaining 99% of communication disorders are functional, and thus are greatly influenced by environmental factors. Children who grow up in non-stimulating environments where they have few good speech and language models, or where they have limited opportunities to communicate, are at risk for communication disorders.

Language disorders may affect receptive or expressive language functions. Receptive language includes receiving and understanding language, while expressive language focuses on using language symbols to formulate and convey thoughts (Lewis & Doorlag, 1999; Smith et al., 2001). Assessment typically targets four important aspects of language:

1. semantics—the meaningful aspects of language
2. syntax—the grammatical aspects of language and the sequencing of ideas
3. phonology—the sound system of language
4. pragmatics—the use of language in context.

A speech-language pathologist conducts the most in-depth assessment of speech and language function. It is important to also assess the student's hearing to determine whether this is a factor in the student's communication challenges. The school nurse, audiologist, and other medical specialists (e.g., an ear, nose, and throat specialist) are instrumental in hearing assessments. Educators and parents also contribute important information about the individual's speech and language in school, home, and community environments.

### Key Issues

a. *Cultural and Linguistic Differences*  Smith, Polloway, Patton, and Dowdy (2001) emphasize the need to distinguish between language differences and language disorders. They note that cultural differences exist in a variety of areas including the use of eye contact, facial expressions, gestures, and physical space between speakers. Educators should familiarize themselves with the cultural backgrounds of their students and the communities in which they teach and be careful to not interpret cultural and language differences as deficits.

As our society becomes increasingly diverse, school leaders must be informed about and model respect for persons of various cultures. All of the ISLLC standards address this issue. Additionally, however, specific resources and programs, such as English as a Second Language (ESL) may be needed to support the learning of these students. If resources are limited for these kinds of programs, administrators may find that they can utilize community resources in the interim while school-based programs are being created. The language departments of local colleges and universities, for example, might have student interns who could serve as translators for students whose first language is not English. The benefits are obvious to the student in the P–12 setting. However, there are also benefits in terms of experience for the university students, and the potential for collaborative relationships between P–12 and post-secondary institutions of learning. ISLLC Standard 4 is relevant here.

*b. Augmentative Communication*   With recent technological advances, numerous assistive devices are available to persons with communication challenges. The speech-language pathologist, in consultation with parents, educators, and other relevant team members, determines the level of aid and type of device needed by a particular student. Community resources may be available to provide devices for students of limited financial means. "Low-tech" supports may be useful as well (e.g., Boardmaker images), and in order to support various learning experiences of students with communication challenges, the educator or language therapist can also individualize these resources.

Technology, as outlined in ISLLC Standard 2, plays a vital role in promoting student learning. When available technology has the potential to open new worlds of learning and communication to students with language impairments, school leaders have an obligation to support its use.


## AUTISM

### Introduction

Autism is a severe, pervasive, developmental disability that affects language, social interactions, behavior, and sensory integration. It is typically manifested by 3 years of age but is difficult to diagnose because many of the characteristics are similar to other conditions (e.g., communication impairments, behavior disorders, mental retardation).

Autism is a low-incidence condition that affects approximately .05% of the school-age population (U.S. Department of Education, 1999). Asperger's syndrome is a condition associated with autism that results in similar characteristics. However, students with Asperger's syndrome generally function at a higher level cognitively and communicatively.

## Identification and Eligibility

IDEA defines autism as a developmental disability that primarily results in significant deficits in verbal and non-verbal communication and social interactions (IDEA, 1997). It is difficult to diagnose because symptoms often mirror other conditions. There is no widespread agreement about the causes of autism and, in most cases, no specific cause can be confirmed (Koegel & Koegel, 1995).

In addition to medical assessments, areas assessed include communication, social skills, behavior, and responses to various sensory stimuli. The assessment team consists of medical professionals, speech-language pathologists, and psychologists, with educators and family members contributing valuable insights about the student's daily functioning in various environments.

### Key Issues

*a. Communication Skills* Communication skills are an important area of emphasis for students with autism. Techniques to focus on these skills may include the use of augmentative communication devices; linking visual prompts with verbal or written information; and facilitated communication, which is a controversial technique wherein an adult physically assists the student in communicating using an augmentative device.

As noted earlier, if specialized technology or the use of additional staff members such as language therapists are needed, administrators can assist greatly in obtaining these resources. ISLLC Standard 3 discusses the administrator's role in managing the organization, operations, and resources of the school to create an appropriate and effective learning environment for students.

*b. Structure and Consistency* A high degree of structure and consistency in the learning environment is important for students with autism and Asperger's syndrome. However, while consistent routines and schedules are important, attempts should be made to gradually introduce changes into the daily schedule to help students with these conditions to acquire greater flexibility. This is important given the flexibility needed to function successfully in community and work settings.

*c. Behavioral Interventions* Behavioral interventions should be utilized to reduce repetitive behaviors displayed by individuals with autism and to encourage social interactions with others. Every school district has policies relative to disciplinary procedures; in addition, the guidelines of the

Individuals with Disabilities Education Act must be followed. Standard 2 of ISLLC would require that school leaders be familiar with the best practices in this area, and Standard 5 reinforces the need for ethical implementation of any interventions utilized with students.

## SENSORY IMPAIRMENTS—VISUAL IMPAIRMENTS (VI) AND HEARING IMPAIRMENTS (HI)

### Introduction

Sensory impairments are conditions that, even after corrective measures are taken (e.g., medical interventions such as medications and surgery; therapeutic interventions; and the use of devices such as eyeglasses and hearing aids), result in significant limitations in vision and hearing. The good news is that, with medical and technological advancements, many conditions previously thought to be uncorrectable can be treated successfully. With cornea transplants and cochlear implants, for example, many individuals have had their vision or hearing restored. In other cases, the conditions persist, and special considerations may be needed in educational environments. The majority of students with vision and hearing impairments are able to participate in general education with appropriate accommodations. However, those with severe sensory impairments or multiple disabilities may require specialized programming. Sensory impairments can interfere with the acquisition of communication skills, considering the role that visual and auditory stimuli play in the transmission of ideas. Thus, early identification and treatment of sensory impairments is of the utmost importance.

In the school-age population, only 0.1% of students are classified as visually impaired, while only 0.11% of students are classified as hearing impaired for special education purposes (U.S. Department of Education, 1998). These figures do not include students with severe and multiple disabilities, because their primary diagnosis may be some other condition, such as mental retardation. (See also the mental retardation section in this chapter.)

Causes of visual and hearing impairments may be congenital, as a result of genetic or developmental anomalies; or adventitious, resulting from accidents, trauma, prematurity, anoxia, drugs, or allergies (Lewis & Doorlag, 1999). In recent years, some risk factors for sensory impairments have been identified and reduced.

### Identification and Eligibility

Both vision and hearing impairments can be mild, moderate, severe, or profound. Visual and hearing impairments are broad terms used to describe the range of impairments. The level of sensory impairment is reflected in some of the terminology used. Students with hearing impairments may be deaf or hard of hearing. Deafness means that the hearing loss is so profound that the auditory channel is not functional and alternate avenues of communication must be used. Hard of hearing means that there is some degree of hearing loss, and augmentative devices may be needed, but the auditory channel serves as the primary vehicle for acquiring communication skills (Diefendorf, 1996). Hearing impairments may be conductive, wherein the transmission of sound through the ear canal is disrupted; or sensorineural, in which there is impairment to the auditory nerve that transmits sound impulses to the brain.

In the same vein, vision impairments are classified as blind or partially sighted. Students who must use Braille are considered to be educationally blind. Other students are classified as legally blind if their visual acuity is 20/200 or less in the stronger eye with correction, or if their field of vision is restricted to an arc of 20 degrees or less. Many students with legal blindness have functional use of residual vision with appropriate supports.

Assessment and diagnosis involves a number of team members ranging from appropriate medical personnel (e.g., physicians, audiologists, school nurses) to educators and parents who contribute useful information about the student's functioning in school, home, and community environments. Identification may begin when an educator or family member suspects that the individual is experiencing difficulty seeing or hearing, or during routine screenings by the school nurse or physician. If screenings indicate that there may be a problem, more in-depth diagnostic procedures are then implemented if the parent or guardian consents. These assessment procedures include not only a thorough diagnosis of the medical aspects of the condition, but identify corrective measures that may be implemented or special accommodations that may be needed.

### Key Issues

a. *Functional Use of Residual Vision or Hearing*   Educators and parents should be alert to signs of vision or hearing loss and the ways that the individual uses vision or hearing to function on a daily basis.

b. *Classroom Accommodations and Technological Supports*   Preferential seating, enlarged print materials, Braille materials, and technological supports (e.g., amplification systems, computer hardware and software) may be needed. Various organizations (e.g., state library for the blind, special education regional resource centers) may be able to assist in providing these materials if the family, school, or district has limited resources.

The technological advances of recent years have resulted in a number of resources for persons with vision and hearing disabilities. Pursuant to ISLLC Standards 3 and 4, school leaders should manage existing school resources in a manner that ensures that they are utilized with students who need them most and, when necessary, school leaders must go beyond the school's existing resources to obtain community resources as needed.

## PHYSICAL AND HEALTH IMPAIRMENTS

### Introduction

Students with physical and health impairments often have conditions that interfere with their mobility, strength, stamina, or endurance. Gollnick and Chinn (1998) assert that the range and variety of conditions related to physical and health impairments are numerous (e.g., asthma, cerebral palsy, traumatic brain injury, diabetes, epilepsy, spina bifida, medical fragility, etc.). Some of these conditions are obvious, while others are invisible; some conditions evoke continuous symptoms, while other conditions symptoms are intermittent. Most are long-term in nature.

Physical and health impairments can have grave, little, or no effect on school performance. Since these students are an extremely heterogeneous group with a wide variety of conditions and diseases, some may require no special adaptations, while others may require modifications to the physical environment or adaptations to instructional activities. (See also the sensory impairments section in this chapter.)

Students whose primary disabilities are physical, functional, or medical in nature represent less than 1% of the school-age population. They comprise about 4% of students with identified disabilities (Lewis & Doorlag, 1999). Students with severe and multiple disabilities may exhibit medical and physical impairments as well, but they are not included in these statistics because their primary disability may be another condition, such as mental retardation. (See also the mental retardation section in this chapter.)

### Identification and Eligibility

Some physical and health impairments are congenital (i.e., present at birth), while others are acquired after birth through disease or injury. Students with physical and health challenges undergo extensive medical diagnostic procedures. However, simply knowing a student's health and medical condition may not provide adequate information for educators working with the student. It is important that team members discuss the impact of the physical or health impairment on learning, social interactions, and life skills. An important focus of assessment of these students is the identification of types of supports needed to enable students to function as fully as possible in typical environments.

Students with physical limitations typically qualify for special education services under the IDEA category of orthopedically impaired, while students with medical and health conditions receive services under the other IDEA category of health impaired (U.S. Department of Education,

1998). Students with physical and health challenges are generally able to participate in general education classrooms for most or part of the school day. Specialized services may focus primarily on physical therapy, occupational therapy, and adapted physical education. Some students may receive assistance in a resource room if those services are deemed necessary by the instructional team.

## Key Issues

a. *Supportive Environment*   We live in a society that places great emphasis on physical beauty and attractiveness. Individuals who deviate significantly from physical norms are subject to possible ridicule and rejection. Administrators must acknowledge the capabilities of these individuals while affirming their efforts as they are included in general education classrooms. Ultimately, the goal is to ensure that these students are able to obtain a quality of life that will allow them to function successfully within the general education setting.

ISLLC Standard 5 is of particular importance, because a climate of acceptance must be modeled for these students with obvious disabilities. This certainly relates to ethical behavior on the part of the school leader and others in the setting. Standard 1 should be considered as well. The administrator's vision for the school setting should be one in which all students are accepted and treated in a humane manner.

b. *Accessibility*   Accessibility of the learning environment should be a top priority for educators and administrators. This includes self-care and safety considerations (e.g., ramps, accessible bathrooms, transportation via wheelchair lift buses, etc.) as well as accommodations within the learning environment (e.g., adapted and augmentative devices, accessible classroom arrangements, etc.). Occupational and physical therapists and other medical professionals should be consulted for guidance in these areas.

The needs of students with physical and health challenges often cause the facility itself, as well as the instructional strategies and resources used in the classroom, to be examined and modified. Administrators need to be both practical and creative in making learning environments accessible to students with physical and health needs. Standard 3 of ISLLC, with its emphasis on management of the operations and resources to create safe, efficient, and effective learning environments applies here.

c. *Maintaining Continuity in the Educational Program During Extended Absences*   Students with certain types of health or medical conditions may be absent from school frequently or for extended periods. Some school districts provide home-based instruction during periods of lengthy absences or hospitalization. There are variations in these guidelines from state to state and between school districts, so it is important for administrators to become familiar with their particular circumstances. At a minimum, the educator should make every effort to keep the student connected with the class through regular communication with the student and family, by sending home work packets for the student to complete if he or she is able, and even through video- and audiotaped classroom experiences.

*d. Fostering Independence*    For students with physical challenges, it is important that educators and families foster as much independence as possible. Physical and occupational therapists can be of great assistance in determining the student's capabilities, assessing important aspects of the physical environment, and designing or acquiring necessary augmentative and assistive devices.

Collaborating with families is stressed in ISLLC Standard 4, as is mobilizing community resources. In order for students with physical and health challenges to live as independently as possible, school leaders should monitor the programming that is provided to their students to ensure that appropriate resources and supports are provided.

## STUDENTS WITH SPECIAL NEEDS NOT COVERED UNDER IDEA

The students in this section do not qualify for special education assistance under IDEA '97 guidelines, but they may experience various challenges in home, school, or community settings that may hinder learning or contribute to the development of behavior challenges. If educators are aware of and sensitive to these conditions, they may be able to effectively address at least some of the needs of these students in classroom and school environments.

## ATTENTION DEFICIT/HYPERACTIVITY DISORDER (ADHD)

### Introduction

Attention deficit/hyperactivity disorder is an invisible disability in that no unique physical characteristics and no definitive psychological or physiological tests differentiate these children from others. Unfortunately, the disabling behaviors associated with attention deficit hyperactivity disorder may be misunderstood and misinterpreted as a sign of being lazy, unorganized, and even disrespectful. The condition can be recognized only through specific behavioral manifestations that may occur during the learning process. Since it is a developmental disability, attention deficit/ hyperactivity disorder becomes apparent before the age of seven; however, in as many as two-thirds of the cases, it continues to cause problems in adulthood. Attention deficit/hyperactivity disorder may have an impact on success in both academic and nonacademic areas, and it occurs across all cultural, racial, and socioeconomic groups. Fowler (1992) notes that it can affect children and adults with all levels of intelligence.

Estimates of the prevalence of attention deficit/hyperactivity disorder in school-age children range from a conservative figure of less than 2% to a more liberal figure of 30%; however, 3%–5% is more probable (American Psychiatric Association, 1994).

## Identification and Eligibility

A variety of terms have been used to identify this disorder, however the current term attention deficit/hyperactivity disorder is most common. The terminology stems from the *Diagnostic and Statistical Manual of Mental Disorders* DSM-IV (4th ed.) (American Psychiatric Association, 1994). Attention deficit/hyperactivity disorder primarily refers to deficits in attention and behaviors characterized by impulsivity and hyperactivity. The DSM-IV classifies attention deficit/hyperactivity disorder as a disruptive disorder expressed in persistent patterns of inappropriate degrees of attention or hyperactivity-impulsivity. It is easy to identify these students within the classroom due to the features of the disorder. Barkely (1991) identifies the features as limited sustained attention or persistence of attention to tasks, reduced impulse control, excessive take-irrelevant activity, deficient rule following, and greater than normal variability during task performance. These behaviors occur to a marked degree and at a higher frequency for students with attention deficit/hyperactivity disorder.

Several theories have been developed to explain the primary causes of attention deficit/hyperactivity disorder. Most professionals agree that attention deficit/hyperactivity disorder is a neurologically-based condition; therefore, the causes might be related to neuroanatomical (related to bone structure), neurochemical (related to a chemical imbalance in the brain), neurophysiological (related to brain function), or any combination of these causes. For the majority of students, the precise cause of the problem may never be understood.

Attention deficit/hyperactivity disorder is more common than any other child psychiatric disorder (Nolan, Volpe, Gadow, & Sprafkin, 1999). Initially the assessment and diagnosis of attention deficit/hyperactivity disorder were considered the responsibility of psychologists, psychiatrists, and physicians. However, the mandates of Section 504 of PL 93–112 as interpreted by the assistant secretary for civil rights (Cantu, 1993) charged public education personnel with responsibility for this assessment. If a school district suspects that a child has a disability that impedes their ability to perform major life activities, such as learning, the district is required to provide an assessment. Attention deficit/hyperactivity disorder is often covered under Section 504, which allows the identified child to be eligible for both assessment and services.

*Key Issues*

*a. Cultural and Linguistic Diversity.*   When attention deficit/hyperactivity disorder coexists with cultural and linguistic diversity, it presents a special set of challenges to the educator. Educators must be cognizant of and sensitive to the needs of this diverse group of students. Problems are exacerbated for these children because of a set of confounding factors (e.g., impoverished background, chaotic home environment, behavioral dilemmas), which can only assist in increased frustration for educators. Therefore, these educators require an arsenal of skills to intervene effectively with the academic and behavioral concerns of these students.

School leaders who are knowledgeable about the external (community-based) factors affecting these students (ISLLC Standards 4 and 6), will have sufficient context for guiding the decision-making process relative to culturally diverse students with attention deficit/hyperactivity disorder. Of course, the commitment to be advocates for the ethical and humane treatment of these students is of great concern here also (ISLLC Standard 5).

*b. Use of Stimulants*   The most commonly prescribed drugs for attention deficit/hyperactivity disorder include Ritalin, Cylert, and Dexedrine, which are stimulants that have serious side effects (e.g., loss of appetite, depression, insomnia, nausea, hypersensitivity, drowsiness, anorexia). Ritalin is the most common stimulant used to treat attention deficit/hyperactivity disorder (Bramlett, Nelson, & Reeves, 1997). Ritalin is prescribed to 93% of all children receiving stimulants. Far too often, stimulants are being used as diagnostic tools for children with attention deficit/hyperactivity disorder. To support this contention, a survey of primary care physicians indicated that the majority relied on observation in their offices and positive response to stimulants as positive diagnoses of attention deficit/hyperactivity disorder (Hyman et al., 1998). A significant danger of stimulant prescriptions is the addictive nature of the substance, and the tendency to abuse it. Educators must be cautious in advising parents regarding the use of stimulants with attention deficit/hyperactivity disorder. It is disconcerting to note that experts estimate that over 2 million children in the U.S. are currently taking psychiatric medication (Sachs, 2000).

As noted in a previous section, Standard 5 on the ethical behavior of educational leaders is most relevant here. Medications should not be viewed as the first or only step in the treatment of behavioral challenges, but as a possible intervention to be used if other interventions prove to be ineffective. They may also be used in conjunction with other strategies, if a qualified medical professional advises that course of treatment.

*c. Educational Interventions*   Interventions that are utilized with the student with attention deficit/hyperactivity disorder should include providing classroom accommodations, managing the classroom environment—utilizing both group and individual contingency plans, physical management, and modifying teacher behavior. Student-regulated strategies (e.g., self-management, self-recording) should be adopted to ensure that students are assuming responsibility for their actions. Interventions that address social skills instruction should also be implemented, thus ensuring that these students will have the requisite skills to be included in general education settings. A key concern is that educators accept these individuals, thus valuing and affirming their contributions to the classroom settings, without utilizing aversive, reactive techniques.

School leaders should be informed about, and when necessary, be advocates of appropriate interventions and instructional supports for these students in accordance with ISLLC Standard 2. Given the large numbers of students identified with attention deficit/hyperactivity disorder in many schools, it may be necessary also for the administrator to provide professional development sessions on the characteristics of these students and effective instructional and behavioral strategies for them (ISLLC Standard 2).

## STUDENTS FROM DIVERSE CULTURAL BACKGROUNDS

### Introduction

Educators are faced with an overwhelming challenge to prepare students from diverse cultural backgrounds to live in a rapidly changing society and a world in which some groups have greater societal benefits than others because of race, ethnicity, gender, class, language, religion, ability, or age (Gollnick & Chinn, 1998). Demographic data confirm that by the year 2002 about 40% of the nation's school age population will be students of color, and students of color already represent 70% of the student population in the 20 largest school districts (Irvine & Armento, 2001). The authors further note that the school failure of culturally diverse students, particularly African American, Hispanic, and Native American students, is well documented. Educators' practices, attitudes, and values, along with the schools' policies and practices, can assist in promoting students' learning, especially for students who have not benefited from their schooling. A critical examination of these practices is warranted.

### Identification and Eligibility

A new study by Harvard University (Council for Exceptional Children [CEC], 2001) substantiates the contention that a disproportionately high number of students from diverse backgrounds are placed in special education. The following information supports that premise:

1. African American children are already three times (2.88) as likely as White children to be identified as mentally retarded, 1.9 times as likely to be identified as emotionally disturbed, and nearly 1.3 times as likely to be identified as having a learning disability.

2. American Indian children are 1.3 times as likely as White children to be identified as mentally retarded, 1.24 times as likely to be identified as emotionally disturbed, and 1.50 times as likely to be identified as having a learning disability.

3. Conversely, Asian Pacific and Hispanic children may be underrepresented in special education.

4. Asian Pacific children are .54 times as likely as White children to be identified as mentally retarded, .29 times as likely to be identified as emotionally disturbed, and 3.0 times as likely to be identified as having a learning disability.

5. Hispanic children are nearly .77 times as likely as White children to be identified as mentally retarded, .74 times as likely to be identified as emotionally disturbed, and 1.7 times as likely to be identified as having a learning disability. (CEC, 2001)

Students from diverse backgrounds in special education are less likely to be returned to general education classes than White children. Additionally, assignment to special education may increase a student's chances of failing high-stakes testing for promotion to the next grade level or graduation.

The Civil Rights Project's papers also note that inappropriate placement in special education limits the success of children from diverse cultures after graduation. Additionally, the report notes that, among secondary aged youth with disabilities, about 75% of African American students, as compared to 47% of White students, are not employed two years out of school. Ultimately, inappropriate assignment to special education or failure to provide appropriate support services to students from diverse cultures may contribute to the large number of adults from diverse cultures in our justice system (CEC, 2001).

### Key Issues

*a. National Attention to the Problem*   In response to the high percentage of students from diverse backgrounds in special education, the Council for Exceptional Children (CEC), which has long been concerned about this issue, passed a resolution calling for the U.S. Department of Education to create a task force to study disproportionate representation, recommend ways to improve practice, and disseminate the information. The CEC also charged the Office of Civil Rights with the tasks of monitoring the disproportionate number of diverse students in special education and, if necessary, changing local policies to conform to those of the task force's recommendations (CEC, 2001).

This recommendation falls under ISLLC Standard 6 in terms of advocacy in the larger political, social, legal, and cultural context. At the school level, administrators should ensure that they model respect for cultural diversity and that they and their staff have knowledge of effective approaches to educating these students. ISLLC Standards 1, 2, and 4 have particular relevance here.

*b. Recognizing and Valuing Individuals First*   It is critical to remember that children are first and foremost children; therefore, schools must focus on adapting either the classroom organization or the curriculum and instruction to meet the instructional needs of individual students. Russo and Talbert-Johnson (1997) suggest that cultural and ethnic differences should be embraced and valued in all forms and degrees as reflections of the contributions that different groups of Americans have made to our society.

As noted above, a number of the ISLLC standards emphasize visioning a supportive learning environment for all students (Standard 1), creating effective learning environments for all students (Standard 2), managing organizational resources to support the learning of all students (Standard 3), responding to diverse community interests and needs (Standard 4), acting with integrity, fairness, and ethical behavior (Standard 5), and understanding, responding to, and shaping the larger context to promote the success of all students (Standard 6).

## STUDENTS AT RISK FOR SCHOOL FAILURE

### Introduction

The term "at risk" is used to describe a multitude of factors that may interfere with school attendance and learning, and that may contribute to inappropriate behaviors and dangerous decisions that could further impede learning. These factors include, but are not limited to, poverty; homelessness; single-parent homes; delinquency; physical, sexual, or emotional abuse; substance abuse; adolescent pregnancy; depression; or suicidal thoughts. Hodgkinson (1993) noted that more than 23% of students in the United States were living below the poverty line and were at risk of failing to achieve their potential. As Haberman (1995) states, "For the children and youth in poverty from diverse cultural backgrounds who attend urban schools, having effective teachers is a matter of life and death" (p. 1).

### Identification and Eligibility

Poverty and homelessness are associated with various types of disabilities, including mild mental retardation, specific learning disabilities, and physical and health problems. There is also a relationship between cultural and linguistic diversity and these risk factors. Due to these factors, it is imperative that educators closely attend to the unique needs of these students. Lewis and Doorlag (1999) posit that:

only 25 states have formally defined the at-risk population. These definitions vary widely, from limiting the group to only dropouts to associating students at-risk with a long list of adverse social and economic conditions (e.g., truancy, absenteeism, drug abuse, delinquency, teenage pregnancy, poverty). (p. 438)

*Key Issues*

*a. Academic Failure*   Educators should strive to hold high expectations for these students and then create supportive learning communities to ensure academic success.

ISLLC Standard 1 promotes a vision of all students as successful learners, regardless of their backgrounds or perceived abilities. This belief is crucial if administrators are going to work to overcome the challenges facing students who are at risk for school failure.

*b. Behavioral Dilemmas*   Keeping students engaged academically in meaningful learning experiences can reduce the incidence of discipline referrals, suspensions, and expulsions. It is vital that educators assist these students in becoming resilient individuals in the face of their challenging circumstances.

As noted earlier, administrators must act with integrity, fairness, and in an ethical manner when dealing with student behaviors (ISLLC Standard 5). Additionally, Standards 4 and 6 of the ISLLC standards stress the importance of school leaders understanding the world beyond school with which these students must cope with on a daily basis, and the need to work in conjunction with families and community members to support the students, and to lead by example or by advocacy for these students in local, state, regional, or national arenas.

*c. School and Community Resources*   Educators should be aware of school and community resources available to support students at risk and their families (e.g., counseling and psychological services, social service agencies, etc.).

This again relates to ISLLC Standards 4 and 6, with emphasis on bringing the entire community's resources to bear on the challenges faced by our youth today.

## RECOMMENDATIONS FOR ADMINISTRATORS

Administrators play a key role in the education of diverse learners, both those served under the Individuals with Disabilities Education Act, and those who may not qualify for special education services, but who nonetheless need alternative strategies and resources in order to learn effectively. Administrators are ultimately responsible for ensuring that all students receive the resources necessary to be educated, contributing members of society. Historically, however, educational administrators have not been adequately prepared for this role. Educational leadership programs have only recently begun including coursework in the areas of special education law and curriculum (Huefner, 2000; Murphy & Forsyth, 1999; Smith & Piele, 1997; Weishaar & Borsa, 2001). The Interstate School Leaders Licensure Consortium (Council of Chief, 1996) created six standards for administrators that emphasize effective learning for all students at all levels. These standards for school leaders stress a comprehensive framework that encompasses visioning effective environments for all students (Standard 1), developing effective learning environments based upon best practices (Standard 2), managing organizational resources to ensure that all students have opportunities to learn (Standard 3), collaborating with families and community members to understand more fully the factors that impact students and the resources available (Standard 4), leading by acting with integrity, fairness, and ethical behavior (Standard 5), and understanding, responding to, and influencing the larger political, social, economic, legal, and cultural context (Standard 6). These guidelines have tremendous potential to transform educational leadership. As the field of education continues to evolve into an increasingly complex endeavor, it is imperative that administrators at both the building and district levels gain a working knowledge of the field of special education, especially as it relates to implementing the provisions of the Individuals with Disabilities Education Act (IDEA), related federal legislation (e.g., Section 504 and ADA), and corresponding state guidelines. On a more personal level, educational leaders must be committed to creating optimum learning environments for *all* students whom it is their responsibility to serve.

## CASES

### Mulanas

Mulanas, a 16-year-old African American male, is being returned to Mrs. Kambon's classroom because of problems in the lunchroom. He typically does not behave well in unstructured settings (e.g., lunchroom; library). He often misbehaves and tries to be the clown of the class. He constantly seeks approval from his peers and will do just about anything to get their attention. Unfortunately, this is a pattern with Mulanas and Mrs. Kambon is concerned because he has already been suspended three times this year. On this particular occasion Mr. Wengate, the principal, brought Mulanas to the classroom. As he enters he states, "Mrs. Kambon, Mulanas was having a problem in the lunchroom and I would appreciate your finding out what the problem is. I have to take care of some other matters, and since he's in your special program, I felt it best to let you handle Mulunas's problem. I figure you understand these troubled youth better than I do; therefore, I'll let you handle your own behavior problems. After all, that is your job as the SBH teacher!" Mrs. Kambon was livid over the insensitive remarks provided by the principal and his inability to see that his comments were offensive to Mulanas.

## QUESTIONS FOR DISCUSSION: MULANAS

1. Communication skills must become part of an individual's repertoire of collaborative interaction skills. Administrators must articulate their disciplinary agendas to teachers in a collaborative dialogue, thus eliminating opportunities for misunderstandings or problems. How can administrators develop their own communication styles in ways that are beneficial to students, teachers, and other constituents in the learning process? In this case, how could Mr. Wengate have communicated with Mrs. Kambon in a more effective manner?

2. Effective discipline continues to be one of the main issues in education today. In the case of Mulanas, is there a clear disciplinary policy that is being followed? If not, what steps can Mr. Wengate take to develop an appropriate policy for the school? Are there special considerations that should be taken into account when students have been identified as having severe behavior disabilities and are receiving special services?

3. School personnel, including administrators, need to critically reflect upon their practice and in particular their personal attitudes and perceptions regarding diverse student populations. In what ways could Mr. Wengate's comments be offensive to Mulanas? What types of professional development opportunities may be available to Mr. Wengate to assist in his understanding of the behavioral repertoires of minority students, in particular African American males?

### Carly

Carly is a 14-year-old female student with moderate mental retardation and autism. She also displays severe aggressive behaviors that appeared around the time she entered puberty. Currently, Carly attends a high school program for students with multiple disabilities in a neighboring school district because her home district has only a few students with similar low-incidence conditions. Her life skills and behavioral needs necessitate individual assistance with most tasks, and close supervision throughout the school day. She can work in small groups or with the entire class only for brief periods with supervision. Working with Carly is intense, and the teacher and paraprofessional take turns working with her. The classroom staff consists of one teacher and one paraprofessional for eight students with multiple disabilities. Only the teacher has had training in the use of severe behavior intervention techniques. The paraprofessional is only in her second year in this position and has no formal preparation. Recently, a student in the class and the paraprofessional were injured during one of Carly's outbursts. After several such incidents, the building principal and special education supervisor for the district requested that Carly's home district provide a paraprofessional to assist in the multiple disabilities classroom. The neighboring school district complied with this request. However, this paraprofessional was inexperienced and untrained as well. Also, the superintendent of Carly's home district was adamant that the full-time paraprofessional work *only* with Carly since her salary was paid by Carly's school district.

## QUESTIONS FOR DISCUSSION: CARLY

1. Despite the increased number of students with special needs who are included in general education classrooms, students with moderate to intensive special needs (low incidence conditions) often require services in self contained special education classrooms, or, in severe cases, services in a specialized program apart from the general education school setting. In the case of Carly, how did the neighboring school districts pool their resources in order to meet her learning and behavioral needs?

2. When the disagreement arose regarding the use of the additional paraprofessional in the special education classroom, the collaboration between the two districts could have been derailed. How did the principal address the situation in an equitable manner, taking into account not only Carly's needs, but also the needs of everyone in this classroom for students with multiple disabilities? Should services needed for a student from a neighboring district be utilized exclusively for that student, or should the teacher, at her discretion, utilize the resources in a manner that takes into account the broader impact of that student's presence in the classroom? What kinds of communication skills are needed by administrators in order to maintain interdistrict agreements such as the one illustrated in the Carly case?

3. What professional development opportunities should be considered by the administrators relative to the severe behavior challenges presented by Carly? What other supports might the classroom staff need in this situation?

### Phil

Phil was the principal of a large high school that was developing a program for students with multiple disabilities. Although the school already provided services for students with mild special needs, such as specific learning disabilities, mild mental retardation, and some physical and health challenges such as muscular dystrophy, neither Phil nor most of his staff had knowledge or experience with students diagnosed with severe or multiple impairments. Prior to the end of the previous school year, Phil worked closely with the district's special education coordinator to prepare his faculty, staff, students, and himself for the new program. Staff meetings were used as a vehicle for disseminating accurate information about special needs populations. Respected colleagues with special education knowledge and expertise in the district provided the information in digestible chunks. General educators at the high school were encouraged to share appropriate information about special needs populations with their students prior to the end of the school year.

Meanwhile, an experienced special educator was recruited and hired to teach the new class for students with multiple disabilities. In one of her conversations with Phil about the program, he made the following comment: "Although I may lack in-depth knowledge about special needs students and programs, I believe that these students deserve a quality education and have a right to be here. I hired you because you are the expert. My job is to support you and obtain the resources you need to meet the learning needs of these students." On the first day of the school year, at the conclusion of his morning announcements over the school's PA system, Phil stated, "I'd like everyone to welcome the multiple disabilities class to our building this year. I want the teachers to take a few minutes to share with you some information about our students with multiple disabilities. They are a part of our school, and I expect them to be treated well here." Phil was true to his word, and he not only worked tirelessly to provide a variety of resources in collaboration with the district's special education coordinator and central administration, but he continued to cultivate a climate of acceptance within the school. Phil also developed a close relationship with the special needs students and began to actively pursue opportunities to learn more about special education students and programs.

Eventually, Phil left the principalship and became an assistant superintendent for student services in another school district, a position that included overseeing all special education services for the district. He is currently superintendent of a county educational services center which has, as one of its major responsibilities, provision of special education services and support personnel to school districts throughout the county. Phil is now something of an expert on special education himself!

This scenario is true. While not all educational administrators would emulate Phil's commitment to acquiring extensive knowledge of special education, his story illustrates key administrative dispositions that are needed in order to provide quality educational programs for students with special needs. First, he displayed an ethic of care and support for inclusion of the students. He believed that they had a fundamental right to be part of a learning community. Second, he participated in professional development opportunities to learn about special needs students and special education processes. Third, Phil realized that special needs students often require additional and unique resources due to their special learning challenges, and that it was his responsibility as the educational leader for the school to provide those resources, whatever they may be. This includes faculty and staff resources; instructional resources, including technology; and community resources. Fourth, he supported his faculty and staff by providing professional development opportunities, respecting their expertise, and participating in collaborative decision making on behalf of students.

## QUESTIONS FOR DISCUSSION: PHIL

1. Effective leadership, and in particular, planning and communication with all stakeholders, is an integral part of effective inclusive education programs. What planning and communication skills did Phil utilize to create a firm foundation upon which to build the new program for students with moderate to intensive special needs in his secondary building? Who are the stakeholders in this scenario?
2. What is the role of professional development in the case of Phil? Please respond in terms of professional development opportunities for the classroom staff, others in the school setting, and for administrators. How might Phil's own pursuit of professional development opportunities have contributed to the success of special education programs such as the one described here?
3. When the new special education program was created in Phil's school building, Phil admittedly had no professional knowledge or expertise in special education. What should be the minimum expectation relative to administrator knowledge of special education programming? How are these expectations reflected in the current standards for school leaders noted at the beginning of this chapter?

## GENERAL QUESTIONS FOR DISCUSSION

1. What professional development opportunities are available to prospective and practicing administrators relevant to diverse student populations, management and discipline concerns, as well as ethical, moral, and peace education dilemmas? How can administrators ensure that they become proactive agents of change in this pluralistic society?
2. What role(s) should administrators assume as team members in schoolwide collaborative problem solving relative to diverse learners? Identify specific IIS-LLC standards (e.g., knowledge, dispositions, and performances) that are vital to collaboration and consensus building.
3. Identify the key stakeholder groups that have an impact on the education of diverse learners. Describe the various ways that they directly or indirectly influence the education of special needs learners. How can administrators develop the communication and interpersonal skills needed to interact effectively with all stakeholders?

## REFERENCES

American Association on Mental Retardation. (1992). *Mental retardation: Definition, classification, and systems of supports* (9th ed.). Washington, DC: Author.

American Psychiatric Association. (1994). *Diagnostic and statistical manual of mental disorders (DSM-IV)* (5th ed.). Washington, DC: Author.

American Speech-Language-Hearing Association. (1982). Definitions: Communicative disorders and variations. *American Speech Language and Hearing Association Journal, 24,* 949–950.

Barkely, R. A. (1991). *Attention deficit/hyperactivity disorder: A clinical workbook.* New York: Guilford Press.

Bender, W. N. (2001). *Learning disabilities: Characteristics, identification, and teaching strategies* (3rd ed.). Boston: Allyn & Bacon.

Bramlett, R. K., Nelson, P., & Reeves, B. (1997). Stimulant treatment of elementary school children: Implications for school counselors. *Elementary School Guidance & Counseling, 31,* 243–249.

Buck, G. H., Polloway, E. A., Kirkpatrick, M. A., Patton, J. R., & Fad, K. (1999). *Developing behavioral intervention plans: A sequential approach.* Unpublished manuscript.

Bullock, L. (1992). *Exceptionalities in children and youth.* Boston: Allyn & Bacon.

Cantu, N. (1993). OCR clarifies evaluation requirements for ADD. *The Special Educator, 9*(1), 11–12.

Council of Chief State School Officers. (1996). *Interstate school leaders licensure consortium: Standards for school leaders.* Washington, DC: Author.

Council for Exceptional Children. (2001). New study verifies the disproportionate number of students from diverse backgrounds in special education. *Today, 7*(8), 7.

Diefendorf, A. O. (1996). Hearing loss and its effects. In F. N. Martin & J. G. Clark (Eds.), *Hearing care for children* (pp. 3–18). Boston: Allyn & Bacon.

Epstein, M. H. (1999). The development and the validation of a scale to assess the emotional and behavioral strengths of children-adolescents. *Remedial and Special Education, 20,* 258–262.

*Federal Register, 42,* 42478.

Foster-Johnson, L., & Dunlap, G. (1993). Using functional assessment to develop effective, individualized interventions for challenging behaviors. *Teaching Exceptional Children, 56,* 44–52.

Fowler, M. (1992). *C.H.A.D.D. educators' manual: An in-depth look at attention deficit disorder for an educational perspective.* Fairfax, VA: CASET Associates, Ltd.

Friend, M., & Bursuck, W. D. (2002). *Including students with special needs* (3rd ed.). Boston: Allyn & Bacon.

Gollnick, D. M., & Chinn, P. C. (1998). *Multicultural education in a pluralistic society* (5th ed.). Upper Saddle River, NJ: Merrill.

Grosenick, J. K., George, N. L., George, M. P., & Lewis, T. J. (1991). Public school services for behaviorally disordered students: Program practices in the 1980s. *Behavioral Disorders, 16,* 87–96.

Grossman, H. J. (Ed.). (1983). *Classification in mental retardation* (Rev. ed.). Washington, DC: American Association on Mental Retardation.

Haberman, M. (1995). *Star teachers of children of poverty.* West Lafayette, IN: Kappa Delta Pi.

Hallahan, D. P., Kauffman, J. M., & Lloyd, J. W. (1996). *Introduction to learning disabilities.* Boston: Allyn & Bacon.

Hodgkinson, H. (1993). American education: The good, the bad, and the task. *Phi Delta Kappan, 74*(8), 619–623.

Huefner, D. S. (2000). *Getting comfortable with special education law: A framework for working with children with disabilities.* Norword, MA: Christopher-Gordon Publishers, Inc.

Hyman, I. A., Wojtowicz, A., Lee, K. D., Haffner, M. E., Fiorello, C. A., Storlazzi, J.J., & Rosenfeld, J. (1998). School-based methylphenidate placebo protocols: Methodological and practical issues. *Journal of Learning Disabilities, 31*(6), 581–594.

Individuals with Disabilities Education Act. (1997). Washington, DC: U.S. Government Printing Office.

Irvine, J. J., & Armento, B. J. (2001). *Culturally responsive teaching: Lesson planning for elementary and middle grades.* San Francisco: McGraw Hill.

Kaplan, P. S. (1996). *Pathways for exceptional children: School, home, and culture.* St. Paul, MN: West Publishing.

Kauffman, J. M., Lloyd, J. W., Baker, J., & Riedel, T. M. (1995). Inclusion of all students with emotional or behavioral disorders: Let's think again. *Phi Delta Kappan, 76*(7), 542–546.

Kavale, A. A., & Forness, S. R. (1996). *Efficacy of special education and related services.* Washington, DC: American Association on Mental Retardation.

Kirk, S. A. (1962). *Educating exceptional children.* Boston: Houghton Mifflin.

Koegel, R. L., & Koegel, L. K. (1995). *Teaching children with autism.* Baltimore: Brookes.

Lerner, J. (2000). *Learning disabilities: Theories, diagnosis, and teaching strategies* (8th ed.). Boston: Houghton Mifflin.

Lewis, R. B., & Doorlag, D. H. (1999). *Teaching special students in general education classrooms* (5th ed.). Upper Saddle River, NJ: Merrill/Prentice-Hall.

Luckasson, R., Coulter, D., Polloway, E. A., Reiss, S., Schalock, R., Snell, M., Spitalnik, D., & Stark, J. (1992). *Mental retardation: Definition, classification, and systems of supports.* Washington, DC: American Association on Mental Retardation.

Malott, R. W., Whaley, D. L., & Malott, M. E. (1997). *Elementary principles of behavior* (3rd ed.). Upper Saddle River, NJ: Prentice-Hall.

Murphy, J., & Forsyth, P. B. (1999). *Educational administration: A decade of reform.* Thousand Oaks, CA: Corwin Press, Inc.

Nolan, E. E., Volpe, R. J., Gadow, K. D., & Sprafkin, J. (1999). Developmental, gender, and co-morbidity differences in clinically referred children with ADHD. *Journal of Emotional and Behavioral Disorders, 7*(1), 11–21.

Oswald, D. P., Coutinho, M. J., Best, A. M., & Singh, N. N. (1999). Ethnic representation in special education: The influence of school-related economic and demographic values. *The Journal of Special Education, 32*, 194–206.

Rosenberg, M. S., Wilson, R., Maheady, L., & Sindelar, P. (1992). *Educating students with behavior disorders.* Boston: Allyn & Bacon.

Russo, C. J., & Talbert-Johnson, C. (1997). The overrepresentation of African American children in special education: The resegregation of educational programming? *Education and Urban Society, 29*(2), 131–148.

Sachs, A. (2000, March 20). When pills make sense. *Time*, F12.

Smith, D. D., & Luckasson, R. (1995). Introduction to special education: Teaching in an age of challenge. Boston: Allyn & Bacon.

Smith, S. C., & Piele, P. K. (1997). *School leadership: Handbook for excellence.* Eugene, OR: ERIC Clearinghouse on Educational Management.

Smith, T. E. C., Finn, D. M., & Dowdy, C. A. (1993). *Teaching students with mild disabilities.* Ft Worth, TX: Harcourt Brace Jovanovich.

Smith, T. E. C., Polloway, E. A., Patton, J. R., & Dowdy, C. A. (2001). *Teaching students with special needs in inclusive settings.* Boston: Allyn & Bacon.

U.S. Department of Education. (1997). New report links fathers' involvement with children's success. *Community Update, 52,* 3.

U.S. Department of Education. (1998*). 20th annual report to Congress on the implementation of the Individuals with Disabilities Education Act.* Washington, DC: Author.

U.S. Department of Education. (1999). *The condition of education.* Washington, DC: Author.

U.S. Office of Education (USOE). (1977). Assistance to states for education of handicapped children: Procedures for evaluating specific learning disabilities. *Federal Register, 42,* 65082–65085.

Weishaar, M. K., & Borsa, J. C. (2001). *Inclusive educational administration: A case study approach.* Boston: McGraw-Hill.

# Chapter 5

# Curriculum Considerations

*Timothy E. Heron, Yvonne L. Goddard,*
*and Matthew J. Tincani*

Every profession—medicine, law, pharmacy, business—has developed, adopted, or adapted a set of assumptions, vocabulary, principles, procedures, and expectations that guide practice within the discipline. Such is the case in education as well. As a result of litigation, legislation, and changing procedures, more students than ever before receive special education services within the general education curriculum. Educational administrators intending to provide useful curriculum-based programs to students with special needs will need to be knowledgeable of these discipline-specific concepts, especially as they relate to curriculum.

There are several reasons for this imperative. First, the final regulations for the Individuals with Disabilities Education Act Amendments of 1997 (IDEA '97) provide that each general and special education teacher and service provider has access to the child's Individualized Education Program (IEP) and is informed of his or her specific teaching or instructional responsibilities under the IEP, and of the specific accommodations, modifications, and supports that must be provided for the child in accordance with the IEP (§ 300.340–300.350). Indeed IDEA '97 also mandates that students receiving special education services be exposed to the general education curriculum to the maximum extent possible.

Second, the data from the 21st Annual Report to Congress on the implementation of IDEA '97 (Policymaking Partnership, 1999) show that almost one half of America's 6 million students with disabilities are educated and spend an increasing portion of their day in general education classrooms.

Finally, a student with a disability integrated into the general education classroom may or may not extend the heterogeneity of the class. For instance, a student with attention deficit disorder (ADD) may require special accommodations with respect to materials, pace of instruction, or number of examples provided during instruction, thereby adding to the multiplicity of the class. However, a student with a specific learning disability (SLD) in math, who participates in the general education classroom for reading, may not require a single accommodation to learn the content, and the diversity of the class may not be extended (i.e., the range of students' abilities and the resulting curricular changes or modifications will not be changed by the addition of this student to the class). Hence, from a regulatory, actuarial, or instructional perspective, administrators will need to be well versed with curriculum more so than their counterparts from past years.

The purpose of this chapter is to (a) articulate key concepts in special education and show how these concepts bear directly on curriculum; (b) outline comprehensive curriculum considerations that enhance instruction, focusing primarily on environmental, teaching, and evaluation strategies; and (c) provide recommendations to administrators to strengthen curriculum delivery for special needs students.

## KEY CONCEPTS FOR EDUCATIONAL ADMINISTRATORS

It is beyond the scope of this chapter to enumerate every key concept that administrators should know regarding special education curriculum. Still, the six concepts that are shown in Table 5.1 are basic to that understanding as they enumerate the relationship to the curriculum, administrator considerations, and related references that underscore their importance.

### Definition of Special Education

The term *special education* means:

specially designed instruction, at no cost to parents, to meet the unique needs of a child with a disability, including—(A) instruction conducted in the classroom, in the home, in hospitals and institutions, and in other settings; and (B) instruction in physical education (Individuals with Disabilities Act Education Amendments of 1997 [IDEA '97] Sec. 602,[25]).

The essential components of this definition rest squarely on the terms *specially designed instruction* and *unique needs*, and the setting (school, home, physical education class). With respect to curriculum, an instructional practice is specially designed if it is based on assessment, codified in the IEP, and implemented in an accommodated manner so as to enhance the learning experience of the identified student. A curriculum would meet a student's unique needs in a similar fashion, adding the proviso that these needs are likely to change as the student grows older or changes settings (class to class or school to home). Finally the administrator must recognize that curricular goals established in the IEP must be addressed even if the student no longer attends the school (i.e., the student is placed on home instruction).

**Table 5.1**
**Relationship of Key Terms to Curriculum**

| Term | Relationship to Curriculum | Considerations for Administrators | Related References |
|---|---|---|---|
| Special Education | • Differing goals and objectives will necessitate different curricula, or implementation of that curricula, for each special needs student, depending on identified need. | • IEP should reflect different goals and objectives for each student.<br>• Annual reviews should show measurable progress towards goals and objectives. | • Heward (2000) Chapter 1<br>• IDEA '97 (Sec. 602, [25]) |
| Disability | • General education teachers will be expected to teach curriculum to students with a variety of disabilities; adaptations are likely. | • Students with disabilities can be identified using differing criteria.<br>• The heterogeneity of the classroom may be expanded considerably given the inclusion of | • ADA (1990, Section 3 [2])<br>• IDEA '97 (Sec. 602,[3]) |

**Table 5.1 (*continued*)**
**Relationship of Key Terms to Curriculum**

|  |  | students with mild, moderate, or severe disabilities. | Rehabilitation Act (1973). |
|---|---|---|---|
|  |  | • Special considerations apply for children aged 3 through 9. Students with disabilities identified through IDEA '97 procedures are eligible for funding reimbursement, while students identified through ADA or Section 504 are not eligible for reimbursement using flow through funds. |  |
| Inclusion | • Curriculum will likely need to be adapted to meet a wider range of student skill levels. • Homework, testing procedures, and | • Inclusive practices should be based on identified need as determined by the multifactored evaluation, not on political expediency. | • Bennett, DeLuca, & Bruns (1997) • Heron & Goddard (1999). |

**Table 5.1 (*continued*)**
**Relationship of Key Terms to Curriculum**

| | | | |
|---|---|---|---|
| | grading practices will likely need to be adapted.<br>• Practices should also focus on prevention approaches, not just remediation or compensation. | • Include all relevant perspectives when deciding inclusive placements (students, parents, teachers).<br>• Keep up-to-date with extant literature on inclusive practices. | • Kauffman & Hallahan, (1993).<br>• Turnbull & Ruef (1997)<br>• Vaughn & Klingner (1998)<br>• Waldron & McLeskey (1998) |
| Least Restrictive Environment | • Environmental factors (seating assignment, pace of instruction, grouping arrangements) must be considered when implementing curriculum.<br>• LRE is a placement; location where the | • LRE can be enhanced by using effective instructional strategies, using trained paraprofessionals, and establishing working relationships with parents.<br>• LRE can be determined by examining benefit to | • Heron & Skinner (1981)<br>• IDEA '97 (Section 612 [5]).<br>• Margolis & Tewel (1990) |

**Table 5.1 (*continued*)**
**Relationship of Key Terms to Curriculum**

| | | | |
|---|---|---|---|
| | student is enrolled. | the student, teacher-student interactions, and socialization opportunities. | |
| Least Restrictive Alternative | ▪ LRA describes the program provided to the student.<br><br>▪ Lesson plans should show evidence of LRA approach.<br><br>▪ Differing instructional methods are likely to be used to teach, and these methods might change across curriculum content.<br><br>▪ Prompting cues and reinforcement contingencies will vary. | ▪ Faculty and staff will need to be well trained in the effective use of prompting and reinforcement techniques.<br><br>▪ During instruction, evidence should exist showing use of least-to-most or most-to-least prompting; stimulus prompts, and response prompts. | ▪ Cooper, Heron, & Heward (1987, Chapter 19).<br><br>▪ Turnbull (1993, Chapter 6). |

**Table 5.1 (*continued*)**
**Relationship of Key Terms to Curriculum**

|  |  |  |  |
|---|---|---|---|
|  | ▪ Focus shifts to adjusting mode of presentation and mode of response. |  |  |
| Best Practice | ▪ Embraces the full range of curriculum, including early education for students with disabilities. | ▪ Practitioners are required by law to use state-of-the-art approaches. | ▪ Heron, Ernsbarger, Tincani, & Harrison (2000).<br>▪ Peters & Heron (1993). |

## Disability

Disability is defined differently depending on whether an IDEA '97 definition is used or the Office of Civil Rights definition is used. For instance, under IDEA '97 disability means:

a child—(i) with mental retardation, hearing impairments (including deafness), speech or language impairments, visual impairments (including blindness), serious emotional disturbance (hereinafter referred to as emotional disturbance), orthopedic impairments, autism, traumatic brain injury, other health impairments, or specific learning disabilities; and (ii) who, by reason thereof, needs special education and related services. (IDEA '97, Sec. 602,[3])

However, under Americans with Disabilities Act of 1990 (ADA), a disability is defined as:

(A) a physical or mental impairment that substantially limits one or more of the major life activities of such individual; (B) [a person who has] a record of such an impairment; or (C) [a person] being regarded as having such an impairment. (Americans with Disabilities Act [ADA], 1990, Sect. 3 [2])

The upshot of differing connotations for the same term is that general education teachers might be expected to teach students who have traditional categorical disabilities (e.g., SLD), while simultaneously accommodating the educational needs of students who qualify for disabilities services under Section 504 of the Rehabilitation Act (e.g., for attention deficit disorder). The level of disability for children under IDEA '97 legislation might range from mild to severe. For children under Section 504 or ADA legislation, the disability may exist in the mild to moderate range. From an administrative or fiscal perspective, services would be reimbursed under IDEA '97, but not reimbursed under ADA or Section 504 of the Rehabilitation Act of 1973.

Instructionally, the teacher would need to implement a curriculum-based program to meet the student's IEP or 504 plan. An administrator, as leader in the school, would be well advised to have ongoing inservice programs that help teachers develop, implement, and evaluate curriculum-based strategies that meet the needs of students eligible for services under varying connotations of disability.

### Inclusion

The term inclusion has broad and narrow connotations (Heron & Harris, 2001). Broadly, it defines classroom environments that integrate the full texture of populations within American society (cultural, religious, ethnic, and disability groups) into one environment. Narrowly, or selectively, it refers to only those students with a disability receiving services within the context of the general education classroom (Banerji & Dailey, 1995; Giangreco, Baumgart, & Doyle, 1995; Vaughn & Schumm, 1995; Winger & Mazurek, 1998).

From a curricular viewpoint, administrators should be aware that multiple perspectives abound on what constitutes inclusion. An administrator who takes the students', parents', and teachers' perspectives into consideration is more likely to be successful implementing a curriculum-sensitive inclusion program than an administrator who operates from a political base (i.e., what is expedient). A collaborative approach is more likely to result in the delivery of a curriculum that meets the needs of all parties involved. Importantly, alliances with key persons, including the regular classroom teacher and parents, are likely to result in higher levels of academic and social success for students (Friend & Cook, 1996; Heron & Harris, 2001). While there have been a host of studies on the effects of inclusion, the research literature is not prescriptive about the benefits (Sabornie & Kauffman, 1986; Sale & Carey, 1995; Salisbury, Gallucci, Palombaro, & Peck, 1995; Waldron & McLeskey, 1998). Still, there appears to be consensus that successful inclusion depends upon collaboration, educational interventions, knowledge of the specialized needs of students, and the appropriate use of a multipronged approach and decision making (Friend & Cook, 1996; Heron, 1978).

## Least Restrictive Environment and Least Restrictive Alternative

In federal law, the least restrictive environment (LRE) is defined as:

To the maximum extent appropriate, children with disabilities, including children in public or private institutions or other care facilities, are educated with children who are not disabled, and special classes, separate schooling, or other removal of children with disabilities from the regular educational environment occurs only when the nature or severity of the disability of a child is such that education in regular classes with the use of supplementary aids and services cannot be achieved satisfactorily. (IDEA '97, Sect. 612 [5])

In brief, LRE means where the students will be educated, and where they will experience the curriculum that is unique and specialized for them. Clearly, the intent is that the student be included with his general education peers to the maximum extent possible, and that the student only be removed from such environments when the student is not able to benefit from the curriculum, even with supplemental learning aids in place.[1] As an outgrowth of *Daniel R. R. v. State Board of Education, Rachel H. v. Board of Education Sacramento City,* and *Roncher v. Walter,* the courts have proposed tests or standards to determine least restrictive environment (Heron, Martz, & Margolis, 1996; Osborne & DiMattia, 1994; Thomas & Rapport, 1998). These tests became known as the inclusion standard, the balancing standard, and the portability standard respectively. Questions that administrators should consider based on these standards are found in Table 5.2.

Table 5.2
A Summary of the "Test" Questions Used to Establish the Standards for Portability, Inclusion, and Balance across Three Court Cases: *Roncker, Daniel R.R.,* and *Rachel H.*

| Roncker | Daniel R.R. | Rachel H. |
|---|---|---|
| Portability Standard | Inclusion Standard | Balancing Standard |
| ➢ Can the services that made a segregated facility superior be provided in the regular | ➢ Can the student be educated in the general education classroom satisfactorily if | ➢ What are the educational benefits available to the child in a general |

**Table 5.2** (*continued*)

**A Summary of the "Test" Questions Used to Establish the Standards for Portability, Inclusion, and Balance across Three Court Cases:** *Roncker, Daniel R.R.,* and *Rachel H.*

| education environment? | supplemental learning aids are provided? | education classroom, supplemented with appropriate aids and services, as compared with the educational benefits of a special education classroom? |
|---|---|---|
| ➤ Can the child benefit from a general education environment? | ➤ If education in the general education classroom cannot occur satisfactorily, is the student placed with nondisabled peers to the maximum extent possible? | ➤ Are there nonacademic benefits of instruction with children who are not disabled? |
| ➤ Are the benefits of a general education placement far outweighed by the benefits gained from services that could not feasibly be provided in general education placement? | | ➤ What effect does the child's presence have on the teacher and other children in the classroom? |
| ➤ Would the child | | ➤ What is the cost of |

The least restrictive alternative (LRA), on the other hand, refers to the program that the child will experience once placed. That is, the instructional method should be the most powerful, but least intrusive, for the individual. The litmus test for administrators is to recognize that different instructional methods, adapted to the specific needs of the student with disabilities, serve as the guiding principle for the least restrictive alterna-

Table 5.2 (*continued*)
A Summary of the "Test" Questions Used to Establish the Standards for Portability, Inclusion, and Balance across Three Court Cases: *Roncker, Daniel R.R.,* and *Rachel H.*

| | | |
|---|---|---|
| significantly disrupt the general education environment? | | educating the child in the general education environment? |
| ➢ Is the cost so excessive as to deprive other children of an education? | | |

*Source*: S. B. Thomas & M. J. K. Rapport (1998), Least restrictive environment: Understanding the directions of the courts, *Journal of Special Education, 32*(2), 66–78. Copyright 1998 by PRO-ED, Inc. Adapted with permission.

tive. Minimally, the LRA methods would dictate that the teacher change the mode of presentation and the expected mode of response for students.

### Best Practice

There are a myriad of alternatives for administrators to consider when planning curricula for their school, including (a) commercially based academic programs in reading, language, math, and social skills; (b) specific instructional methodologies (e.g., the Lovaas method); and (c) the overarching philosophy of the school (Direct Instruction, Developmentally Appropriate Practice, Whole Language, Immersion, and so forth). To navigate these options, a standard for comparative evaluation must be applied; otherwise, the administrator may be lulled into believing that any avant-garde method that is published or popular is as good as any other. In effect, the administrator might ignore a superior instructional practice and adopt one for his school that is not based on research or effective outcome data (Kameenui, 1994). According to Peters and Heron (1993), best practice hinges on answering five questions:

- Does the practice have a sound theoretical base?
- Is the methodological integrity of the research convincing and compelling?
- Is there consensus with existing literature?
- Is there evidence that desired outcomes are consistently produced?
- Is there evidence of social validity?

These factors are important to consider, given that educators have so little time within a school day and school year to intervene with students with disabilities. The time spent educating these students must incorporate effective instruction that will help students learn. In a summary of decades of reading research, Lyon (1998) concluded that if intervention is delayed until age nine (which is when most children with significant needs begin to receive services), approximately 75% of the children will continue to have difficulty learning to read throughout high school. These facts should be a clarion call for all administrators to adopt effective, research-supported methods for all learners.

## Curriculum

Broadly defined, curriculum means the sum of the planned learning experiences that have intended educational outcomes (Hoover, 1988). The key words within this definition are *planned*, *intended*, and *outcomes*. Such a definition embraces generalized and maintenance outcomes that should be programmed (Baer, Wolf, & Risley, 1968). However, curriculum does not embrace incidental learning that may take place. While such learning is universally welcomed, it is not part of the definition per se because it was not planned or intended. A planned, intended, and outcome-oriented learning experience presupposes that the teacher develop a lesson plan based on the student's IEP that delineates the objective for the lesson, the criterion for success, and the evaluation system for measurement (Rosenberg, O'Shea, & O'Shea, 1998). Wood (1998) concurs when she states: "Curriculum [should be] based on student outcomes and should be student appropriate" (p. 138). Furthermore, the outcome would be based on a standard for acceptable performance. For instance, if reading orally at a fluent level was the target behavior, the lesson plan might read: the student will read 180 words correctly, with fewer than five errors, using the basal reading series at grade level 3.1.

In addition to being planned, intended, and outcome-oriented, Polloway, Patton, Payne, and Payne (1989) indicate that the curriculum must be dynamic, and it must reflect the changing developmental, academic, social, vocational, and life-skill needs of students as they advance through grades or levels. Minimally, the curriculum for special needs students should reflect the changing dimensions of remedial, tutorial, learning strategies, and functional curriculum orientations. Importantly, it should change based on individual students' progress and needs.

Still, there is not unanimous consensus in the field on what forms the curriculum for special needs students. For example, Sands, Adams, and Stout (1995), reporting on a statewide survey of the nature and use of curriculum in special education, found that teachers believe that the IEP itself constitutes the curriculum. Teachers did not view the scope and sequence of skills often associated with the general education course of study as their template for designing curriculum.

Likewise, their data suggest that special education teachers as a group would prefer to switch their emphasis of instruction from academics to life-skill, functional, and vocational areas, especially as students progress through school. Of course, the challenge for these teachers and the administrator is to balance the legitimate IEP needs of the student with the expectations of the general curriculum when the student is integrated into this setting, a point supported by Polloway et al. (1989).

Wood (1998) states succinctly the challenge that administrators face when considering curriculum issues with students with disabilities:

Administrators are faced with finding money for unfunded mandates and allocating the necessary resources, materials, and manpower to support educators. New technology and teaching curriculum must be investigated. Business as usual can no longer exist. Administrators are faced with challenges in the emotional climate of the school as students with disabilities are increasingly being integrated into general education settings. The focus of inservice programs must change; encouraging work for the benefit of the child is a high priority. Communicating administrative support to all parents, students, teachers, and the community is necessary considering the growing number of mandated changes. In addition, accountability for student learning outcomes has become a focus, and restructuring is a necessary element now that general and special education have become alienated. (p. 21)

## Curriculum Considerations

This section will define and provide relevant exemplars of a comprehensive special education curriculum. Also, Wood's SAALE model (1998) will be featured as a way for administrators to calibrate how curriculum is delivered in the special education settings.

According to Polloway et al. (1989), a comprehensive special education curriculum:

- Is responsive to the student's needs in the current situation
- Balances maximum interaction with general education students against critical curriculum needs
- Relates to the continuum of services options
- Derives from a realistic appraisal of adult outcomes
- Focuses on transition during the life span
- Is sensitive to graduation goals

In addition, we believe that it should incorporate research-supported methods and use student data to determine progress. Taken as a whole, these seven points provide a blueprint for administrators to follow when implementing comprehensive curriculum.

*Is Responsive to the Student's Needs in the Current Situation*

A curriculum can be considered responsive to the current situation when there is a match between the skill level of the student, the mode of presentation of the task, and the expected mode of response (Heron & Harris, 2001). Further, a curriculum is responsive when it changes, depending upon the focus of instruction (e.g., basic skills, remedial, tutorial, or vocational). For instance, teaching subtraction to a student with developmental disabilities at the elementary level may involve concrete objects, pictures, or symbols in an effort to teach the basic skill. At the middle school level, a tutorial approach might be used to assist the student with passing a test in mathematics, while simultaneously keeping him or her in the general education classroom (Polloway et al., 1989). At the high school, a student who continues to experience skill deficits with subtraction should be exposed to occupational or vocational examples (balancing a checkbook, cutting a length of material from a bolt of cloth, and so forth).

*Balances Maximum Interaction with General Education*
*Students against Critical Curriculum Needs*

Some skill deficits that students with special needs experience may require more intensive instruction than can be provided in the general education classroom, even with supplemental aids in place. In these cases, a balance will need to be achieved that reconciles the student's maximum interaction with general education peers with the curricular goals delineated in the IEP or expressed in the curriculum guide. Consistent with IEP goals and objectives, a student with special needs may be fully integrated and enjoy maximum interaction with peers for some subject areas (e.g., reading and language arts), but experience a "pull-out" program for other subjects (e.g., math).

*Relates to the Continuum of Services Options*

The continuum of services model outlines the linear arrangement of placement options that exist for students with special needs (Heward, 2000). At one end of the continuum, the entire curriculum would be delivered in the general education class. At the opposite end, services would be provided in an institutional setting. Between these parameters is a host of options (e.g., general education with tutorial services, self-contained special education classrooms, resource rooms, day-treatment centers, and so forth). The point is that every attempt should be made to deliver the curriculum in the most appropriate, powerful, and least intrusive of these settings.

## Derives from a Realistic Appraisal of Adult Outcomes

Ultimately, the curriculum should focus on outcomes, including the student performing skills at an independent level. The outcomes, of necessity, need to be based on accuracy (how correct is the response), rate (how fast is the response), generality (does the response appear elsewhere), and maintenance (can the student sustain new learning over time). Ideally, the curriculum should provide ample opportunities to respond (Greenwood, Delquardri, & Hall, 1984) and multiple active student response opportunities (Barbetta, Heron, & Heward, 1993) so that accuracy, rate, and generality can be programmed, practiced, mastered, and maintained. If a special needs student takes a horticultural class in high school, he or she should be able to identify plants accurately, quickly, and under differing conditions (e.g., flowers have not bloomed, but leaves present). Moreover, the standard for performance should be established relative to an adult worker in a nursery, florist shop, or garden supply store. In cases where the student can perform part of the behavioral repertoire (i.e., name the plant accurately) but not name a group of plants quickly, a shaping process can be integrated in the curriculum to reinforce closer and closer approximations to the target behaviors (Cooper et al., 1987).

Important considerations for students with mild to moderate disabilities involve an assessment of the relevance of academic tasks. For instance, having a student with mild mental retardation identify prepositional phrases in a middle school language arts class may not be functional for that child's future. A more relevant, but related, task might be for the student to write a cohesive sentence containing a subject carrying out an action.

## Focuses on Transition during the Life Span

Transition is a natural part of the life cycle. Students transition from preschool to kindergarten, kindergarten to first grade, elementary to middle school, middle to high school, and from high school to post-secondary environments. At each of these junctions, a step up in requirements usually occurs, meaning that behaviors must become more established, refined, generalized, or maintained (Wehman, 1996). A comprehensive curriculum recognizes that these life changes occur and provides experiences at each step to ease the transition to the next level. West et al. (1992) offer excellent recommendations for including specific features of transition programming in the IEP.

## Is Sensitive to Graduation Goals

All states set minimum standards for the completion of a course of study leading to a high school diploma. Included in these standards are such items as required credits, completion of a literacy or proficiency test, and requisite number of days in school. Students with special needs may fall short of meeting some of these standards, but still fulfill the major goals on their IEP. In such cases, Wood (1998) correctly reminds administrators that alternatives are available (e.g., certificate of attendance), and that the curriculum for students with disabilities can be planned so as to achieve a modified diploma.

### Systematic Approach for Adapting the Learning Environment (the SAALE model)

Wood (1998) offers the SAALE model for curriculum use and adaptation. In her view, three principal components embrace curriculum delivery: adapting the total environment (social, behavioral, physical), adapting the instructional environment (lesson plans, teaching, format, and media), and adapting evaluation components (student evaluation and grades).

*Adapting the Total Environment.* Adapting the total environment means that the administrator sets the occasion for the teacher to create a risk-free setting in which students with special needs are respected, trusted, and appreciated, despite their disability. Furthermore, when adapting the total environment, the behavioral aspects of classroom management, rule making, student discipline, and expectations for performance are firmly and fairly applied. If the class structure varies inconsistently from room to room where students with special needs are integrated that they will be faced with insurmountable challenges trying to discriminate these differences. Finally, when adapting the total environment, administrators can render an invaluable service to teachers by ensuring that the curriculum is delivered on a schedule that is accommodating to the student's disability, and by using materials that have appropriate stimulus control features (Vargas, 1984). For example, where scheduling is concerned, if the student has an attention deficit, it would not be wise to schedule repetitive classes where attention to detail, heavy content, and sustained attention would be required. To the contrary, it would be efficacious to divide the school day with art, music, physical education, or a study hall to allow the student with special needs to space heavier and lighter content classes.

With respect to stimulus control, if students can respond to text-based questions after having read only marginal notes, the stimulus control features of the text would be suspect and would warrant change. Once a teacher determines instructional objectives for students, tasks that the students are required to complete should relate directly to the objectives and should require students to practice the target skill. Answering comprehension questions based on reading marginal notes in a chapter is not likely the skill or the task that the teacher intended for students to practice. Grouping strategies should also be considered at this point. That is, the judicious use of large, small, dyadic, or cooperative learning groups can enhance the delivery of the curriculum (Heron & Harris, 2001; Wood, 1998).

*Adapting the Instructional Environment.* To adapt the instructional environment, administrators can render assistance to teachers by helping them link IEP goals and benchmarks (short-term objectives) with the daily lesson plan. The plan should include not only the objectives for the lesson, but also the strategy for using audio, visual, or technological media (computers) with appropriate evaluation protocols. Considering the student's present level of functioning, the goal of the lesson, and available resources, a decision can be made about whether the lesson would be best taught using teacher-directed, peer-mediated, or semi-independent methods. Finally, administrators can ensure that different levels of evaluation occur depending on whether the skill is at the acquisition or fluency levels (see Mercer & Mercer, 2001, for details regarding stages of learning and requisite criteria for student outcomes). Briefly, learner performance during acquisition stages of learning may increase from 0% to 100% accuracy. In the next stage, proficiency, automaticity is the goal, with performance becoming fast and accurate. Maintenance, generality, and adaption (i.e., problem solving) follow. Teachers' instruction and assessment of student progress should vary depending upon students' stages of learning.

*Adapting Evaluation.* Because students with disabilities may have difficulty processing directions, responding within specific timeframes, or responding in a way similar to their general education peers, accommodations to evaluation and grading need to be factored into their programs. So, basic items like test directions (written versus verbal), time factors (one-half more allocated time), and the physical layout of the test (e.g., larger font for students with visual impairment) are germane. Moreover, a shift in emphasis from summative evaluation (formal reporting of grades) to curriculum-based measures (the student's progress with respect to the actual curriculum or IEP objectives) should be applied on a case-by-case basis. The administrator needs to be comfortable with the principle that different students need different evaluation standards. Where students are to receive summative grades, and where they are included in the general education curriculum, administrators facilitate fair and equitable grading by developing a policy that the final grade reflects the general and the special education teachers' perspectives.

**Recommendations for Administrators**

The following recommendations serve as a guide for administrators who would like to become more competent with curriculum delivery issues as they relate to special needs populations.

*Participate Fully in IEP and IFSP Processes*

Administrator input into the IEP and IFSP serves several functions. First, it signals to all participants—teachers, parents, students—that the IEP/IFSP is important and worthwhile. Second, by engaging in this process, administrators gain a more complete understanding of the curricular issues that face parents (i.e., tasks that are too difficult for their child; homework assignments that are too long and that require prerequisite skills that their child does not have; implementation strategies that do work and that should be continued; teachers who are either unwilling or unable to make accommodations for students with special needs). Finally, the administrator can use the IEP/IFSP process as a stepping stone to conduct an internal audit of the process within the building, asking questions like: Who is being referred? What services are missing from our continuum that if in place would enhance the education of our students? How are IEP/IFSP goals and objectives being met on an annual basis? Are students making progress against stated IEP/IFSP goals and objectives? Are relevant, accurate, and timely data being collected to examine student progress?

*Comply with IDEA '97 Provisions that Provide for Improved Access to the General Education Curriculum for Students with Disabilities*

IDEA '97 contains several provisions directed at providing students with disabilities greater access to the general education curriculum and calls for a broader focus in educational planning. For instance, if a child's history suggests that management issues might surface, then a behavior implementation plan (BIP) should be included in the IEP (regardless of disability), and the teacher should be knowledgeable about how to implement the plan. Second, access to the general education curriculum is dependent, in part, on (a) pedagogically skilled educators, (b) instructional materials that are available to students (i.e., build in success), and (c) the effective delivery of instructional strategies. The goal for the administrator is to find ways to change the environment and the methods that teachers might use within classrooms, instead of making a preemptive decision that the setting is inappropriate. Heron (1978) provided a

decision-making model for achieving this purpose. Finally, joint participation of general and special educators in curriculum development, professional enhancement, resource allocation, and instruction are critical in
helping students with disabilities (a) access the general education curriculum and (b) acquire skills that will prepare them better for life after
school. The school-based administrator can enhance such collaborative
efforts through supportive measures such as common planning times for
teachers.

### Schedule Regular Meetings with Faculty and Staff Who Teach Children with Special Needs (Including Regular Educators) and also the Parents of Children with Disabilities

Regular face-to-face meetings with teachers and parents will set the
occasion for the administrator to take a proactive stance with respect to a
wide range of issues facing children, teachers, and family members. Such
meetings should have a theme and be open to a wide range of individuals.
Ideally, they should be times for the administrator to listen to others and
to plan a joint approach to meet real or perceived needs. If the data of
Sands, Adams, & Stout (1995) are to be believed, the administrator might
arrange a series of forums with teachers and parents to discuss their views
on the focus of the curriculum. As Sands et al. state:

> If IEPs are the curriculum, we must have avenues to both define and ensure com-
> prehensive educational opportunities for students with disabilities. Special ed-
> ucators would need comprehensive skills in teaching the whole curriculum,
> especially at the secondary level. Alternatively, if IEPs highlight the value added to
> the school curriculum, special educators will need to know how to analyze and
> then translate that curriculum to make it accessible for their consumers (students).
> (p. 80)

### Keep Abreast of Professional Developments

Margolis (1998) provides administrators with valuable insight with
respect to knowing relevant procedures and keeping up-to-date. He states:

> It is essential to understand the concepts and directives...with the IDEA Amend-
> ments of 1997, case law, and related laws and ensure a high standard of profes-
> sional practice....This information defines and governs the nature of special
> education at the macro and micro levels. (p. 249)

Attending conferences, hosting colloquia, and conferring regularly with
colleagues at professional meetings are but a few methods that administrators can use to stay current.

*Frequent the NAESP and NASSP Web Pages*

The National Association of Elementary School Principals (NAESP) and the National Association of Secondary School Principals (NASSP) have useful web pages that include links to curriculum (see www.naesp.org and www.nassp.org). Administrators can access timely information on-line. Of course, a major benefit of on-line access is that documents of common interest can be downloaded, saved, e-mailed to colleagues, and aggregated for special use (e.g., developing a compendium of best practice procedures).

*Enroll in Formal Course Work*

While on-line courses and web sites offer novel, exciting, and convenient alternatives for maintaining professional skills, they are not a substitute for formal course work. Clearly, administrators need to come into contact with university-based faculty and their students. One way for this to happen is for the administrators to enroll in courses on curriculum, inclusive methods, or consultation offered at the university. In doing so, they are more likely to understand the full range of issues that affect educating students with disabilities within integrated classrooms.

*Understand the Unique Responsibilities of Special Educators*

The flagship international organization for special education, the Council for Exceptional Children, conducts frequent surveys of its members, including practitioners (Council for Exceptional Children, 1999). The consistent refrain from special education teachers regarding working conditions centers around burdensome paperwork requiring significant time and high student caseloads. Additional issues include lack of adequate planning time (planning time is often spent completing paperwork and setting up meetings rather than planning for instruction), resources, and instructional staff. All of these factors may lead to high rates of teacher turnover (i.e., burnout) in special education. Administrators can provide support to special education teachers through measures such as common planning times with general educators, additional time during the school day for paperwork, reduction of school-wide duties (e.g., cafeteria duty), and careful control of caseloads.

## CONCLUSION

Historically, special education students and their teachers were relegated to separate classrooms and isolated schools, requiring only the attention of administrators with direct responsibility for those programs.

Over the past three decades, education for students with disabilities has changed drastically. As a result, the roles that administrators play in the education and lives of children with disabilities are vastly different and highly important.

Issues pertinent to the population of special needs students demand the focused time of concerned and knowledgeable administrators. Through an awareness of key concepts in special education and important curriculum and environmental considerations that enhance instruction, administrators can create a climate to support all students. These are important points, because administrators play a pivotal role in setting the climate in schools (Goddard & Goddard, 2000; Hoy & Miskel, 2001). A supportive school climate can be enhanced when administrators set the occasion for teachers to have mastery experiences with the curriculum and with students' progress in the curriculum (Bandura, 1997). Administrators who are knowledgeable about the curricular needs of students with disabilities and how special education and general education curricula intersect will be better prepared to face the challenges of educating all students successfully.

This knowledge begins with an awareness of special education issues, both existing and emerging. Other important considerations include an awareness of best practices in special education, effective instructional presentation strategies, curricular adaptations that support individual student progress, and a variety of summative and formative evaluation methods. There are a host of ways that administrators can become familiar with current and emerging issues in special education. This chapter can be viewed as a springboard for administrators to increase their awareness and sensitivity with issues that affect their interaction with students with special needs, their teachers, and their parents.

## NOTE

1. Supplemental aids are not equal in definition to classroom aides, but extend to a variety of supports that may be used to make inclusion successful for students.

## REFERENCES

Americans with Disabilities Act, 42 U.S.C.A. § 12101 *et seq.* (1990).

Baer, D.M., Wolf, M.M., & Risley, T. (1968). Some current dimensions of applied behavior analysis. *Journal of Applied Behavior Analysis, 1,* 91–97.

Bandura, A. (1997). Self-efficacy: The exercise of control. New York: W. H. Freeman.

Banerji, M., & Dailey, R.A. (1995). A study of the effects of an inclusion model on students with specific learning disabilities. *Journal of Learning Disabilities, 28*(8), 511–522.

Barbetta, P., Heron, T., & Heward, W.L. (1993). Effects of active response during error correction on the acquisition, maintenance, and generalization of sight words by students with developmental disabilities. *Journal of Applied Behavior Analysis, 26*(1), 111–119.

Bennett, T., DeLuca, D., & Bruns, D. (1997). Putting inclusion into practice: Perspectives of teachers and parents. *Exceptional Children, 64*(1), 115–131.

Cooper, J. O., Heron, T. E., & Heward, W. L. (1987). *Applied behavior analysis.* Columbus, OH: Merrill.

Council for Exceptional Children (1999). Update of special education teaching conditions forum. *CEC Today, 5*(5), 10.

Daniel R. R. v. State Board of Educ., 874 F. 2d 1036 (5th Cir. 1989).

Friend, M., & Cook, L. (1996). *Interactions: Collaboration skills for school professionals* (2nd ed.). New York: Longman.

Giangreco, M. F., Baumgart, D. M. J., & Doyle, M. B. (1995). How inclusion can facilitate teaching and learning. *Intervention in School and Clinic, 30*(5), 273–278.

Goddard, R. D., & Goddard, Y. L. (2000). *A multilevel analysis of teacher and collective efficacy.* Unpublished manuscript.

Greenwood, C. R., Delquardri, J. C., & Hall, R. V. (1984). Opportunity to respond and student achievement. In W. L. Heward, T. E. Heron, D. S. Hill, & J. Trap-Porter (Eds.), *Focus on behavior analysis in education* (pp. 58–88). Columbus, OH: Merrill.

Heron, T. E. (1978). Maintaining the mildly handicapped student in the regular class: The decision-making process. *Journal of Learning Disabilities, 11,* 210–216.

Heron, T. E., Ernsbarger, S., Tincani, M., & Harrison, T. (2000, September). *Early literacy considerations for individuals with special needs: Best practices, research and policy issues, and future directions.* Address to the Statewide Literacy Conference hosted by the Ohio Coalition for Children with Disabilities, Columbus, OH.

Heron, T. E., & Goddard, Y. (1999). Secondary prevention: Applications through intervention assistance programs and inclusive education. In C. R. Reynolds & T. B. Gutkin (Eds.), *The handbook of school psychology* (3rd ed., pp. 800–821). New York: Wiley.

Heron, T. E., & Harris, K. C. (2001). *The educational consultant: Helping professionals, parents and students in inclusive classrooms* (4th ed.). Austin, TX: PRO-ED.

Heron, T. E., Martz, S. A., & Margolis, H. (1996). Ethical and legal issues on consultation. *Remedial and Special Education, 17*(6), 377–385, 392.

Heron, T. E., & Skinner, M. E. (1981). Criteria for defining the least restrictive environment for learning disabled students in the regular classroom. *Learning Disability Quarterly, 4,* 115–121.

Heward, W. L. (2000). *Exceptional children* (6th ed.). Upper Saddle River, NJ: Prentice Hall.

Hoover, J. J. (1988). *Teaching handicapped students study skills.* Lindale, TX: Hamilton.

Hoy, W. K., & Miskel, C. G. (2001). *Educational administration: Theory, research, and practice.* Columbus, OH: McGraw-Hill.

Individuals with Disabilities Education Act. 20 U.S.C. §§ 1400 *et seq.* (1997).

Kameenui, E. (1994). Measurably superior instructional practices in measurably inferior times: Reflections on Twain and Pauli. In R. Gardner, J. O. Cooper, T. E. Heron, W. L. Heward, J. Eshleman, & D. Sainato (Eds.), *Behavioral analy-*

sis in education: Focus on measurably superior instruction (pp. 149–159). Mon-
terey, CA: Brooks-Cole.

Kauffman, J.M., & Hallahan, D.P. (1993). The illusion of full inclusion. Austin, TX:
PRO-ED.

Lyon, G.R. (1998). Overview of reading and literacy initiatives (Report to Committee
on Labor and Human Resources, U.S. Senate). Bethesda, MD: National
Institute of Child Health and Human Development, National Institutes of
Health.

Margolis, H. (1998). Avoiding special education due process hearings: Lessons
from the field. Journal of Educational and Psychological Consultation, 9(3),
233–260.

Margolis, H., & Tewel, K. (1990). Understanding least restrictive environment:
A key to avoiding parent-school conflict. The Urban Review, 22(4),
283–296.

Mercer, C.D., & Mercer, A.R. (2001). Teaching students with learning problems (6th
ed.). Upper Saddle River, NJ: Merrill.

Osborne, A.G., Jr., & DiMattia, P. (1994). The IDEA's least restrictive environment
mandate: Legal implications. Exceptional Children, 61(1), 6–14.

Peters, M., & Heron, T.E. (1993). When the best is not good enough: An examination of best practice. Journal of Special Education, 26(4), 371–385.

Policymaking Partnership for Implementing IDEA. (1999). The 21st annual report to
congress on the implementation of the Individuals with Disabilities Act [On-line].
Available: www.ideapolicy.org/twentyfirst.htm

Polloway, E.A., Patton, J.R., Payne, J.S., & Payne, R.A. (1989). Strategies for teaching learners with special needs (4th ed.). Columbus, OH: Merrill.

Rehabilitation Act. P.L. 93–112, § 504 (1973).

Roncker v. Walter, 700 F. 2d 1058 (6th Cir. 1983), cert. denied, 464 U.S. 864 (1983).

Rosenberg, M.S., O'Shea, L., & O'Shea, D.J. (1998). Student teacher to master teacher:
A practical guide for educating students with special needs (2nd ed.). Upper Saddle River, NJ: Prentice Hall.

Sabornie, E.J., & Kauffman, J.M. (1986). Social acceptance of learning disabled
adolescents. Learning Disability Quarterly, 9(1), 55–60.

Sale, P., & Carey, D.M. (1995). The sociometric status of students with disabilities
in a full-inclusion school. Exceptional Children, 62(1), 6–19.

Salisbury, C.L., Gallucci, C., Palombaro, M.M., & Peck, C.A. (1995). Strategies that
promote social relations among elementary students with and without
severe disabilities in inclusive schools. Exceptional Children, 62(2), 125–137.

Sands, D.J., Adams, L, & Stout, D.M. (1995). A statewide exploration of the nature
and use of curriculum in special education. Exceptional Children, 62(1),
68–83.

Thomas, S.B., & Rapport, M.J.K. (1998). Least restrictive environment: Understanding the directions of the courts. The Journal of Special Education, 32(2),
66–78.

Turnbull, A.P., & Ruef, M. (1997). Family perspectives on inclusive lifestyle issues
for people with problem behavior. Exceptional Children, 63(2), 211–227.

Turnbull, H.R., III. (1993). Free appropriate public education: The law and children with
disabilities (4th ed.). Denver: Love Publishing Company.

Vargas, J. (1984). What are your exercises teaching? An analysis of stimulus control in instructional material. In W. L. Heward, T. E. Heron, D. S. Hill, & J. Trap-Porter (Eds.), *Focus on behavior analysis in education* (pp. 126–141). Columbus, OH: Merrill.

Vaughn, S., & Klingner, J. K. (1998). Students' perceptions of inclusion and resource room settings. *The Journal of Special Education, 32*(2), 79–88.

Vaughn, S., & Schumm, J. S. (1995). Responsible inclusion for students with learning disabilities. *Journal of Learning Disabilities, 28*(5), 264–270, 290.

Waldron, N. L., & McLeskey, J. (1998). The effects of an inclusive school program on students with mild and severe learning disabilities. *Exceptional Children, 64*(3), 395–405.

Wehman, P. (Ed.). (1996). *Life beyond the classroom: Transition for youth with disabilities* (2nd ed.). Baltimore, MD: Brookes.

West, L. L., Corbey, S., Boyer-Stephens, A., Jones, B., Miller, R. J., & Sarkees-Wircenski, M. (1992). *Integrating transition planning into the IEP process.* Reston, VA: Council for Exceptional Children.

Winger, M. A., & Mazurek, K. (1998). *Special education in multicultural contexts.* Upper Saddle River, NJ: Prentice-Hall, Inc.

Wood, J. W. (1998). *Adapting instruction to accommodate students in inclusive settings* (3rd ed.). Upper Saddle River, NJ: Merrill.

# Chapter 6

# Administration of Programs and Services

*Stephen B. Richards and Steven C. Russell*

## INTRODUCTION

In this chapter, a number of issues critical to administrators who are responsible for programs serving students with disabilities are addressed. First, we will examine the possibilities for and effects of various methods of school and individual scheduling. Scheduling becomes a critical factor in service delivery and opportunities for collaboration among educators. Second, the purposes and best practices of intervention assistance teams (IAT) will be reviewed. IATs often include the initial, systematic efforts to address learning difficulties of students in the general education classroom and curriculum. Intervention based assessment/multifactored evaluations (IBA/MFE) are addressed. These multidisciplinary teams are convened when the efforts of the IAT have resulted in a documented suspicion that the student may have a disability. Parental participation at this point becomes mandatory and the due process rights guaranteed by the Individuals with Disabilities Education Act become critical in ensuring that students and their families are treated fairly. We recommend in this chapter, as does the state of Ohio, that parents be informed and involved at the IAT level as well. A key feature of the IBA/MFE team is that it is a collaborative problem-solving process that focuses on specific concerns that are mutually defined, analyzed, and addressed through measurable goals and interventions that are monitored for effectiveness on an ongoing basis. When students are discovered to have a disability, parental permission is obtained to develop an Individualized Education Program (IEP) and determine the student's least restrictive environment (LRE). If no determination of disability is made, students may be referred back to the IAT or there may be a decision to provide services under the provisions of Section 504 of the Rehabilitation Act of 1973 (504 Plans). Both IEPs and 504 Plans will be examined for content and intent. Under federal rules and regulations are the possibilities of providing related and/or auxiliary services that we will also consider. Finally, we will include case scenarios to illustrate aspects of these necessary but sometimes complicated processes.

## SCHEDULING

Of great importance in any school is what schedule is used. The overall schedule of the school may facilitate or discourage collaboration and consultation among the teachers. Clearly, scheduling considerations may differ to some extent between elementary and secondary levels, although there are some common considerations. We will discuss overall scheduling concerns, those that affect special and general educators in particular, issues related to the elementary and secondary levels, and concerns with the individual student.

### Overall Scheduling Concerns

Perhaps of greatest concern is the degree to which the scheduling plan affords teachers (and students and their families) opportunities to discuss issues, plan curriculum and instruction along with adaptations or accommodations, and evaluate the outcomes of the instruction. The school administrator sets the tone and transmits to all concerned whether these are of importance within the school and district. For inclusive education to be successful, these processes are mandatory. In developing the schedule, educators should begin with this in mind. Another critical consideration is the representation of students with disabilities within each class. These students should be scheduled into classes prior to those without disabilities. This ensures that no inclusive class contains an overrepresentation of students with disabilities. Natural proportions suggest that a class should include students with disabilities at about 10% of its overall enrollment. Maintaining natural proportions also helps general education teachers in that no one is given extraordinarily more or less responsibility for educating students with diverse needs.

### *Considerations for General and Special Educators*

The administrator can provide guidance and assistance in scheduling to all teachers by following a few guidelines offered here. First, general educators need direct assistance in coordinating services that are delivered in their classrooms. Keep in mind that speech and language pathologists, psychologists, instructional aides, and reading specialists may all provide services in the inclusive classroom. One way to streamline services is to consider whether one educator (e.g., speech and language pathologist or reading specialist) can perform functions that might typically be performed by another (e.g., recording a student's on-task behavior, checking a student's planner). This can minimize the number of professionals present in the classroom at any given time as well as provide all concerned with knowledge about what others are doing to assist the student (i.e., a transdisciplinary model for service delivery).

Special educators might be assigned to work with a particular team of teachers based on grade level or content areas. In this way, general educators have a direct relationship with a source to whom they can turn when scheduling or other types of assistance are needed. Additionally, the team can address issues regarding planning time for collaboration better than the individual special educator trying to adjust to half a dozen different schedules of general educators (Friend & Cook, 2000). Friend and Cook also outline two additional issues regarding scheduling.

When special education services are delivered to each student individually each day in inclusive classes, the unfortunate result may be that each student on an IEP receives a brief (perhaps 10–30 minutes) amount of attention. This method often results in a sense that special educators are not teaching but monitoring, and students are receiving help in a piecemeal rather than systematic fashion. Time should be included for general and special educators to co-teach. Co-teaching need not occur each day, but regularly scheduled time periods in which both teachers are present and responsible for instruction and adaptations or accommodations provides for shared ownership and responsibility and mutual understanding of the roles and responsibilities of each.

Administrators should assist special educators in retaining some degree of flexibility within their schedules. If every minute of each day is scheduled, when emergency meetings or parent conferences are called or an assessment is needed, some other service is cancelled. This may be annoying to general educators who are depending on the special educator and may weaken relationships between them. Friend and Cook suggest that one alternative might be to plan for four days of co-teaching, leaving a fifth day for other service options. Another possibility is to have special educators' lunch and planning periods scheduled back to back so that they can be switched if the need arises. Finally, some special educators keep perhaps two 1-hour time periods available each week to accommodate duties beyond planning and co-teaching (Friend & Cook, 2000).

Clearly, some students may continue to be served in resource rooms and other special education settings. Administrators should be aware that when students move in and out of general and special education settings on a given day, the schedules for that student and those serving that student are increasingly complicated (Olson & Platt, 2000).

### Considerations for the Elementary Level

Friend and Cook (2000) note two important issues to consider in scheduling at the elementary level. First, many general educators prefer co-teaching during language arts. If this is the case, then the times at which this subject is taught by different teachers must be staggered throughout the schedule so that co-teaching can be achieved. If all general educators teach specific language arts between 10:00 and 11:00 A.M., clearly scheduling co-teaching becomes problematic. Second, "specials" such as art, music, and physical education can be scheduled at the same time for grade levels or teams of teachers. This provides an opportunity for team planning during the school day.

### Special Considerations for the Secondary Level

Of concern at the secondary level is that there are typically more teachers working with each individual student. Therefore, the assigning of teachers to teams becomes critical to avoid the problems outlined earlier. Many secondary schools have moved toward block scheduling. Santos and Rettig (1999) offer suggestions for scheduling of students with disabilities within either an A/B (all courses are taught each week but alternated on days of the week) or 4/4 block schedule (courses are staggered across two semesters).

In A/B schedules, resource classes are scheduled during single daily periods opposite lunch or other activity periods (rather than during full blocks), if available, so that special educators can have daily contact with students. Resource periods and classes in which the student is struggling are scheduled on alternate days. Systems to lessen confusion about the schedule should be created for each student (e.g., color coding days and posting that code at the entrance to school each day or when there is a schedule change).

For 4/4 schedules, try to include resource room services each day opposite lunch or activity periods. Balance course workloads across semesters. If a self-contained class is available in a core area (e.g., special education math class), pair it with a resource class and a general education class across the entire school year, as that allows a greater array of changes in service delivery options as students improve performance.

### Special Considerations for the Individual Student

Mastropieri and Scruggs (2000) offer a number of suggestions regarding overall scheduling issues for students with disabilities. First, they recommend that administrators and teachers ensure from the first day of school that all students know how to locate rooms and important areas within the school. Using peer assistants, buddy or mentor systems may assist in this process. Teachers should ensure students know the schedule and how to follow individual schedules and be aware that students with disabilities may have some difficulty with the building layout and the schedule, but be too embarrassed to ask for assistance.

Students should have accessibility to and know the procedures for use of lockers or personal storage space from the outset of school. Students can be asked privately to demonstrate they understand the use of this personal space.

Changes in schedules should be clearly posted and warnings given in advance. Some students with disabilities have difficulty with change, especially unforeseen change. Teachers should establish clear expectations of students regarding routines (e.g., getting to class, coming in from recess, and being seated when the bell rings). The more consistent these expectations are from teacher to teacher, the better.

Finally, students should be taught to maintain calendars for both short- and long-term planning as developmentally appropriate. Adults use these regularly, and the development of personal planning skills is functional for all students (Mastropieri & Scruggs, 2000).

## CASE STUDY

*The Issue: How do you schedule students with disabilities into classes?*

Mr. Evans is a new principal of Wherever Middle School. He was a teacher for eight years and has been an elementary school assistant principal for two years. Before the end of the present school year, he heard from a number of teachers at the middle school regarding their opinions about the effectiveness of inclusive education. Some teachers felt they were given too many students with disabilities in their classes because they were or had been supportive of inclusion. Many expressed concern that other teachers were avoiding having students with disabilities in their classes because they expressed negative opinions about inclusion. Several teachers believed students with disabilities were receiving less help than they had when they were in resource rooms each day. Special educators were primarily "checking" on students once a day for about 30 minutes and often saw several students during that time. Special educators complained they had to adjust their schedule to all the general educators, making it nearly impossible to satisfy everyone. Mr. Evans knew he had to do something.

## QUESTIONS FOR DISCUSSION

*What might be the first step that Mr. Evans could take?*

Form a committee of teachers, parents, and other concerned individuals who will collaborate in planning the schedule for next year.

*Should teachers be able to avoid the challenges and rewards associated with inclusive education?*

While teachers' attitudes do affect the way a school operates, all educators must recognize that students' needs come first. Students with disabilities should be assigned somewhat equally across inclusive classes. However, the administrator should take into account the level of training teachers have had in inclusive strategies. This could also be a means for identifying teachers in need of additional in-service.

*What are some considerations for how many students with severe disabilities Mr. Evans might schedule into a class versus how many students with mild disabilities?*

Typically, the administrator would assign only very small numbers of students with severe disabilities to any inclusive class. Larger numbers of students with milder disabilities might be assigned. Overall, no more than about 10% of a class enrollment should have disabilities to maintain the generally accepted ratio that exists in the overall school-age population.

*What steps might Mr. Evans take to assign teachers to teams and to schedule their planning periods?*

Each grade level would have two teams numbering from four to five general education teachers who taught various content areas. Each team could be assigned a special educator. The planning periods of all teachers on a team should be at the same time each day. Planning periods could be staggered by teams.

*How might Mr. Evans complete the scheduling of special educators?*

Special educators could spend entire teaching periods each week with each of their team members. One afternoon per week could be kept free for special educators to arrange meetings, do observations, conduct assessments, and document IEP progress. Special educators assigned to work with students in more restrictive settings could still be assigned to teams appropriate to the students they would be serving.

Scheduling is a complicated but critical aspect of school planning. Once students are appropriately scheduled and classes are in session, inevitably difficulties will emerge. When these do occur, the IAT is likely to become involved.

## INTERVENTION ASSISTANCE TEAMS

Prior to the formal referral of a student for identification of a disability, teachers use assessment information that has been obtained as a part of regular instruction and information that has been obtained in the effort to evaluate any special provisions made in the general education classroom to make judgments regarding a student's difficulties in academic or behavioral skill acquisition. If it is found that satisfactory progress is not realized in spite of any special provisions being made, the teacher may then require the support of an intervention assistance team (IAT). Involving general education teachers as well as others, the team—on occasion referred to as the prereferral team, the mainstream assistance team (MAT), the schoolwide assistance team (SWAT), the intervention assistance team (IAT), or the teacher assistance team (TAT) (Salvia & Ysseldyke, 1998)—endeavors to assist teachers with the development and suggestion of methods to teach those students having difficulty in the general education classroom.

Kirk and Chalfant introduced the concept of teacher assistance teams in 1984 and suggested that such efforts had helped many teachers to reduce the number of inappropriate referrals for special education and disability identification, as well as address many of the student problems that teachers were experiencing in the general education classroom. Kirk and Chalfant (1984) suggest that the teams be comprised of at least three elected teachers, the teacher requesting the assistance, and the parents and others as required. The Ohio Department of Education (1988, 1990) suggests that the school principal serve on the team as well, allowing the school principal to assume the role of instructional leader. In this capacity, the school principal can assist the team by obtaining access to instructional resources, improve his or her knowledge of curriculum and instructional strategies, and develop a long-term view of individual progress by students. Whatever the case, it is important to recognize the need for team members who have both breadth and depth in their understanding of curriculum and instructional methodologies, as well as the resources necessary to implement curriculum and instruction. The members of the IAT should be representative of the instructional leadership within the school. It will be their responsibility to suggest alternative instructional strategies and curricular means to assist with learning difficulties being experienced by students in the general education classroom.

As suggested by the Ohio Department of Education (1988), IATs, as they are referred to in Ohio, "are school-based problem-solving groups whose purpose is to assist teachers with intervention strategies for dealing with the learning needs and interests of pupils. Such groups seek creative ways to maximize the use of available resources" (p. iii). As such, IATs can assist school personnel in addressing the needs of at-risk students, be a means of accountability and documentation of efforts meant to address individual learner needs, be used to facilitate a more cooperative and collaborative learning environment in the school setting, serve as a mechanism to encourage parent participation, enhance staff development, and respond to special education concerns of over-identification.

In operation, an IAT is convened after a general education teacher has attempted, without success, to address the needs of a student experiencing a learning difficulty during general classroom instruction. The general education teacher should have attempted several methods to accommodate the learning difficulty. In addition, he or she should have kept detailed information on the different methods attempted and their respective outcomes. If all attempts have failed to alleviate the difficulties, he or she then contacts the chair of the IAT to arrange for a meeting. As indicated above, the chair may be the school principal, or it may be another teacher. The chair will then call a meeting of the IAT, and will, in many cases, include the parents of the child experiencing the learning difficulty. At the meeting, the general education teacher will present the information gained to date. This should include a description of the learning tasks, all methods that have been used to instruct the student, and the outcome of each instructional method. The IAT will then consider all of the information presented, and, in short, make a recommendation to the general education teacher of a method or methods that might alleviate the learning difficulty being experienced by the student. If necessary, members of the IAT may be needed to provide instructional support to the general education teacher as he or she learns and implements the suggested new methodology. Again, the general education teacher is encouraged to keep systematic and detailed notes concerning the use of the new methodology and how it affects the learning of the student. After an implementation phase of appropriate length, the general education teacher will again need to evaluate the success of the instruction. If the student is now responding to the method and succeeding in learning the skills, the IAT has been successful in assisting the general education teacher, the specific student, and his or her parents, and has avoided an inappropriate referral to special education. In the event that the methodology is not successful in assisting the student with the learning difficulty, it may be appropriate for the next step to be referral for special education services.

## CASE STUDY

*The Issue: What expectations might you have for the IAT in assisting teachers to educate students who are having difficulty with the typical methods of instruction?*

Ms. Shafer has been struggling to make progress with a student, Michelle, in her third grade reading class. Though Ms. Shafer has attempted to utilize the basal reading series and its instructions for the reading lessons, she has been unsuccessful in helping Michelle to read and learn the new vocabulary words introduced in each story. Ms. Shafer has provided Michelle with a word-ring for the purpose of practicing the new vocabulary words at home and during study periods throughout the school day. This, too, has not seemed to assist Michelle in learning and retaining the new vocabulary. As another tactic, Ms. Shafer has had a more proficient reader in her third grade reading class become a peer reader; she and Michelle read the new stories together again after they have been introduced and read with the entire class. Here, Ms. Shafer thought that the extra practice with an able reader would give Michelle another opportunity to learn the new vocabulary. This, too, has not been successful.

At this point, Ms. Shafer is not sure what she might do next to assist Michelle in being more successful with the new vocabulary being introduced in each story. Moreover, she is becoming alarmingly concerned as each new story is introduced and Michelle gets farther and farther behind in learning the new vocabulary in the basal reading series. Consequently, Ms. Shafer contacts her principal, Ms. Rowe, and asks her for the assistance of the intervention assistance team (IAT).

## QUESTIONS FOR DISCUSSION

*Who should Principal Rowe involve in the building's IAT?*

The principal, the instructional leader of the building, should most likely chair the IAT. Membership on the IAT might be determined through election by peer teachers in the building. The membership should be the very best teachers, two or three, who can provide others with curricular and instructional leadership.

*What should Principal Rowe do to begin meeting Ms. Shafer's request?*

First, Ms. Rowe should ask Ms. Shafer to prepare materials for the IAT that would help them in understanding the instructional expectations that Ms. Shafer has for Michelle; the difficulties Michelle appears to demonstrate in meeting these instructional expectations; the various and different methods Ms. Shafer has attempted in order to assist Michelle in meeting the instructional expectations; and a critical analysis of each of the methods attempted, the outcomes of the attempts, and any additional information that might assist the team in understanding the situation.

*What should Principal Rowe expect from the IAT?*

First, it is expected that the IAT will meet with Ms. Shafer and allow her to present her material to the team. This should permit the team to gather the kind of information that will be helpful to them in making positive and productive educational recommendations. Further, the principal should expect that the team will actively participate in this initial meeting by asking questions, probing deeper, gaining new insights and additional information from Ms. Shafer that will help them in making the best recommendations possible. It may be that at this first meeting the team will be able to make sound, educationally relevant recommendations to assist

Ms. Shafer in meeting Michelle's instructional needs. However, it is doubtful. It is more likely that, following this initial introduction to the issues presented by Ms. Shafer, the team members will want time to reflect, to research, and to consult before they make recommendations. Following such a time for these activities, it is expected that the team will again meet with Ms. Shafer and render their recommendations. Moreover, it may be expected, especially where a new methodology is recommended—one with which Ms. Shafer is unfamiliar—that a member from the team will assist Ms. Shafer with the implementation of the recommendations either through one-on-one consultation, peer-teaching, or any of a number of other possible avenues.

*What follow-up steps might Principal Rowe expect of the IAT?*

It certainly should be the expectation of the principal that the IAT will also recommend a timeline for evaluation of the success of the recommendations made to Ms. Shafer for assisting Michelle with reading instruction. After sufficient time for implementation of the recommendations, if it is found that they are not resulting in the desired outcome, then the team may need to reconvene and consider other recommendations. If all recommendations fail to assist Ms. Shafer in meeting Michelle's instructional needs, then, and only then, might the team recommend that Michelle be referred to, and evaluated by, the intervention based assessment/multifactored evaluation team.

## INTERVENTION BASED
## ASSESSMENT/MULTIFACTORED EVALUATION

If the IAT finds documented suspicion that a disability may exist, parents are notified that the district wishes to provide an Intervention Based Assessment/Multifactored Evaluation (IBA/MFE) or Multifactored Evaluation (MFE). The MFE is planned and conducted by a team of professionals to determine first if a disability exists that qualifies the student for special education and related services. If there is no determination of disability, the student may be referred back to the IAT for additional efforts at mediating whatever difficulties exist. Here, we will focus our attention on the assumption that there is a determination of disability at an eligibility meeting. In that case, the multidisciplinary team convenes to write an IEP and determine the LRE for that student. We will discuss IEPs and 504 plans later in this chapter.

As the process begins to determine eligibility for special education and related services, administrators need to be aware of the steps involved to ensure due process rights are protected and the MFE is conducted in a nondiscriminatory manner. Administrators should identify a professional within the school or district who is familiar and comfortable with all forms, policies, and procedures outlined by the state of Ohio in *Model Policies and Procedures for the Education of Children with Disabilities* (Ohio

Department of Education [ODE], 2000). The administrator, as well, should have a copy of and be familiar with this vital manual that governs many of the processes discussed in this chapter. Here, we will summarize the major steps outlined in this manual for the MFE.

Each district must have written procedures governing the conduct of the multidisciplinary team in conducting MFEs. Additionally, procedures must be written to ensure reevaluations at least once every three years (more often than that if conditions warrant) following determination of initial eligibility. These procedures (for when there is a suspected disability) must include the following.

(a) Parents are given notice of the intent to conduct the MFE and the evaluation plan within 30 days of the referral by the IAT. Notification must be in the parents' native language or primary mode of communication (e.g., American Sign Language) and attempts to obtain consent of parents must be documented (e.g., by registered mail).

(b) Parents are provided with a full explanation of procedural safeguards governing the evaluation of their child and provision of special education and related services if eligibility is determined. If consent is not given by parents to evaluate the child, the district must implement other due process procedures to obtain consent. Parents have the right to obtain independent evaluations and have those data reviewed. Consent for reevaluations is not required if reasonable attempts are documented to obtain consent and the child's parents have not responded.

(c) Provided consent is obtained, evaluation activities are implemented with assurances that they are nondiscriminatory (e.g., not biased due to linguistic, cultural or racial diversity). Many areas of evaluation are possible (e.g., hearing, vision, general intellectual functioning, achievement, behavioral characteristics, etc.) and technically sound methods are required and outlined in the evaluation plan determined by the multidisciplinary team. No single procedure (e.g., intelligence testing) may be used to determine eligibility for special education and related services and assessment procedures should be related to the suspected disability (different disability categories require documentation of deficits in different areas; e.g., for a diagnosis of developmental handicap, deficits in adaptive behavior must be documented).

(d) The qualified professionals on the multidisciplinary team prepare a report that summarizes the data obtained and includes whether there has been a determination of eligibility and the reasons for that determination. Members of the team shall include the child's teacher, as appropriate an individual familiar with the child's diverse background, at least one individual qualified to administer appropriate diagnostic assessments, and one or more individuals familiar with the suspected disability, typical child development, intervention design, and the general education curriculum.

(e) A copy of that report, which is usually given at an eligibility meeting with the parents and student as appropriate, is provided for parents and for the development of the IEP.

The state of Ohio Department of Education is currently developing the IBA/MFE, a collaborative, problem-solving process that focuses on a specific concern that affects a learner's progress. The purpose of the IBA/MFE is to involve professionals, the learner, and the learner's family in defining and analyzing the concern, developing measurable goals to address the concern, designing and implementing interventions to accomplish those goals, and using on-going performance data to monitor the effectiveness of the interventions. The IBA/MFE will very possibly become the standard procedure used in determining the eligibility of students for special education and related services. Why might this be necessary? IATs are not uniformly effective in every school. The IBA/MFE will more likely guarantee systematic efforts at interventions prior to referral for evaluation and maintain a direct link between the referral concerns and the development of the IEP. Administrators should be familiar with this process that emphasizes collaboration among all concerned parties. Due process procedures such as those previously outlined remain unchanged. Rather, the IBA/MFE stresses that improved outcomes stem from early parental involvement, delivering services specific to the problem and where the problem occurs, assessments that support teaching and learning, and creation of high expectations as an outgrowth of shared goal setting. The preceding discussion is paraphrased from the *Model Policies and Procedures for the Education of Children with Disabilities* (ODE, 2000).

## CASE STUDY

*The Issue: What steps need to be taken to safeguard the rights of the student and the family and to ensure the school is in compliance with the IDEA?*

Mr. Evans has now begun the new year and things are moving along well. However, Ms. Roberts, a seventh grade general education teacher, has expressed that she is having problems with a new student named Chris. Chris has been "acting out" in her class for the better part of two months, talking out inappropriately, getting out of his seat, refusing to complete work and participate in class activities, and making inappropriate comments to other students. She has asked Mr. Evans for help.

First, Mr. Evans visits the daily teacher team meeting. He asks if other teachers are experiencing the same problems. Two are reporting very similar behavior; two others report they have seen the problem but inconsistently. Mr. Evans asks if they have contacted the IAT for the school. The teachers report they have and have implemented a behavior management plan and altered some instructional techniques. Also, they have begun to keep frequency counts on Chris's disruptive behavior. Mr. Evans asks if they have knowledge of Chris's background that might give clues as to why he is having these difficulties. He asks that the special education teacher review all available records and for Ms. Roberts to contact Chris's parents again about the continued problems to discern if they have any clues to explain his behavior. Mr. Evans states he will ask Chris's school counselor to make an appointment with Chris to attempt to address what might be bothering the young man.

One month later, the teachers on the team are reporting that Chris's problems have continued despite the behavior management plan, instructional changes, and counseling. They feel Chris might have an emotional or behavioral disorder or perhaps a learning disability that is preventing his keeping up in classes, which in turn is exacerbating his behavioral difficulties. His parents reported he had always had problems in school and that the problems were only getting worse. His grades had dropped to failing levels in two of his classes and well below average in the others. The counselor reported that Chris had revealed little to her other than that he hates school. Mr. Evans does not like to refer students for an IBA/MFE without good cause but he agrees it appears justifiable. The special education teacher fills out the necessary paperwork to begin the process with the team's approval. Chris's parents are notified of the team's intention and tentative approval is obtained.

## DISCUSSION QUESTIONS

*Who should be assigned to the multidisciplinary team?*
The multidisciplinary team could include anyone who is knowledgeable about the student and concerned about his learning and behavioral outcomes. There should be at a minimum a special education team member, a school psychologist or appropriate individual with a background in diagnostic assessment and emotional and behavioral disorders, and a learning disability specialist in Chris's case.

*What next due process steps school should the school take after the multidisciplinary team is formed?*
The team devises an evaluation plan and that plan, along with a consent form and a pamphlet describing Chris's and his parents' due process rights must be sent home. The special education teacher or other professional should follow up with a home visit, telephone call, or conference to ensure the parents understand their rights and responsibilities. Consent is obtained and the team can begin its work of determining whether Chris has a disability.

*Once consent to evaluate is obtained, what is it the team wants to discover aside from whether or not Chris qualifies for special education and related services?*
They should attempt to describe and analyze concerns, identify measurable goals and interventions, and develop methods for evaluating the effectiveness of those interventions.

## INDIVIDUALIZED EDUCATION PROGRAMS (IEPS)

Once a student has been determined to be eligible for special education and related services, the multidisciplinary team must develop an IEP. The IEP is the cornerstone of educating students with disabilities. The *Model Policies and Procedures for the Education of Children with Disabilities* (ODE, 2000) outlines the major procedures in developing IEPs.

The IEP must be developed within 30 calendar days of initial determination of disability. In the prior case study, the multidisciplinary team would have to ensure that the IEP was written within 30 days of the completion of the IBA/MFE. If more time is needed, an agreement must be reached with parents. Once the IEP is written, it must be implemented immediately following the IEP meeting. To that end, all service providers should be given copies of the child's IEP. However, all recipients should be aware of their obligation to respect privacy and confidentiality.

At the IEP meeting, the following individuals should be in attendance: the parents of the child, the general education teacher or teachers (when more than one works with the student, one or more may be designated to attend), a special educator or service provider (e.g., a physical therapist) who is or will be responsible for implementing the IEP, a representative of the district, someone who can interpret instructional implications of the evaluation results, other appropriate individuals, and the student as appropriate. The administrator has an obligation to take measures that all required participants can attend the meeting and that each is sent notification. When students are 14 years of age or older, transition plans for post-school life must be made and the student is invited to attend. If the student cannot attend, measures must be taken to determine his or her preferences and interests. Also, any adult service agencies (e.g., Bureau of Vocational Rehabilitation) may be invited to meetings when transition plans are to be addressed.

Parental notification must be made in timely fashion by conference, telephone, or mail. The scheduled meeting time should be mutually agreed upon and the notification should include the purpose of the meeting (e.g., to determine eligibility, to review the existing IEP), time, location, who will be in attendance, and the right of parents and school personnel to invite others to be a part of the team. The district should invite the student. Efforts to contact parents should be documented. If an interpreter or translator is needed, the district arranges this service. Parents should receive a copy of the IEP and if they are unable to attend, the results of the meeting should be included with the copy of the IEP. Additionally, when a student reaches the age of majority (18 years in Ohio), he or she must be informed of his or her rights under the IDEA and provided with the same information concerning those rights that parents receive for younger children. The student should sign a statement of transfer of rights on the IEP when this occurs.

In developing the IEP, several considerations should be taken into account. The team should consider

(a) a plan to address behavioral issues that significantly interfere with the student's or others' learning;
(b) the language needs of a student with limited English proficiency;
(c) whether Braille instruction is appropriate for students with visual impairments;
(d) communication needs and mode of communication;
(e) whether the student needs assistive technology;
(f) the student's physical education needs;
(g) whether extended school year services are needed;
(h) a plan for the transition from preschool to school-age programs (if the child is a preschooler);
(i) transition services needed for movement from school to postschool environments;
(j) how to ensure participation in state and district-wide assessments and testing to the maximum extent appropriate.

The actual steps to develop the IEP are as follows:

(a) discuss vision: future planning;
(b) discuss present levels of performance;
(c) identify specialized needs for this IEP;
(d) identify measurable goals, objectives, and assessment procedures;
(e) identify needed services;
(f) determine the LRE (ODE, 2000).

The manual includes expansions on each of the above steps and special considerations with which the administrator and school level special educators should be familiar. Once the IEP is implemented, the district and all district personnel are obligated to follow the provisions and maintain accurate documentation of progress toward goals and objectives. In rare instances when the IEP will be implemented in a different school or agency than that which develops the IEP (e.g., a student will receive services in a psychiatric facility), the district of residence remains responsible for ensuring compliance with the IDEA. For students served in chartered nonpublic schools, the district must make provisions for the participation of those students in using Title VI-B Flow-Thru Funds.

Additionally, administrators should be aware that training opportunities in complying with the IDEA are available through Special Education Regional Resource Centers (SERRCs) and other professional development agencies. Each district will participate, as required, in school improvement reviews conducted by the Division of Special Education and monitoring of licensed center-based classrooms for early childhood special education services.

### Section 504 Plans

Mastropieri and Scruggs (2000) note that students with Attention Deficit Disorder (with or without hyperactivity) may be served under Section 504 if not eligible under the IDEA. These authors note other children that might be served under this law have conditions such as asthma, AIDS, tuberculosis, diabetes, drug or alcohol addiction, and behavioral problems. Section 504 uses a broader definition of disability that encompasses individuals who might not meet the state requirements for special education and related services under IDEA. Section 504 requires the disability substantially limits learning or other major life activities (e.g., ambulation) while the IDEA requires conditions adversely affect educational performance.

*Section 504 of the Rehabilitation Act of 1973* (Ohio Coalition for the Education of Children with Disabilities, 1999) is a manual to provide guidance to school districts in providing services under this act. The Coalition notes several important points. Section 504 is a civil rights act that at its core requires public schools to provide a free appropriate public education to each qualified individual in the district. Section 504, which also requires nondiscriminatory evaluation and education for students with disabilities, recognizes that equal treatment sometimes means different treatment from that provided to people without disabilities. Section 504 requires that students may be provided general or special education and related aids and services to meet individual needs. Finally, the Act requires schools to

(a) identify and locate students who qualify for services;

(b) notify parents of the opportunity of the student to receive a free, appropriate public education;

(c) evaluate any student, because of a disability, who needs accommodations in the general education program, special education, related aids or services;

(d) use a multidisciplinary team knowledgeable about the student to determine appropriate placement; and

(e) develop a plan to meet the needs of the student as adequately as the needs of peers without disabilities are met.

The determination of the student's LRE should consider what modifications are needed. Can these be made in the general education classroom? What are the benefits of a particular setting? What are methods for minimizing the impact of the student being placed in general education settings?

Procedural safeguards include that the district must provide written assurance of nondiscrimination. A "504 Coordinator" is appointed who coordinates compliance. Grievance procedures are in place to resolve complaints. Notice of nondiscrimination and access to programs and activities must be included in a student-parent handbook. Annually, the district must locate and identify students who qualify who are not receiving a free appropriate public education. Annually, the district must notify students and parents of the district's responsibilities under Section 504. Finally, parents are provided with procedural safeguards, including notice of their rights; opportunities to review relevant records; impartial hearings with participation by parents, students, and representation by counsel; and an opportunity to appeal decisions.

The Individualized 504 Plan generally is less involved than an IEP. Components of typical plans might include demographic information; the reason for meeting (e.g., new plan, periodic review, change in plan); accommodations for state- and district-wide testing; the student's educational needs and expected student outcomes, interventions, or adaptations needed to meet those needs; evaluation procedures to determine the effectiveness of those interventions, responsible persons, and date of review of progress (Ohio Coalition, 1999).

## CASE STUDY

*The Issue: How might you resolve a conflict between a teacher's beliefs about how students should learn and be assessed and the provisions in a student's IEP?*

Mr. Evans is now in the spring of his first year as principal. Ms. Elliot, a seventh grade teacher, has three students with IEPs who have been scheduled in her language arts class. All three are behind their peers in reading comprehension and written expression. The special educator on the team has assisted other team members in developing adaptations and accommodations in their classes that allow students with disabilities to obtain the knowledge and skills they need to perform adequately in those classes. These teachers were participants in the development of the IEPs for these students. For various reasons, Ms. Elliot was not able to attend those meetings.

The team has tried to resolve a problem that has arisen but is having little success. Ms. Elliot feels strongly that students on IEPs should be treated the same as everyone else in the class. If they cannot learn like everyone else, she notes, they should be in special education classes.

Mr. Evans has scheduled a conference with Ms. Elliot. At the meeting, he listens to her concerns about the students in her class. After reflecting on her comments, Mr. Evans knows that he has some challenges ahead.

# DISCUSSION QUESTIONS

*What might Mr. Evans tell Ms. Elliot about the meaning of a district represen-tative signing and agreeing with a student's IEP?*

First, he must pass on to all his teachers that IEPs are signed by a district representative, meaning that all faculty and staff must follow their provi-sions. They may disagree with the provisions, but they must provide the adaptations and accommodations promised.

*What might be some areas for additional training for Ms. Elliot and other teachers who have had less involvement in IEP development?*

One area to be considered is the need for teachers to understand what comprises an IEP, what their responsibilities are in the process of develop-ing an IEP, and that they should be very much involved in developing IEPs. Some teachers may need inservice training and on-going assistance in providing adaptations and accommodations to students with diverse learning needs. Teachers still need development in the collaborative pro-cess for team problem solving.

*What is a fundamental issue in scheduling that Mr. Evans should address?*

He needs to ensure that all teachers and parents who want or need to participate in IEP meetings should attend.

Either IEPs or 504 Plans may require schools to provide related and aux-iliary services. Administrators and teachers, in general education espe-cially, understandably are concerned with the provision of educational services. However, related and auxiliary services may be needed for a stu-dent to achieve access to environments or programs (e.g., ramps, Braille plaques around the school, special transportation) or to benefit from edu-cational services (e.g., physical therapy, speech and language services, occupational therapy).

## RELATED AND AUXILIARY SERVICES

As indicated above, in order for planned programs for students with disabilities to achieve the expected levels of success, it may be necessary that support from other professionals, programs, or services will be required. Federal laws mandate that such related professionals, programs, and services must be made available when it is deemed appropriate. The related services are identified in the *Federal Register* (1992) as

transportation and such developmental, corrective, and other supportive services as are required to assist a child with a disability to benefit from special education, and includes speech pathology and audiology, psychological services, physical and occupational therapy, recreation, including therapeutic recreation, early iden-tification and assessment of disabilities in children, counseling services, including rehabilitation counseling, and medical services for diagnostic or evaluation purposes. The term also includes school health services, social work services in schools, and parent counseling and training. (§300.16, 44803)

These services, both related and auxiliary, may be very important to the success of a child's educational program. The school has the responsibility to find and provide those services when the evaluation team deems them necessary. Moreover, in planning the best educational program for a student, the evaluation team should ensure that, where necessary, related and auxiliary services are included in the plan. After all, the educational success of the student is at the heart of the decision-making here. The evaluation team must do everything possible to ensure the educational success of the student. Further, it should be noted that these services must be provided at no cost to the child or parents. When these services are deemed appropriate by the evaluation team, they are the financial responsibility of the school to provide.

It might be helpful to examine some of these related and auxiliary services in more detail. For example, *counseling services* might include both group and individual counseling. If determined to be necessary for the student under consideration, counseling might be directed toward rehabilitation counseling that would prepare the student with regard to career development, employment, achieving independence, or integration into the workplace. Counseling services might also include psychological counseling or parent counseling. *Transportation,* while being the one related service not provided by highly skilled professionals, may seem fairly simple. However, such factors as needing additional personnel to assist in the transportation (e.g., having a driver *and* an attendant for a student) and traveling long distances between home and the school determine where the child's education will occur and increase the cost to the school for a specific child's education. As with other related services, if these types of transportation services are necessary for the child to achieve success, the cost must be borne by the school and the school has the responsibility to provide such services. *Psychological services* might include observation, testing, and consultation, and *physical and occupational therapy* might include therapies to improve independent functioning. *Recreational therapy* is likely to include general recreation programs, therapeutic recreation, and assistance with leisure planning. *Speech pathology and audiology services* are likely to include speech correction, language development, hearing amplification, and conservation programs. *Early identification and assessment of disabilities in children, medical services for diagnostic or evaluation purposes, school health services,* and *social work services* all appear to be fairly obvious as to what they might include.

Thus, schools are required to provide those services typically available to all students who attend, as well as related and auxiliary services that may be necessary to ensure the educational success of the student with a disability. Most often, the need for these related and auxiliary services will be established by the evaluation of a specialist. The school or the parent will seek the evaluation by the specialist, and the specialist through the evaluation procedure will establish the specific service that would be successful and benefit the student. Consequently, professional opinion will play a role in determining the viability of related and auxiliary services for an individual child. When it is determined that a child needs services provided by a related or auxiliary area, an invitation is made to a representative specialist of that related or auxiliary service to be a part of the planning team charged with developing the child's individualized education plan.

One overriding factor that must be particularly mentioned is that of cost. Related and auxiliary services are often found to be quite costly. However, cost is not a factor in determining whether or not a related or auxiliary service is provided. If the evaluation team and the specialists involved in planning the educational program for a specific child deem that that child will benefit from specific related or auxiliary services, then, according to the law, the school must provide those services *at no cost to the parent or child.*

## SUMMARY

In this chapter, we have discussed a number of critical issues. We have discussed the role that scheduling may play in the successful delivery of services for specific children and the role that scheduling may play in assisting school personnel to be able to collaborate. We have also discussed intervention assistance teams (IATs) and how such an approach can help ameliorate the difficulties experienced by a child when pursuing defined educational objectives, as well as the assistance IATs can provide the general educator in meeting the educational demands of the classroom for specific students. Multidisciplinary teams and intervention based assessment/multifactored evaluations have also been explored. These teams and evaluations become particularly critical in the identification and planning that is completed to ensure the educational success of students who have been found to have disabilities. Finally, we have included discussion of related and auxiliary services, and the educational role that they play in developing a complete Individualized Educational Program or Individualized 504 Plan. Scenarios illustrating many of these aspects have also been included to ensure that users will have real-life experiences in which to better understand the function of each of these factors in quality educational programming.

## REFERENCES

*Federal Register.* (1992). §300.16, 44803.

Friend, M., & Cook, L. (2000). *Interactions: Collaboration skills for school professionals* (3rd ed.). New York: Longman.

Kirk, S. A., & Chalfant, J. C. (1984). *Academic and developmental learning disabilities.* Denver: Love.

Mastropieri, M. A., & Scruggs, T. E. (2000). *The inclusive classroom: Strategies for effective instruction.* Upper Saddle River, NJ: Prentice-Hall, Inc.

Ohio Coalition for the Education of Children with Disabilities. (1999). *Section 504 of the Rehabilitation Act of 1973.* Marion, OH: Author.

Ohio Department of Education. (1988). *Intervention assistance team models: Sharing the responsibility for success.* Columbus, OH: Author.

Ohio Department of Education. (1990). *Secondary-level intervention assistance team models: Sharing the responsibility for success.* Columbus, OH: Author.

Ohio Department of Education [ODE]. (2000). *Model policies and procedures for the education of children with disabilities.* Columbus, OH: Author.

Olson, J. L., & Platt, J. M. (2000). *Teaching children and adolescents with special needs* (3rd ed.). Upper Saddle River, NJ: Prentice-Hall, Inc.

Salvia, J., & Ysseldyke, J. E. (1998). *Assessment* (7th ed.). Boston: Houghton Mifflin Co.

Santos, K. E., & Rettig, M. D. (1999). Going on the block: Meeting the needs of students with disabilities in high schools with block scheduling. *Teaching Exceptional Children, 31,* 54–59.

# Chapter 7

# Resource Utilization

*Kevin L. Bright*

In any discussion of the best utilization of resources in administering special education programs, there is an overriding philosophy to which administrators and all staff must subscribe. This is, that special needs students will receive service as needed, where needed, in the most appropriate setting.

At the same time, philosophically speaking, each individual school district and each respective building must decide the level of service needed and the level of service which will be provided by the staff on an individual student basis, in accordance with the law in the form of federal and state regulations, and in response to each student's individualized educational program (IEP).

A continuum of services, if you will, must be developed, and all staff must embrace beginning each student's service level in the least restrictive environment and moving from that level accordingly to find that which works best in meeting each individual student's needs.

In this chapter, we will analyze how to best serve the needs of individual students with disabilities in such areas as transportation, extended school year, assistive technology, related services, and faculty utilization. Once again, the purpose is to provide assistance in effectively administering the utilization of resources for students with identified disabilities.

## TRANSPORTATION

Richards (2000) states that with respect to transportation, a district's duty to students with disabilities is twofold. First, a student with disabilities should not be denied access to transportation that a similarly situated non-disabled student can access. If the district provides bus transportation to students who live a certain distance from the school or who must cross a dangerous road to get to school, that service must be offered equally to students with disabilities. Second, even if transportation services are not available to a population of students because they live too close to school, a child with a disability may require the district to provide transportation services.

The Individuals with Disabilities Act (IDEA) of 1997 expressly requires school districts to furnish students with disabilities necessary transportation as a related service. Ohio school districts must also furnish transportation to students with disabilities who attend private schools, if transportation is necessary for the student to receive a free appropriate public education.

Transportation, as defined within the IDEA, includes

(1)  travel to and from school and between schools;

(2)  travel in and around school buildings; and

(3)  specialized equipment (such as special or adapted buses, lifts, ramps), if required to provide special transportation for a child with a disability.

In Alabama, the 11th Circuit Court of Appeals ruled

In determining whether a student with disabilities needs transportation as a related service, the court must consider the student's age, the distance the student must travel, the nature of the area over which the student must travel, the availability of private assistance, and the availability of public transit and crossing guards. (Oakstone, 2000, p. 193)

Overall, Burns (1999) states that transportation is a related service under the IDEA (1997) when it is "required to assist a child with a disability to benefit from special education." She goes on to say that two laws— the Rehabilitation Act of 1973, Section 504, as well as the Americans with Disabilities Act (ADA)—require that reasonable modifications be made to existing policies, practices, or procedures so that individuals with disabilities may participate in services, programs, or activities in a manner equivalent to that of their non-disabled peers. These two federal laws are pertinent when claims are made that one individual has been treated differently than another simply because he or she has a disability.

## Accommodations within the Realm of Transportation

Just as in any other situation involving special needs students, the transportation needs of students with disabilities must be determined on an individual, case by case basis, in consideration of each student's unique disability related needs. If transportation is necessary for students with disabilities to benefit from education, it must be provided as a related service. The key question, then, is whether a student's disability makes it difficult for the child to get to school in the same way as typical students.

Transportation, as a related service, can take many forms, depending on the situation and the child's unique disabilities. When traveling to and from school, various vehicles may be utilized. Traditional "yellow" school buses are utilized when disabilities are less severe or there is a greater perceived need to include the student with disabilities with typical students. Mini-buses, vans, mini-vans, and private cars are other modes available.

Within the use of these five modes of transportation, there are several different types of specialized equipment required, depending upon a student's disabling condition. For younger and smaller students, car seats and seat belts are required. Preschool students with disabilities, typically aged three to five in most states, would qualify for this type of equipment. Two-way radios and cellular phones today have become standard equipment on any vehicle transporting students. This communication capability becomes that much more important when the students with a life-threatening disability are involved. Climate control and air conditioning have likewise become standard equipment when transporting students with disabilities.

For the more seriously impaired students, several accommodations are instituted. On mini-buses and in some vans, lifts for wheelchairs and for students unable to climb steps due to leg braces are available. At the same time, harnesses, restraints, and brackets are required to keep students securely in place while on the vehicle. Upon arrival at the school, curb cuts and ramps must be made available for students with orthopedic impairments. In some situations, school districts have been asked to provide restrooms en route to and from the school building.

Just as specialized equipment is necessary to provide appropriate accommodations to students with disabilities when transportation is required as a related service, so too is specialized personnel. Assistants are often required for students with severe disabilities. If such personnel are needed within the classroom, a case can be made that they will be needed on the vehicle to and from school as well. Frequently, bus monitors are needed for students with hearing impairments, deafness, or visual impairments. Nurses are provided to administer medical care and to provide catheterization. Aides are enlisted to attend to students en route and assist with escorting and directing students from the vehicle to the building.

Once at school, based upon the provisions of IDEA (1997), transportation as a related service expands to include access, navigation, and travel in and around the school building. Mechanical devices such as elevators, lifts, and Stair Tracs assist students in negotiating stairs and multiple floor buildings. As with transportation outside the building, aides and monitors are required for travel inside the building where the disability demands them. Additionally, provision of wheelchairs and ramps allows students with severe orthopedic handicaps the ability to move around well within the school.

## Least Restrictive Environment As It Relates to IDEA and Transportation

Pitasky (2000) examines the least restrictive environment requirement of IDEA (1997) as it applies to transportation. The provision states:

Local school districts are required to develop procedures to ensure that, to the maximum extent appropriate, children with disabilities, including children in public or private institutions or other care facilities, are educated with children who are not disabled and that special classes, separate schooling, or other removal of children with disabilities occurs only when the nature or severity of the disability is such that education in regular classes with the use of supplementary aids and services cannot be achieved satisfactorily. (p. 15)

However, when it comes to transportation, school districts are always wise to give serious consideration to mainstream transportation, and if they reject this option, it should be because the mainstream option would not be considered appropriate for that student.

The relevant factors to consider in determining whether or not a student with disabilities will ride on a "yellow" bus are:

*Safety and Health:* Will the student be exposed to dangers on a regular education school bus? Can the regular education bus be suitably adapted or outfitted with proper equipment and features as required by the student's disabling condition?

*Economic Factors:* If the regular education bus can be suitably adapted with proper equipment and features required by the student's disabling condition, will the costs of doing so be prohibitive, or are they relatively inexpensive, minor, one time changes?

*Feasibility:* Would accomplishing a mainstream transportation arrangement be feasible from an administrative viewpoint? Would the schedules of non-disabled students have to be disrupted or altered or bus routes changed significantly?

## Formalizing Transportation Provisions within the Individualized Educational Program

Transportation provisions and decisions are made by the IEP team during IEP meetings and should be determined on an individualized, case-by-case basis. Once formalized in writing within the IEP, this creates a student entitlement which the district is then obligated to fulfill. Within the IEP where transportation is listed as a related service, the following information should be delineated:

a. First of all, the nature and extent of the transportation service to be provided should be explained. Here, the degree of door-to-door consideration and any special arrangements should be discussed.

b. Next, what are the specific circumstances under which transportation service will be provided? Special consideration should be given to off-campus educational activities.

c. What type of vehicle will be utilized to provide the transportation?

d. What personnel will be needed to provide the service, if any?

e. What specialized or adaptive equipment will be needed, if any?

f. What are the goals and objectives of the service, if there is a purpose other than accessing a fair and appropriate education (i.e., increased opportunity for socialization and independence within the community)?

## Extent of Transportation Service

IDEA (1997) and other federal regulations are silent on the exact point at which the duty to transport begins and ends. Because the issue is open to interpretation, schools should review pertinent state law provisions, as well as local policies. As with any portion of a program for a special needs child, the extent of transportation provided is based upon the unique needs of each child on an individualized, case by case basis.

Policymakers generally agree that a school district's obligation to transport begins and ends outside the house. Districts are not required to go into the house to pick up or drop off the child. Beyond this, once again, IDEA (1997) is silent on transporting students to and from bus stops instead of from home.

Pitasky (2000) lists considerations which are relevant for the actual writing of the IEP. These include:

• What type of disability(ies) does the child have? Does the disability affect the reasoning skill of the child in making appropriate decisions regarding bus travel, following directions, and traveling to and from a pick-up point safely?

• What is the child's age and maturity level in understanding potential hazards, such as traffic conditions, and peer influences?

• Is the child mobile or non-ambulatory? Can the child move from one location to another without difficulty? Students with orthopedic handicaps and other mobility impairments are of particular concern here.

• What is the distance to be traveled and the nature and conditions of the route? Is it particularly arduous for a child to navigate, given age and disability considerations?

• Is there access to private assistance? Is there a parent or other person, including classmates, available to help the student access the transportation?

- Is there any availability of public assistance en route to transportation, such as crossing guards or public transportation?

- What are the student's supervisory needs? If supervision and attention is required during the school day, there is a good argument that similar provisions must be made in transportation service as well. (p. 8)

Additionally, the school's transportation responsibilities do not change due to road conditions or lack of proper road maintenance. At the same time, a student's disability-related transportation needs may change with the weather, and the district must be prepared to respond accordingly, even though such transportation-related needs may be temporary in nature.

## Additional Considerations for Schools Regarding Transportation As a Related Service

- Extracurricular activities fall into the same category as a regular education program. Transportation must be provided to create opportunities equal for students with disabilities as for those students who are not disabled.

- There can be no adverse effects from a student with disabilities spending an exorbitant amount of time on the bus or missing extensive class time. In either case, the district must compensate or correct the situation(s).

- Based upon a 1999 Cedar Rapids School District case, school districts must now provide medical treatment on the school bus to students whose medical condition requires this level of continuous care and attention.

- Due process hearings extend beyond the IEP process or mediation and often address transportation eligibility, adequacy, extent, and reimbursement.

- Office of Civil Rights interventions often focus on such things as bus ride length, missed class time, accommodations and accessible availability of service without interruption due to weather, breakdowns, and extracurricular and field trip opportunities through transportation availability.

- Remedies for transportation violations include: reimbursing parents for costs they have incurred as associated with providing their own transportation or securing an alternative form, compensating for lost instructional time by awarding additional educational service, or revising the provision of transportation service so that discriminatory conditions and denial of a free and appropriate public education are eliminated.

- Based upon Section 504 and ADA requirements, schools, as public agencies, must make reasonable accommodations to meet the needs of students with disabilities, provided they don't cause "undue hardship." This can be interpreted to mean financial strain or administrative inconvenience. Examples of enforcement of this rule could pertain to making building entrances accessible and using specialized mechanized equipment such as lifts and Stair Tracs to move mobility-impaired students without lifting or carrying them.

- Equal transportation services must be provided to both students with disabilities and typical students, even in the face of work stoppages, equipment failure, and inclement weather. One group should not be singled out over another for interruption of service. Both groups should be treated the same. Crisis transportation plans must be maintained to effectively deal with the aforementioned situations.

- The primary obligation of the school is to provide transportation in and around the building. This includes effectively navigating interior corridors and classrooms by providing necessary services, equipment, and assistance.

- School districts may contract out to private providers for provision of transportation as a related service. This may be appropriate for out of district placements or for smaller school districts lacking their own resources.

- Due process procedural safeguards must be invoked when adjusting the provision of transportation service in response to students misbehaving.

- It is up to each school district to ensure appropriate safety when transporting disabled students. Transportation provisions and equipment must be safe based upon industry regulations and standards. As such, lifts and ramps should be installed and utilized, as opposed to manually carrying students. Equipment must be in good condition and properly inspected on a regular basis, this includes the actual restraints to secure students on the bus.

- Additionally, personnel working with students should undergo proper training. Personnel should also be knowledgeable in the operation of equipment.

Pitasky (2000) states that

- Schools are not required to supply transportation to a student who has a free and appropriate education available in a nearby school but elects to attend another school outside of the geographic area based upon personal preference. Schools are also not required to accommodate the lifestyle preferences and domestic arrangements associated with individual parents and students in the transportation that is provided.

- It is sometimes appropriate for the school district to reimburse parents for expenses associated with transportation of students with disabilities. Once again this should be decided on an individual, case-by-case basis. Examples of when reimbursement may be appropriate in transporting a student with disabilities for a free and appropriate public education:
    (1) When a school district and the parent of a child with disabilities mutually agree that due to a lack of resources on the district's part, the parents will provide the transportation service on their own.
    (2) When the transportation the district is providing is inadequate.
    (3) When the school district doesn't recognize the student's need for transportation services. (p. 26)

Meanwhile, reimbursement is not appropriate when the school district realizes that a student with disabilities is in need of transportation services, makes a reasonable offer of services, and the parents refuse that reasonable offer of services.

Reasonable is the key word in provision of transportation services, as well as with the payment to parents in the form of reimbursement. To take it a step further, in any situation where a school district or an administrator is taken to court for acts of omission or commission of negligence, the court will primarily attempt to determine whether the action taken or not taken was reasonable.

Specifically, with regard to transportation services for a student with disabilities where reimbursement to parents for transportation expense is appropriate, parents may be paid for mileage or fuel, time and effort (particularly if the transportation service has taken the parents from their own jobs), and even for meals, lodging, and airline tickets for both parents and families or the student's trips home when housed in a residential facility far from home (visits, pickups, and dropoffs may be included in the reimbursement).

For a private school student with a disability to benefit from or participate in services under the IDEA (1997) regulations, the child must be provided transportation from the child's home or school to a site other than the private school, or from the service site to the private school or the child's home. However, under these regulations, transportation service is not required from the child's home to the private school.

For publicly placed private school students, where the public school lacks the appropriate resources for effective service for the student, and thus places the student in a private facility, the public school district has the same basic duty to transport as if the student remained within the public school system.

Beyond regular day schools or day treatment programs in residential and overnight facilities, because the IDEA (1997) regulations are silent on minimum numbers of family visits and student trips home, state policies should allow for individualized, case-by-case determination of frequency of trips and visits. Whenever the private school is closed, the student must be transported to and from the facility. Family visits are determined in each situation.

## TRANSPORTATION SUMMARY

Obviously, there are some recurring principles that act as guides for administrators of special education programs.

(1) Determine whether transportation, as a related service, is necessary as a part of the right of the child with disabilities to a free and appropriate public education (FAPE).

(2) Evaluate each student's situation on an individualized, case-by-case basis when determining any services offered.

(3) Act reasonably. Determine a reasonable extent of service, and a reasonable amount of reimbursement as payment to parents.

(4) Remember to provide service as needed, where needed, in the most appropriate setting.

Beyond these four guiding principles, here are some additional hints:

- Utilize the transportation supervisor or director in IEP meetings where transportation as a related service will be discussed.
- Whether your school district offers the program or not, if you've recommended a placement within or outside the district, the district must provide transportation. Transportation is provided because the placement is seen as the most appropriate for that particular student.
- The school district is not required to provide transportation beyond 30 minutes. In these instances, the district may provide parents reimbursement (often called payment in lieu of transportation service).
- The district is ultimately responsible for doing whatever it takes to safely transport the student to the appropriate destination.
- It is appropriate to contract with a private transportation firm when a school district's transportation organization cannot provide the necessary service.

## EXTENDED SCHOOL YEAR SERVICES

Extended school year (ESY) services regulations are delineated within IDEA (1997). Accordingly, extended school year services must be provided only if a child's IEP determines on an individual basis that the services are necessary for the provision of a free and appropriate public education to the child.

Extended school year services means special education and related services that are provided to a child with a disability beyond the normal school year of the school district, in accordance with the child's IEP, at no cost to the parents of the child, and meets the standards of the State Education Agency.

The provision of extended school year services to a child with a disability shall be determined on an individual, case-by-case basis, based upon the judgment and decision-making process of the participants in the IEP meeting.

The IEP team members shall consider the following:

a. Whether ESY services are necessary, not just beneficial, components of a free appropriate public education (FAPE). To take it a step further, are ESY services

essential for the student to fulfill the goals of his or her IEP? Thus, is it a requirement for which the school district is responsible?

b. Whether extended school year services are required to prevent significant
regression of skills or knowledge due to interruption of instruction between
years. Every time there is a break in the child's instruction, there is regression in
achievement, virtually back to where the child began the previous year. It is
crucial that such a trend be documented by factual data, rather than by guess-
work.

c. Whether extended school year services are required to prevent significant regression of skills or knowledge retained by the child that cannot be recouped in a reasonable amount of time so as to seriously affect his or her progress toward
self-sufficiency. Here, the regulations discuss related services as well as academics. Thus, the regression could occur in such areas as speech, large or small motor
dexterity, and the school district would be obligated to provide extended school
year services in speech therapy, physical therapy, or occupational therapy.

In making the determination as to whether or not a student should
receive extended school year services, the IEP team should consider the
following:

a. Without extended school year services, will the student receive benefit(s)
appropriate to his or her relative ability and disability?

b. Is the child failing to achieve short-term instructional objectives on the IEP due
to interruption of instruction between school years?

c. Is the child likely to fail to achieve short-term instructional objectives on the IEP
due to interruption of instruction between school years?

d. Will the child regress during interruption of instruction between school years to
the extent that skills and knowledge cannot be recouped in a reasonable
amount of time?

e. Is the regression caused by interruption of instruction between school years, or
does the child regress periodically throughout the school year?

f. Is the regression caused by interruption of instruction between school years, or
are other non-school factors related to the regression?

If the IEP team members determine that a child with a disability
requires extended school year services, they should:

a. Identify the extended school year services needed

b. Design ESY services to meet the child's unique needs. In determining what services are needed, the IEP team should consider the following:

    (1) Services can be the same as, or a portion of, the services provided during the regular
        school year.
    (2) Extended school year services may be different from a child's regular school year
        services.

(3) Services may be provided by another agency or by the school district.

(4) Services may include an extension of related services.

Extended school year services should be documented on the IEP. The original IEP may be used with modifications in services, setting, initiation, and duration of services, or the team may develop a new IEP. Additionally, the provision of extended school year services to a child with a disability is not automatic year after year and is determined through the IEP process.

## ESY HINTS

1. Try to keep emotion out of it. Don't obligate the district to extended school year services because a child would make more progress. ESY should only be offered because it is essential for a child to fulfill the goals of his or her IEP.
2. Base the decision on fact. Actions should not be based on teacher intuition or "feel."
3. Keep accurate, well-charted data throughout the year.
4. Develop the art of letting teachers know that not every student is going to receive ESY services.
5. ESY decisions must match school district and building mission and resources. There is an art here as well. Helping parents understand the availability of district resources and getting them to accept ESY services offered is important.
6. Balance doing the right thing for the child with doing so in a cost effective manner.

## ASSISTIVE TECHNOLOGY

A school district is responsible for ensuring that assistive technology (AT) devices and services are made available to a child with a disability if required as part of the child's special education, related services, or supplementary aids and services.

### Definitions According to IDEA (1997)

Assistive technology is defined as follows:

"Assistive Technology Device" means any item, piece of equipment or product system, whether acquired commercially off the shelf, modified, or customized, that is used to increase, maintain, or improve the functional capabilities of a child with a disability.

"Assistive Technology Service" means any service that directly assists a child with a disability in the selection, acquisition, or use of an assistive technology device. Such term includes

(A) The evaluation of the needs of such child, including a functional evaluation of the child in the child's customary environment;

(B) Purchasing, leasing, or otherwise providing for the acquisition of assistive technology devices by such child;

(C) Selecting, designing, fitting, customizing, adapting, applying, maintaining, repairing, or replacing assistive technology devices;

(D) Coordinating and using other therapies, interventions, or services with assistive technology devices, such as those associated with existing education and rehabilitation plans and programs;

(E) Training or technical assistance for such child, or, where appropriate, the family of such child; and

(F) Training or technical assistance for professionals (including individuals providing education and rehabilitation services), employers, or other individuals who provide services to, employ, or are otherwise substantially involved in the major life functions of such child.

## EXAMPLES OF DEVICES

| Technology Type | Disability |
|---|---|
| *FM sound systems* | Hearing impaired |
| Sound field FM systems | Hearing impaired |
| Personal FM systems | Hearing impaired |
| | |
| *Computers* | All disabilities and types |
| Touch screen computers | Students with small motor |
| Intellikeys (expanded keyboard with highly | disability |
| sensitive keys) | Often used for students with |
| Alpha smart keyboards (miniature computers | cerebral palsy |
| with limited word processing capabilities) | All higher incidence disability |
| | types |
| | |
| *Boardmaker* (computer software for communication | For students having difficulty |
| and scheduling) | with verbal communication skills |
| *Closed circuit television systems* | Visually impaired |
| *Books on tape* | Poor readers |
| *Books on compact disk* | Visually impaired |
| *Writing tutorial compact disk* (interactive introduction | High incidence students for |
| to speech recognition) | writing improvement |

Harding (1999) states that "recognizing that consideration of assistive technology for every student with an IEP is not a best practice, but rather a federal statutory mandate, may be the first and most productive admission an administrator can make" (p. 7). Harding also maintains that AT decisions should be made on an individual, case-by-case basis by qualified teams of professionals with a modicum of AT knowledge.

## Assistive Technology Helpful Hints

(1) Make assistive technology decisions on an individual, case-by-case basis.

(2) Ask whether assistive technology is essential for the student with disabilities to fulfill the goals of his or her IEP.

(3) Determine what resources the Special Education Regional Resource Center can provide in making any assistive technology decisions.

(4) Utilize such outside agencies as the Association for the Blind or Hearing Impaired.

(5) Make decisions, as with those made in relation to transportation and extended school year services, based upon reasonable costs and reasonable provision of equipment that support the student's needs.

(6) Provide AT equipment and service as needed, where needed, in the most appropriate setting.

## RELATED SERVICES

Under IDEA (1997), related services are those services that are necessary for the child to benefit from special education.

Related services include but are not limited to:

- Transportation
- Such developmental, corrective and other support services as:
  - Speech-language therapy and audiology services
  - Psychological services
  - Physical and occupational therapy
  - Recreation, including therapeutic recreation
  - Social work services
  - Counseling services, including rehabilitation counseling
  - Orientation and mobility services
  - Medical services for diagnostic and evaluation purposes only
  - Early identification and assessment of disabling conditions in children
  - Parent counseling and training
  - Work-study
  - Orientation and Mobility

Other developmental, corrective, or supportive services required to assist a child with a disability to benefit from special education in order for the child to receive a free and appropriate public education may also be included as related services.

For one of these areas to be considered a related service, the lack of such service would have to be seen as having an adverse effect on a child's fulfillment of his or her IEP goals. Such a lack of service would actually hinder the student from fulfilling the goals. Related services are associated with those listed above and such services are integrated throughout the regular school day.

In cases where a student's disability is obvious and an existing IEP is in place, the decision to provide the related service(s) is easy. With out-of-state cases, in particular, where the disability is less obvious, a good practice is to take three to four weeks to observe the child within the regular classroom setting.

For all students moving into the school district, the designated team should meet, review the IEP, and perform a multifactored evaluation of the need for related services. October 1 is the deadline for deciding to either provide or withhold services.

### Helpful Hints on Provision of Related Services

- Have the full team meet with both parents to discuss the child's need or lack of need for related services.
- Understand going in to this meeting that there will be give and take.
- Develop an atmosphere of partnership where collaboration and compromise exist.
- Select great people to be part of the team. This goes back to the initial recruitment and selection process. Great people offer great responses to parents.
- Remember the four-way test previously outlined:
    (1) Look at each student's need for related services on an individualized, case-by-case basis.
    (2) Is the request for related services essential for the child to receive a free and appropriate public education?
    (3) Is the request for services reasonable from the standpoint of cost and resource deployment by the district?
    (4) Are you, as a school district, providing related service as needed, where needed, and in the most appropriate setting?

## FACULTY UTILIZATION

In devising any plan to best utilize faculty to provide service for students with disabilities, consideration needs to be given to provision of a comprehensive continuum of services. This continuum should provide service as needed, where needed, in the most appropriate setting, while beginning each student within the least restrictive environment and moving to a more restrictive environment as needed.

Known as IDEA, in the true spirit of least restrictive environment, as outlined within Public Law 94–142, now special education teachers could serve as "co-teachers" (special education teachers who both support the students with disabilities and provide whole group instruction) with the typical teachers in the regular classroom setting. Here, the special educator assumes more responsibility for the instruction than merely "supporting" the needs of the students with disabilities. The co-teacher divides the overall teaching responsibility with the typical teacher and, between them, they take turns supporting the needs of both the students with disabilities and those students having difficulty mastering certain concepts. When the co-teacher teaches a unit to the entire class, the typical teacher may be seen circulating around the room providing additional assistance to any students in need. The reverse occurs when the typical teacher provides the whole group instruction.

Of all the designs for utilizing faculty, the co-teaching model is one of the more progressive because it elevates the special education teacher to a status equal with that of the typical teacher. Here, the special education teacher is no longer seen as the subordinate to the typical teacher. The co-teacher no longer assists or intervenes. The special education teacher is responsible for actually teaching, as well as providing support and intervention to the students with disabilities.

The next level, as far as least restrictive faculty utilization is concerned, would be "support educators." Support educators provide support and educate within the typical classroom environment; however, they do not assume equal shared responsibility for the classroom instruction. They might teach a unit here or there, but for the most part, they are providing support for those students in need, and primarily the students on IEPs, although they might cross over and assist typical students having some difficulty as well.

Another group of special educators are identified as "intervention specialists." As the title suggests these teachers specialize in intervening. They focus on assisting with remediation efforts for students. Ideally here, a plan is put into place that helps each student with disabilities meet his or her IEP objectives in the most appropriate setting.

Intervention specialists often provide their services in both typical classrooms, and in segregated resource room settings. Today, the vast majority of service from a special educator takes place within the regular classroom setting. However, there are those times when a more quiet, separate resource room setting can assist in providing an environment where a student with disabilities might better concentrate and master concepts. Some today still embrace the concept of the resource room as an effective tool because it offers a "place of recluse" for students in need.

Individual small group instructors end up being tutors that work with students on IEPs individually or in small groups to assist them with concept mastery in any or all of the disabled students' subjects. These instructors typically meet with the student(s) in an office and help with learning and review anywhere from 30 to 60 minutes per day.

Yet another type of faculty utilization occurs with home instruction. This instruction is utilized when a student is going to be out of school for an extended or an indefinite period of time due to injury, illness, childbirth, or because the student simply cannot cope with the rigors of a typical school day. Faculty selected for this type of program are often either part-time teachers hired on a service contract, or full-time teachers within the district who pick up some additional home instruction time after normal school hours during the week.

Beyond these types of faculty utilization then, and once again based upon a continuum of services, students could be placed in a partial or full-time day treatment facility. Further restriction would see full institutionalization 24 hours a day and seven days a week.

Below is a possible continuum of services for students with disabilities starting from least restrictive to most restrictive environments.

(1) Full inclusion in the regular classroom setting

(2) Full inclusion in the regular classroom and partial tutoring assistance by the individual small group instructor one period each day

(3) Partial inclusion in the regular classroom setting and partial attendance in the resource room as a place of recluse

(4) About half-time in the typical classroom and half-time within the resource room

(5) Full-time enrollment in the resource room

(6) Half-time enrollment in the resource room and half-time home instruction

(7) Full-time home instruction phased out as a student is capable of returning to the demands of a normal school day

(8) Half-time home instruction, half-time day treatment

(9) Full-time day treatment

(10) Full-time institutionalization 24 hours a day and seven days a week

Remember, it is up to each school and its staff to provide the most appropriate continuum to progress from the least to the most restrictive environment. The overall goal is to provide service as needed, where needed, and in the most appropriate setting.

### Staff Development and Meeting Time to Enhance Faculty Utilization

Particularly in the realm of special education, we, as administrators, never seem able to provide enough opportunity for high-quality staff development and meeting time. Listed below are a few ideas that I've seen work over the years.

(1) Consider revamping your bus schedule to provide 30 to 40 minutes of time before school starts. This seems to work well at the elementary level.

(2) Consider a late start or early release one time per week or one time per month. Make the length anywhere from 60 to 90 minutes. This seems to work particularly well at the middle and high school levels.

(3) Implement a working lunch. Hire additional playground, recess, and lunchroom aides and relieve all the teachers of these duties one day per week. Depending on the situation, up to an extra half hour of time may be attached to teacher lunches to discuss special needs students or programming. This is effective at the elementary level.

(4) Designate a day or a half-day for intervention based multi-factored evaluation (IBMFE or problem solving). Provide five substitutes who cycle through teachers' typical schedules and support assignments to free them up to attend meetings. This works for all levels.

(5) Divide your staff into fourths or eighths. For example, if your building has 40 staff, you'd have 4 groups of 10; 80 staff would be 8 groups of 10. Then, hire 10 substitutes for two days each month to cycle through the classrooms of the 10 teachers as follows:

| Day 1 | Day 2 |
|---|---|
| Team A 8–10 A.M. | Team E 8–10 A.M. |
| Team B 10–12 P.M. | Team F 10–12 P.M. |
| Team C 12–2 P.M. | Team G 12–2 P.M. |
| Team D 2–4 P.M. | Team H 2–4 P.M. |

Develop your topics ahead of time and use the two-hour block wisely. Of course, each group would have at least one special educator with them. Here again, this concept works for all levels.

(6) Build team planning time into the regular school day. Not only would a teacher and team receive up to 45 minutes of individual planning time, they would receive team planning time as well. Here again, each team would have at least one special educator assigned to them. This is effective with the middle grades.

## CASE STUDY #1

### Extended School Year Service

### Cambridge Public School, Massachusetts, August 20, 1996

The parents of an 8-year-old student with a language-based learning disability and attention deficit disorder requested a due process hearing to determine whether the student was entitled to extended school year services during the summer and sought reimbursement for the costs of a private tutor they had arranged for during that period. At a team meeting, district personnel considered whether the student needed ESY and determined it was not necessary to prevent regression. The district did recommend the student practice his reading and writing skills over the summer.

Issue: When is extended school year service appropriate?

Q   (1) How does a school district determine if ESY services are appropriate?

A   (a) Without extended school year services, will the student receive benefit(s) appropriate to his or her relative ability and disability?

  (b) Is the child failing to achieve short-term instructional objectives on the IEP due to interruption of instruction between school years?

  (c) Is the child likely to fail to achieve short-term instructional objectives on the IEP due to interruption of instruction between school years?

  (d) Will the child regress during interruption of instruction between school years to the extent that skills and knowledge cannot be recouped in a reasonable amount of time?

  (e) Is the regression caused by interruption of instruction between school years, or does the child regress periodically throughout the school year?

  (f) Is the regression caused by interruption of instruction between school years, or are there other factors related to the regression?

Q   (2) Does expert testimony help a district show a need or lack of need for ESY services?

A   (2) Yes, this case shows how experts or specialists in their field can help substantiate the need or lack of it for ESY services.

## HELD: For the Parents

The hearing officer concluded the student was eligible for extended year services, as there was a strong possibility he would substantially regress during the summer. In reaching this conclusion, the hearing officer stated that a majority of the witnesses indicated the student's need for continued, one-on-one reading instruction. Moreover, the one district witness was unable to give an opinion as to whether the student's reading ability would regress over the summer, as the witness was not a reading teacher. Since an extended school year program was necessary to prevent the student's regression, the hearing officer ordered the district to reimburse the parents for the costs of the private tutor. This is a case of the use of expert testimony provided by three different individuals that this student would very possibly substantially regress over the summer without ESY.

## CASE STUDY #2

### Metropolitan Nashville, Tennessee, Public Schools
### December 4, 1995

The parent of a 12-year-old student with multiple disabilities filed a complaint with OCR alleging the student was denied FAPE and discriminated against due to her race. The complaint alleged the district did not provide the student with occupational therapy (OT) and visual therapy during her extended school year program, as required by her IEP, and did not provide the parent with a notice of her due process rights. The alleged racial discrimination occurred when the student was not given "the most improved award" and when the parent was required to wear an identification badge during visits to the student's school.

Issue: How are related services for ESY determined?

## DISCUSSION QUESTIONS:

Q  (1) How are related services for a student involved with ESY determined?

A  (1) As with any other special needs situation, determine (1) on an individual, case-by-case basis, (2) whether to provide a free and appropriate public education, the related services are essential, (3) whether the request for services is reasonable for the district from the standpoint of cost and resource deployment, and (4) whether the services are provided as needed, where needed, and in the most appropriate setting.

Q  (2) How is discrimination for a special needs student or minority student proven?

A  (2) Typically, no matter the race or disability or lack thereof, all students and their parents should be treated the same. If there is some type of different treatment occurring, it could be grounds for discrimination.

### HELD: For the district

OCR concluded the district did not provide OT and visual therapy to the student because her IEP committee determined these services were unnecessary due to the student's progress evaluations and observations. OCR determined that the parent had been made aware of her due process rights through her receipt of a district booklet, which contained an explanation of parental rights, and her signature on the student's IEP acknowledging her rights had been explained. As to the allegations of racial discrimination, OCR noted the student's teacher had awarded the most improved award to another student the teacher felt was the most deserving, and there was not evidence this decision was based on race. Moreover, since all school visitors were required to wear identification badges at all times during any visit, without exception, the district did not discriminate against the parent based on race when it required her to adhere to this policy. Accordingly, OCR determined the district had not violated any regulation.

## CASE STUDY #3

### Cedar Rapids, Iowa, 1999

The IDEA (1997) expressly requires school districts to furnish necessary transportation as a related service to students with disabilities. School districts must also furnish transportation to students with disabilities attending private schools if necessary for the student to receive a FAPE.

An Iowa student with severe disabilities, including cerebral palsy and spastic quadriplegia, participated in the special education program at her regularly assigned, neighborhood school. She was transported there with a lift bus that traveled a special route for her. Her parents sought to transfer her to a different school under the intra-district transfer program and asked for special transportation despite the program requirement that they furnish their own transportation. The district approved the transfer but denied the transportation request. An administrative law judge held that the parents had established no need for special transportation beyond parental preference for placement at a specific school. A federal district court reversed the administrative decision, ruling that the district had impermissibly limited the student's opportunity to participate in the transfer program.

Issue: With a change of school building attendance within a school district, is the district required to provide transportation for the child with disabilities if the parents make the request for a change in building attendance?

## DISCUSSION QUESTIONS

Q  (1) When does a district need to provide transportation for a student with disabilities to a different school building within the same school district?

A  (1) A district must provide transportation for a student with disabilities to a different school building within the same district when the child is unable to access the necessary services, personnel resources, or supports in their initial designated building. The district then becomes obligated to provide transportation to the new building.

Q  (2) When is it inappropriate for the district to provide such transportation?

A  (2) When a building change occurs simply due to parental preference and the change is not linked to necessary improved service, a district can decline the provision of transportation service. Additionally, if a case can be made by the district that providing transportation service is unduly burdensome or causes financial or administrative hardship to the district, here again, the district need not supply transportation service.

Q  (3) Can a case be made that the child was discriminated against on the basis of her disability?

A  (3) Not in this case, but discrimination on the basis of a disability is something, as administrators, that we must all guard against.

Q  (4) Should school districts create a policy in intra-district transfer programs which requires parents to provide their own transportation, should they decide to participate?

A  (4) Without question! Any such program should establish procedural guidelines and requirements for parents who participate.

## HELD: For the District

The district appealed to the Eighth Circuit, which observed that in § 504 cases, students complaining must demonstrate that there has been discrimination on the basis of disability. A defendant school district is entitled to show that the requested accommodation is unduly burdensome. This may be demonstrated by proof of undue financial and administrative burdens to the district, or by showing that the requested accommodations require the fundamental alteration of a school program. The court found that the student was not denied the benefit of participating in the intra-district transfer program, since she was allowed to participate in it on the same terms as other applicants. There was no evidence of discrimination in the administration of the transfer program, and the student was not denied access to it on the basis of her disability. Instead, her parents did not wish to comply with "the main condition of the program applicable to all students who wish(ed) to participate—parental transportation," Requiring the district to spend additional funds on transportation to the transfer program would fundamentally alter this requirement, creating an undue burden on the school district. The court reversed and remanded the district court decision. *Timothy H. and Brenda H. v. Cedar Rapids Comm. School Dist.*, 178 F.3d 9688 (8th Cir.1999).

## REFERENCES

Americans with Disabilities Act, 42 U.S.C. A. § 12101 *et seq.* (1990).

Burns, P. A. (1999). *Special needs transportation law: 1998 in review.* Lafayette, CO: Education Compliance Press.

Harding, J. (1999). Assistive technology: What administrators need to know. *The Special Educator, 14* (14), 6–7.

Individuals With Disabilities Act. 20 U.S.C. §§ 1400–1485 (1997).

Oakstone Legal & Business Publishing. (2000). *Students with disabilities and special education* (17th ed.). Birmingham, AL: Author.

Pitasky, V. (2000, May). *Transporting students with disabilities: It's not just your typical school bus anymore!* Paper presented at the Legal Issues Conference, New Orleans, LA.

Richards, D. (2000). Take caution when transporting students with disabilities. *The Special Educator, 16* (10), 3.

# Chapter 8

# Collaborative-Based Leadership

*Bridgie A. Ford and Susan G. Clark*

Across the nation, state and local education systems' demand for higher standards and greater accountability for public school performance has drawn administrators, teachers, parents, and community organizations into new innovative collaborative networks. A primary aim of these partnerships is the improvement in school outcomes for all youth, including those with disabilities. This recent trend toward systematic collaboration by the public educational system focuses attention on the fact that concentrated efforts by *all* stakeholders is required to help ensure excellence in educational programming for all youth.

Shared decision making within site-based managed schools, collaborative programming among teachers, and school and community partnerships are advocated as important components of restructured schools that make a difference, those that optimize educational service delivery (Banks, 1997; Comer, 1989; Cummins, 1986; Ford Foundation and John D. & C.T. MacArthur Foundation, 1989; Goor, 1995; Hatch, 1998). These collaborative professional practices are manifested in Ohio's school districts in varied capacities: the increased emphasis on teacher assistance teams (TAT), the awarding of many *Ohio Reads* grants to school districts that train and support community volunteer involvement in reading with students, principals opening the doors to institutions of higher education to use college students from all disciplines to provide intensive one-on-one work with students, and in some instances the housing of community counseling and health agencies. In addition, partnerships with the business community abound; work cooperatives and internships link students to career opportunities. Also, more special and general education teachers, curriculum specialists, and principals are now analyzing proficiency test data together to realign curriculum and make important instructional changes to improve student achievement.

The shift from "charitable" relationships to authentic system-wide collaborative efforts to improve conditions for all students and their families is a significant realignment in the approach to the organization and administration of a school's operation (Bradshaw, 2000). It requires role changes of building level administrators (i.e., principals). For many administrators who have the responsibility for administrating special education programs, this shift may entail the acquisition of an expanded professional knowledge base, skills, and dispositions (Bradshaw, 2000; Foley & Lewis, 1999; Goor, 1995). Some of these would include an adequate knowledge of federal laws and state statutes, proficiency in team building, coordination between general and special education, creation of effective communication and organizational structures that enhance cooperation, knowledge of appropriate instructional learning environments for students with disabilities, skills in monitoring special education procedures, and skills in developing staff in-service training.

## FACTORS THAT MUST BE TAKEN INTO CONSIDERATION WHEN PRINCIPALS FACILITATE COLLABORATION

Following are listed specific elements cited by an Ohio administrator about factors that must be taken into consideration for the facilitation of collaborative networks (within and beyond the school).

- Board of education policies supporting collaboration
- Teacher and paraprofessional contract language supporting collaboration
- Visionary leadership that is positive, optimistic, and supportive of collaboration
- Development of a plan of action with stakeholders outlining collaborative efforts throughout the entire collaborative process regarding:
  1. Why and the conditions under which the collaboration was entered into
  2. Existing levels and areas of collaboration
  3. Strengths
  4. Needs
  5. Ongoing staff development plan
  6. Goals with specific timeframes
  7. Objectives with specific timeframes
  8. Assessment process
  9. Evaluation process
  10. Crisis prevention and intervention for collaboration participants who experience problems and have questions as the collaborative process is implemented
  11. Pre-training and post-training schedules

- Stakeholder buy in
- Stakeholder attitude, fears, and misconceptions
- Stakeholder past experiences with collaboration
- Staff participation in the collaboration voluntary
- Facilities planning and space issues
- Room location
- Scheduling consideration
- Joint planning times for collaboration participants
- Release time for teachers and paraprofessionals built in to attend training
- Staff mobility
- Student needs are IEP driven
- Staff student match
- Development of unique forms needed to implement the collaboration
- Responsibility clarification regarding:
    1. Discipline
    2. Grades
    3. Parent teacher conferences
    4. Curriculum modifications and adaptation
- Staff awareness of multi-ability level teaching strategies and classroom needs

The levels of administration responsible for administering special education programs are multilayered and include directors and assistant directors of special education or cooperatives, coordinators or supervisors, superintendents, and principals (Goor, 1995). In addition, in some Ohio school districts, school psychologists (and other school personnel) may have some administrative responsibility for special education (Ford, 1998). Each administrative level is associated with varying responsibilities. A collaborative leadership style, however, is required in order to promote equitable educational service delivery for youth with disabilities and their families. The experiences described by an Ohio principal in the vignette in the following case study illustrates the multidimensional challenges associated with appropriate service delivery for youth with disabilities when collaborative-based leadership and planning is not the framework.

## CASE STUDY

Mrs. Jackson, the principal of Green Leaf Elementary School, received a phone call two days prior to the start of the school year. The call came from the district's Facilities Management Office indicating that they had underestimated the projected number of first grade students who would be attending Green Leaf Elementary. Instead of the projected two first grade classes, now the enrollment figures supported the need for three.

Initially, Mrs. Jackson was panicked, the scheduling process involving room assignments and time of room usage had already been completed. Furthermore, Green Leaf Elementary School had a classroom shortage issue. Every available space in the building was allocated and used. The stage area, the janitor's old closet, and even the lunchroom were all being used for programming. Several teachers had even agreed to team teach in light of the space shortage. Readjusting the schedule and room assignments was next to impossible with only two days remaining until the first day of school.

Mrs. Jackson reviewed her list of teachers looking to find the names of two teachers who might be willing to team teach, freeing up a classroom for the third first grade class. As she went down the list she came across Mr. Perry's name. Mr. Perry was the special education teacher at Green Leaf Elementary School. He taught students with specific learning disabilities and developmental handicaps (SLD/DH) in a self-contained unit or classroom. Mr. Perry averaged between 12 and 13 students a year. He had been successful with mainstreaming several of his students. Suddenly, Mrs. Jackson had a fantastic idea. About six months ago, Mr. Perry attended a workshop about inclusion. Mr. Perry spoke very positively about the workshop and the inclusive practices discussed. He had suggested to Mrs. Jackson that Green Leaf try some of the ideas presented. With that thought, Mrs. Jackson found a solution to her classroom shortage problem. Including Mr. Perry's students in the regular classrooms would give her an available classroom and the location for the additional first grade class. Mrs. Jackson called Mr. Perry at home that evening and told him the situation with which the building was faced and he eagerly agreed to her proposal of including all of his SLD/DH students in regular classes.

The following day when the teachers arrived for their first day of school, Mrs. Jackson informed them during the morning staff meeting that due to the addition of a third first grade class, Mr. Perry's students would now be included in their classes providing the building with a much needed additional classroom. They were also informed that the inclusion process would begin the following day, the first day of school for students.

Immediately, hands went up and Mrs. Jackson was flooded with questions from the staff. She informed them that all of their questions would be answered the following Wednesday at a staff meeting where the special education coordinator would be available to answer their questions. The building secretary rushed into the staff meeting informing Mrs. Jackson that the fifth grade science book order had just arrived and that the order was incomplete for the second time. Mrs. Jackson adjourned the meeting and rushed off to contact the warehouse regarding the fifth grade science book order. With the staff meeting adjourned, everyone left filled with questions and concerns but preoccupied with placing the finishing touches on their classrooms in preparation for the students' arrival the next day.

Following the meeting, four staff members placed calls to their union representatives regarding what the contract language said about them (regular teachers) accepting special education students in their classrooms. The fourth and fifth grade team teachers met during lunch. Collectively, they felt that they were not equipped with the necessary skills or training to meet the needs of special education students and decided to file a grievance. Meanwhile, Mr. Perry made calls to parents of his students. He informed them of the need to reconvene in order to modify their children's IEPs due to the implementation of inclusion. After receiving calls from Mr. Perry, five parents made calls to the special education office and the superintendent's office to voice their concerns. The parents felt that they should have been consulted and informed of this change sooner. Furthermore, several parents indicated that their children had already experienced failure in regular classrooms; placing them back into the regular classrooms was setting them up for failure.

After speaking with the parents, Mr. Perry placed a call to the union representative to discuss his inability to work with so many teachers and provide them with support. He had never done inclusion before; he had only attended one workshop about inclusion. He felt that if another teacher or educational assistant was assigned to the building, he might be able to make this inclusion thing work. Furthermore, he shared a planning period with only two of the six teachers who would be receiving his students. How could he and the other teachers work together and plan for the students' needs if they could not plan together? Mr. Perry just wanted to know what his options were at this point; he reluctantly filed a grievance.

As aforementioned, within the organizational structure of the public school system, various administrators have differing levels of responsibilities for youth with disabilities. However, it is the principal who plays a particularly critical role in the implementation and management of quality special education services. The literature (Goor, 1995; Sage & Burrello, 1994) documents that the success of special educational programming within individual schools is directly influenced by the principal's attitude. To this end, this chapter examines the challenges to effective collaboration confronted by principals. First, collaboration as an essential framework for special education service delivery is discussed. Next, five critical barriers to effective collaboration are explored: (a) organizational cultural barriers, (b) knowledge barriers, (c) communication barriers, (d) professional associations barriers, and (e) systemic barriers. Highlighted during the discussion about these impediments are constructive ways and strategies in which principals can affect the processes and outcomes of collaborative efforts among those working on behalf of *all* students (with and without disabilities).

When principals incorporate the strategies offered, they become what is called a "collaborative principal"; one who provides equitable and quality educational services for youth with disabilities by collaborating with educators and parents (and others) as co-equal team members, establishing mutual goals, and solving problems to design and support innovative programs (Goor, 1995). Collectively, this administrator advocates that special education is a vital component of the total system.

## COLLABORATION AS A FRAMEWORK FOR QUALITY SPECIAL EDUCATION SERVICE DELIVERY

Collaboration connotes the desirable working relationships within and beyond the school setting. It is a method of solving the problems of educational practice in partnership with others that can improve the quality of teaching and learning in any school, for all students, including those who historically have received inadequate service delivery, (i.e., young children and youth with disabilities). The educational importance of collaborative networks is inherent within recent special education federal legislation (Individuals with Disabilities Education Act [IDEA], 1997); publications from educational reform groups (e.g., Carnegie Forum on Education and the Economy, *A Nation Prepared: Teachers for the 21st Century*, 1986; and the Holmes Group, *Tomorrow's Teachers*, 1986); and our national education goals (e.g., Goals 2000 Educate America Act [1994]). The three concepts of community, collaboration, and collegiality are cited as essential elements in the implementation of the diverse reform initiatives (Dorsch, 1998).

Site-based managed schools are a professional recommendation advocated by proponents of the education reform movement. Within this organizational structure, the locus of decision making shifts from centralized bureaucracies to more local districts and school levels (Cook, Weintraub, & Morse, 1995). Teachers (both general and special educators) and principals collaborate in their decision making. When properly operationalized, this professional framework helps create the cultural climate within the school for collaborative networking to improve educational outcomes for all youth.

Through IDEA 97, Congress wanted to ensure that educators and parents have the tools to improve educational results for students with disabilities. To achieve this goal, in part, the law expects that parents, students, educators, and even future employers and agency representatives participate in planning an education that will lead students with disabilities to employment, self-sufficiency, and independence. For principals, this entails an understanding that collaboration between schools and public community agencies, such as the Bureau of Employment Services or Vocational Rehabilitation, also is needed (and expected under IDEA) to increase the coordination of services to students with disabilities. The establishment of collaborative networks in the home communities of multicultural students must also become systemic.

## Multiculturalism and Students with Disabilities

Dramatic changes in student and teacher demographics support the need to establish collaborative partnerships with significant resources in the communities of multicultural youth with disabilities. The number of Americans commonly referred to as ethnic minorities is rising in proportion to the number of White Americans. Over one-third of the students in our nation's schools are likely to be from multicultural backgrounds. The three fastest growing groups are African Americans, Hispanic and Latino Americans, and southeast Asian Americans (Grossman, 1998). Currently, 23 of the 25 largest school systems in the United States are heavily composed of multicultural students, with approximately 75% of them being African Americans. This significant increase in the population of multicultural students exists in many of Ohio's urban school districts.

Along with this increase in multicultural students in the nation's schools, there has been an increase in the number of multicultural group members identified for special education services. The controversial issue of disproportionate representation (over- and underrepresentation) of ethnically and culturally diverse students in special education services and programs remains alive (Artiles & Trent, 1994; Harry, 1994). Furthermore, governmental reports (e.g., the 18th Annual Report of the U.S. Department of Education, 1996) continue to indicate that the disproportionate representation of racial and ethnic minorities occurs not only in the disabilities categories that require professionals to make more complex judgments about placements, such as mental retardation, serious emotional disturbance, or learning disability, but also in such categories as deaf-blind, visual impairments, and orthopedic impairments. The issue of representation is further compounded by the fact that multicultural youth now constitute the majority in many inner city school systems. Despite this demographic shift, data consistently evidence disproportionate representation of ethnic minority youth in special education programming (Harry, 1994).

## Multiculturalism and Educators

Existing concurrently with the increase in multicultural student population is the significant decline in the number of teachers and administrators from multicultural backgrounds. Wald (1996) noted the diminished supply of teachers from multicultural groups (with 86% of the teachers being White, 10% Black, 2% Hispanic, and 2% other). Combined with this is the dramatic shift toward a female teaching force (68%). Compounding these phenomena is the realization that the majority of these teachers and administrators do not reside in the communities of the multicultural students they serve. The potential for a disconnectedness between the school and the community becomes heightened. Ethnically diverse teachers (and administrators) often serve as accessible role models and mentors to many youth. One way to supplement the loss of these critical role models is by schools connecting with not-for-profit significant community resources within the home communities of multicultural students. Not-for-profit significant community resources are defined as service or social organizations, clubs or agencies, religious groups or churches, and individuals that local community residents perceive as providing valuable services. These services may include educational, advocacy, financial, legal, or empowerment assistance. A defining attribute of significant community resources is participation by local residents (i.e., parents). These familiar significant community resources have established mutually trusting relationships with residents (Ford, 1998; Ford & Bessent-Byrd, 2000). Significant community resources generally offer numerous types of services to impact the various developmental needs of multicultural youth (U.S. Department of Education, 1994).

Scholars Hurley (1995) and Wilderson (1995) elaborate on the importance of school personnel gaining personal experiences with the communities of African American learners and schools facilitating partnerships with respected community leaders to help optimize the schooling process for African American youth with disabilities. Ford and Reynolds (2001)

delineate six ways that connecting with significant resources in multicultural communities can assist school personnel in improving educational outcome for multicultural youth with disabilities: (1) reinforcement of school-related skills, (2) improved sensitivity to culturally responsive programming and information needed by parents, (3) accessible adult role models, mentors, and advocates, (4) increased parental involvement, (5) enhancement of a friendly school environment for family and community, and (6) dissemination and collection of information. (p. 214)

In spite of the federal mandates and professional practices advocating for systemic collaborative-based program planning, its incorporation into the daily schooling process remains challenging. The following sections discuss these challenges as well as illuminate strategies to assist principals in eliminating or reducing the barriers to effective collaboration.

## COLLABORATIVE PROGRAMMING: CHALLENGES AND STRATEGIES

Principals not only need to be aware of the opportunities for collaboration, both inside the school and in the broader community, they need to make strategic decisions about utilizing those opportunities. Collaboration can be developed to benefit students with partners from the family, from within the classroom, and from the building, the district, and the community. Planned collaboration with these various sectors permits educators to open decision making to those persons most closely involved in implementing services to students and to those most interested in the outcomes of that work.

The process of collaboration requires shared thinking, a kind of interactive teaming engaged in by those who have knowledge to meet the needs of all students. However, effective collaboration does not occur spontaneously. Without a clear recognition of the challenges and barriers to effective collaboration, the principal, as the building administrator, may be inadequately prepared to serve in the role as a collaborative principal. Consequently, the teams may be without the tools to sustain active partnerships. As stated previously, the challenges to collaboration will be identified as (a) organizational cultural, (b) knowledge, (c) communication, (d) professional associations, and (e) systemic.

## ORGANIZATIONAL CULTURAL BARRIERS

Cultural barriers are those tacit or acknowledged beliefs, norms, behaviors, and expectations that are embedded in school practices that may impair collaborative efforts. Welch (2000) refers to these as the effects of socialization into a profession that is built upon autonomy, isolation, history, and tradition. Goor (1995) cites five forces available to administrators (e.g., principals) to transform schools into quality-focused organizations: technical, human, educational, symbolic, and cultural forces. Of these, *symbolic* forces (defining values and continually focusing the attention of others on what is important) and *cultural* forces (helping educators reshape beliefs and attitudes toward students with special needs) are stated as the most powerful aspects of leadership in bringing about educational excellence.

Traditionally, students with disabilities have been segregated, first in separate schools (if schooling was provided at all), and later in separate classrooms. This historical removal from the mainstream educational program entrenched the notion that the general classroom was not the place where students with disabilities could learn.

Furthermore, historically, teachers (both general and special educators) generally have worked alone in the classroom. They are accustomed to the role of sole decision maker in designing instruction, selecting materials, implementing projects, managing groups of children, grading and assessing, and correcting and rewarding behavior. Compounding this autonomy are student codes of conduct, which often make clear that the teacher is responsible for the rules and norms of the classroom; seeking assistance from the principal's office may be codified as an option only after classroom consequences have been unsuccessful.

There even may be preconceived notions embedded in the cultural climate about asking for help and doing so may be considered a weakness, a failure. Indeed, an attitude of helplessness can derail any collaborative effort even before it begins (i.e., "Why try? Things are as they have always been. Nothing will change"). Sarason (1990) equated this attitude with teachers' limited power to make systemic change and with administrators' power to support (or not to support) change efforts. Unless a transformation occurs in the hierarchical working relationships between teachers and principals, efforts at team building and creating a shared, deliberate culture of inclusiveness will fail. The principal's responsibility is to remove organizational cultural barriers that keep people isolated from one another.

Even in situations where new models of service to students with disabilities are being used, there are cultural expectations about how those services will be delivered in the general education settings. One study involving general educators, special educators, and principals found that special educators were expected "to be 'super teachers,' that is, in addition to...providing direct instruction to students [with disabilities], they are expected to confer with general education teachers, observe students in mainstream settings, conduct inservice training, and so on" (Friend, 1984, p. 249).

To counter the cultural forces that drive teachers into deeper isolation from one another or set up unrealistic expectations, the principal must assume and practice the role of instructional leader for *all* students. As mentioned, research demonstrates that the principal's attitudes and behaviors directly influence teachers' attitudes and behaviors and, ultimately, the success of special education programming (Sage & Burrello, 1994).

Indeed, in order to have a coordinated educational program, the principal must maintain administrative responsibility for *all* faculty and staff in the building. Principals can exert this influence by ensuring that new hires espouse philosophies of integration. Furthermore, principals need to provide ongoing program and staff development in curriculum and academic interventions, positive interventions associated with different perspectives, team building, and teaching strategies. Principals need to make use of central office resource staff as direct service providers to teachers, not just consultants. For example, psychologists can be collaborators with teaching teams, speech therapists can be collaborators in language arts skill development, and curriculum supervisors can be collaborators in modifying and adapting courses of study. The literature (Bradshaw, 2000) documents the importance of principals providing teachers with both *emotional supports* (e.g., maintaining open communication, showing appreciation) and *instrumental supports* (providing opportunities to participate in in-service workshops) because these are considered significant predictors of teachers' commitment to the school.

Principals, as instructional leaders, must implement a system of clear instructional objectives for monitoring and assessing the performance of all students. This requires knowledge of the vast array of best practices in curriculum, and student (and program) monitoring. Lastly, and perhaps most important, is that research shows that principals, elementary and secondary, view collaboration with parents and organized groups of parents (i.e., advocates) in general as meaningful and that they have a positive impact on their instructional services to students with disabilities (Sage & Burrello, 1994). The research also discusses unfortunate discrepancies in the views of school personnel (e.g., administrators) of parents from multicultural or poor backgrounds. Despite the evidence supporting the positive impact of parental involvement for multicultural learners, schools traditionally have not embraced the wealth of knowledge and skills these parents may afford. Collaborative principals must possess an inclusive paradigm and establish collaborative networks that permit and empower the involvement of *all* parents, including those from socioculturally diverse backgrounds.

Collaborative principals empower others (e.g., professionals, parents, and community leaders) to address student needs. By placing the principal in the role of instructional resource to others, the opportunities to work together increase. Creating a culture and climate of responsiveness to student needs places a demand on the principal to (a) facilitate a vision of child advocacy, (b) share this vision with everyone, (c) enlist their assistance in making change, and (d) use action research to improve learning.

## KNOWLEDGE BARRIERS

### Knowledge of Self

Collaborative teams are built upon knowledge and understanding of one's own skills and abilities (Cramer, 1998). At most, a teacher's performance is evaluated once or twice per year; this process is largely feedback on limited observations of a few teaching episodes. These limited evaluations, coupled with a culture of teacher isolation in the classroom, do not suffice as means for teachers to become aware of the nature and quality of their own interpersonal relationships that constitute teaching or of the instructional challenges that need to be solved. Ongoing discussion of the challenges of instruction are needed; teachers need to work with one another, with principals, and with families, as well as with other human resources in facing this primary task. Principals must understand the integral humanness embedded in curriculum and possess a deep knowledge of instruction. In order to help accomplish this, principals need to visit classrooms and listen to teachers, their team members.

Most important, principals need to understand themselves and how others view them. Kirby and Blase (1991) state that teachers who perceive their principals as inaccessible, authoritarian, unsupportive, inconsistent, indecisive, and ambiguous are likely to be wary of any efforts toward increased collaboration. Teachers either insulate themselves from these principals and avoid interactions with them and other staff or use strategies to ingratiate themselves by offering support or extra effort only in exchange for material goals such as supplies. The perception teachers have of their principals creates barriers that can encourage or discourage communication and increase or decrease autonomy and isolation. Principals can begin to assess how they are perceived by noticing if teachers remain alone in their classrooms before or after school, whether many teachers volunteer for committee work or if the same few teachers come forward, if teachers seek out their professional advice, or if there are factions of teachers that refuse to work together. If any of these conditions exist, team building and climate enhancement are in order. *Collaboration and community engagement* with staff cannot occur unless principals are aware of their effect on others.

### Knowledge of the Law

By examining a number of studies on principals' knowledge of various instructional issues for students with disabilities and giftedness, Sage and Burrello (1994) report that principals acquire their knowledge base either through on-the-job experiences or through self-study. They concluded that principals felt constrained by mandates, rules, laws, regulations, and central office directives, and that they were limited in their responses to those mandates; frustration and concern about due process and litigation issues caused further limitations. Lawmakers did not anticipate that the delivery of services to students with disabilities would be constrained further by economic forces.

While limited knowledge of the law can create barriers to service and collaboration, adequate knowledge can be empowering in crafting alternatives to service delivery for students. To better ensure quality service delivery, the principal should have sufficient knowledge of the mandates and procedures surrounding the legal basis for special education programming (e.g., the referral process, determination of eligibility through a multi-factored nondiscriminatory evaluation, development and implementation of an individualized education plan or individualized transition plan, placement into the least restrictive environment, evaluation and monitoring of students' progress, due process procedures, parental involvement, and related services).

The principal's key role is one of leadership through support—to understand the requirements of the law and to empower the team's creativity that can abound when several minds come together to address the unique needs of the student. When essentially 12% of a school district's student population is identified with disabilities, *professional ethics and integrity* require that every school leader be an advocate for meaningful education for students with disabilities.

The term *special education,* as defined in the IDEA implementing regulations, means specially designed instruction, at no cost to parents, to meet the unique needs of a child with a disability. The provision of specialized instruction necessitates that the content, methodology, or delivery of the general education curriculum (i.e., its content, scope, sequence) adopted by the school board that applies to all children without disabilities be adapted in ways that allow students with disabilities to learn in large groups, small groups, or individually in a variety of settings (Clark, 2000a).

If student outcomes are to demonstrate meaningful progress, the principal can model to a team that opportunities can be generated for creative decision making and that risks involving professional practices can be taken. Being proactive rather than reactive is a choice that allows principals to work collaboratively to create individualized programming and a climate of acceptance. When the student reaches the age of 16, the IEP planning needs to include any individuals from external agencies or schools that will be serving the student after schooling ends. Partnerships can be developed with area colleges, employers, or housing authorities. Such interdisciplinary collaboration is understood commonly as a critical element of educators' work and as the primary way of delivering effective and educational support services to students with disabilities (Mostert, 1998). The results of a national study (Foley & Lewis, 1999) about the self-perceived competency of secondary school principals indicated that principals held lower levels of self-perceived competency for guiding a school's collaboration with community service providers. According to the authors, the failure of school administrators to recognize the role and responsibility of school participation in such a system prohibits the provision of needed services to youth with disabilities.

If the principal does not have access to these resources, a knowledgeable special educator can be empowered to seek out the parent and community services that can be of important value to the student with disabilities. Ford and Bessent-Byrd (2000) detail a three-phase training model to prepare school personnel in how to connect with and utilize significant community resources. Administrator Leverett (1999) uses the phrase "mining the community" in his discussion about the importance of schools connecting with the strengths and assets of the communities of youth from socioculturally diverse backgrounds.

## Knowledge of All Students

The knowledge a principal has about students, learning styles, and differences is key to addressing the unique needs of diverse learners. Nationwide the diversity of the student population is growing in ways that require attention to cultural, ethnic, language, and social needs of learners; to academic readiness and preparedness; to group behavior; to the nutritional and health needs of children. The principal plays a key leadership role in espousing the shared responsibility for *all* and in shaping instructional programming. Understanding the public that the school serves, including the broader community, is critical.

Darling-Hammond (2000) and others have found that "high stakes" assessments seem to have the potential to alter instructional emphases and the decisions made in schools about how to respond to students who are having learning difficulties. The findings indicated that high stakes testing resulted in greater numbers of students identified with disabilities and an increased use of retention. In the past, exemptions from achievement testing have removed students with disabilities from the public accountability inherent in the state proficiency test reporting. Allington, McGill-Franzen, and Schick (1997) found that principals did not respond to learning difficulties by suggesting general classroom program interventions; rather, the principals spoke of the need for more federal and state funding, and without such funding they were unable to provide remedial interventions, especially in the early grades. No principal in the study suggested the need for summer intervention or extended day programs; rather, they suggested special education, even if not tailored to the individual needs of the students, or waiting to see what happened was a preferred alternative.

With the requirement that students with disabilities have access to the general education curriculum in the least restrictive environment to the maximum extent with nondisabled peers, the law makes clear that students with disabilities are not to be unilaterally segregated. Any exclusion from general education must be justified in writing; sound pedagogical reasons should dictate any such recommendation. Furthermore, many students who are unsuccessful in passing the proficiency test are not students with disabilities. The conclusion that some, most, or all students with learning difficulties require special education is unrealistic.

Generally, when considering the needs of students who have learning difficulties, principals do not discuss the need for strategies to strengthen the expertise of teachers and the general education system to better meet the needs of harder to teach students (Allington et al., 1997). Collaboration among those who have knowledge of students and their needs has the potential to create meaningful change in the way teachers teach and students learn. Studies of nondisabled peers learning alongside students with disabilities show that there is no statistically significant effect on their academic outcomes. Instructional time was not lost and they did not acquire undesirable behaviors from their peers with disabilities. "All children learn best in regular classrooms when there are flexible organizational and instructional patterns in place and material supports for those with special needs" (Tanner, Vaughn Linscott, & Galis, 1996, p. 4). The responsibility for responding to student learning needs by setting a tone of acceptance and inclusiveness and by providing human and other supports rests with the principal. The principal establishes the quality and nature of school culture and instructional programming.

## COMMUNICATION BARRIERS

### Language

Jargon and technical language can impair collaborative efforts by creating obstacles to communication. Parents, teachers, and other professionals may not be communicating in ways each understands. A principal can model the desire for clear communication by reminding team members and invited guests to use lay language wherever possible.

Recognition of and adequate response to *language variations* is also an important element in positive collaborative relationships. Language variation refers to differences or variations in a person's language due to sociocultural characteristics (e.g., cultural backgrounds, geographical location, social class, gender, or age) (Wolfram, Adger, & Christian, 1999). Principals must assist school personnel with their attitudes about language variations and their skills in effectively interacting with students, parents, and other stakeholders who manifest language variance.

### Skills

People use a variety of communication styles in their interactions. Sometimes these conflicting styles cause difficulty in coming to an understanding or agreement. Rather than leave any collaborative effort to chance, a principal will ask (not tell) faculty how they plan to run their meetings. As with any good meeting, the team uses an agenda and a process to set that agenda; all meetings have a purpose and set of objectives. Leadership should be distributed so that no one person is "in charge." Should problems arise, the team will carefully identify the problem by listening to one another, rephrasing what is heard, creating alternatives through exhaustive brainstorming, selecting a data-based strategy from the alternatives, and implementing formal and informal feedback through monitoring and evaluation. Depending on the formality of the collaborative meeting, these processes may be written and followed as guides to practice. Friend and Cook (1996) state that listening is an especially critical part of collaboration. It is cited as a primary means for gaining information as well as conveying interest in the messages communicated (by parent, community representative, or other individuals involved in the collaborative process). Effective listening is used to establish rapport. Inherent in good teaming is accountability for decisions made, follow-through, and the functioning of the team itself.

Teachers, parents, and other team members want to experience collaboration that is productive, purposeful, and meets their needs. Each has a need for a sense of belonging to the team and being vital to the team's work (i.e., to counter the "Why am I here?" puzzle). Each member desires to exert power and worth by being heard and by having input valued. Each wants enough freedom to contribute and choose among options, rather than being told what to do. Each prefers a comfortable collaborative meeting, not a painful or useless effort (Bodine, Crawford, & Schrumpf, 1994).

Yet when conflict and disagreement arise, professional behavior must prevail through principled negotiation, not aggression or avoidance of the issues (Fisher, Ury, & Patton, 1991). In fact, Huefner (1991) found that one of the reasons school districts end up in due process is because administrators were not adept at managing conflict. Just as administrators practice negotiation skills in collective bargaining and mediation, these same skills need to be identified and used by teams working collaboratively. Principals cannot assume that these skills are inherent; rather, negotiation skills need to be taught through staff development and modeling and are essential in managing the organization. Modeling and symbolic behaviors are key functions recognized by principals.

### Nonverbal Skills

The behavioral attributes associated with how something is said, is at times, equally as important as what is said. The productive use of nonverbal behaviors is considered an essential element in communicating attitudes necessary for establishing and maintaining positive relationships (Friend & Cook, 1996). These include (1) body movement (e.g., facial expression, eye contact, posture, and gestures, (2) vocal cues such as quality of voice and the pacing or flow of speech, (3) spatial relations—the physical distance between the participants, and (4) minimal encouragers, including both verbal and nonverbal components. Given the large number of students from culturally diverse backgrounds and their families who may exhibit differences in verbal and non-verbal language styles, professional practices dictate that principals and teachers gain knowledge about these differences and respond appropriately during collaborative situations.

## PROFESSIONAL ASSOCIATION BARRIERS

Professional teacher unions, associations, and organizations can play a key role in issues that impact general education when students with disabilities are included in those settings. Although by its nature, a collective bargaining agreement restricts administrator discretion, a study of Ohio collective bargaining agreements that contain provisions addressing special education revealed that teacher associations anticipated some of the important elements of the 1997 IDEA (Clark, 2000b). These contracts allowed for the general educator to be an invited member of the IEP team, identified responsible parties for the provision of medication and health-related services, reduced class size when students with multiple needs were included without an assistant or aide, and developed joint study teams to examine the overall implementation of services to students in general education settings. Administrators can forego the need to include such provisions in master agreements if they discuss teachers' needs with them and respond to them by behaving proactively. Although guidelines exist, conflicts regarding instruction, placement, related services, and other critical areas occur. To this end, principals should facilitate collaborative decision making based on laws, policies, and ethical deliberations.

## SYSTEMIC BARRIERS

### District Context

Murphy (1988) argues that there are district-wide organizational forces that play a critical role in how principals manage their buildings. He believes that these forces shape principal behaviors and that the climate of the district itself affects the instructional program and creates opportunities and constraints on principal behavior. Sage and Burrello (1994) found that contextual differences affected the way principals used their time, rather than their attitudes about acceptance of students with disabilities; a principal's personal beliefs has more impact on his or her behavior toward special education than the context of the district or overall community. Hence, no matter the context of the district, whether rural, urban, or suburban, the *ethics and integrity* of the principal play a key role in how students are educated and in how the school climate supports a community capable of collaborating to solve the problems of teaching and learning.

## Time

Without sufficient time to share formal and informal information about students and instruction, collaboration can become a burden and not a benefit. Time has been defined as a commodity, "a finite resource or means that can be increased, decreased, managed, manipulated, organized, or reorganized in order to accommodate selected educational purposes" (Cambone, 1995, p. 514). However, because teachers' work is context-dependent and individualized, a quick solution will no doubt prove inadequate (e.g., scheduling per administrative need rather than instructional need). Studies report that teachers need time to learn and develop collaborative strategies and ways to create modifications for students (Tanner et al., 1996). Principals can work with teachers to remove these barriers by altering the schedule, determining policy, and assigning roles and tasks. Removal of systemic barriers can be demonstrated by the active participation of faculty, staff, principal, and others in owning when, what, how, and why certain activities occur in schools.


## Support

Most studies on collaboration identify the lack of administrative support as the greatest barrier to successful collaboration. Support can be defined as the creation of an environment of safety, one in which teachers and students are free to be innovative and take risks in order to facilitate learning, one in which community members and parents are welcome to be a part of the education of students. Principals that allow for individualized instruction, cooperative and peer mediated instruction, and teacher collaborative models build communities of learners. Teams can create new models of instruction unique to the context of the building and district. Substitute teachers can be used to permit teachers to engage in professional development, to build instructional teams, to free teachers to build relationships with community agencies, and to permit educators and others to analyze proficiency and other achievement and instructional data collected.

Analysis of student achievement scores shows that students receiving a combination of direct and support services exhibited small, but significantly greater gains in achievement than did students receiving pull-out resource room instruction one period daily (Schulte, Osborne, & McKinney, 1990). Furthermore, Sage and Burrello (1994) reported that principals who allowed teachers to discuss integration of students with disabilities in light of consensus values and belief statements and to create special support groups of faculty and staff for the purpose of brainstorming creative alternative teaching and learning strategies and facilitating integration were more effective than principals who did not allow those meetings. Existing structures in schools cannot support creative reconsideration of boundaries, relationships, and benefits (O'Brien & O'Brien, 1994). The work of true collaboration will lead to changes in job descriptions, supervisory arrangements, and, in some cases, conditions of employment.

Inadequate communication, misgovernance, and poor allocation of resources are frequently cited as reasons students with disabilities do not do well in general education. The collaborative teaching model has emerged as the preferred method of addressing the curricular needs of *all* children. Numerous models should be explored by faculty to understand the relationships that can be developed to serve students. Some of the many models are the co-teaching or team teaching model; the complementary model; parallel teaching; team model; team approach to mastery; and the methods and resources teacher model.

## CONCLUSION

Collaborative principals make no distinction between the expectations set for special and general education students, faculty, staff, and programs. Research suggests that the most effective instructional interventions for students with disabilities are those developed through a collaborative team approach to decision making, resulting in intensive and reasonably individualized teaching combined with very close cooperation between general and special education teachers, which is monitored carefully and frequently for progress or revision (Hocutt, 1997). In addition, the complex problems confronted by youth with disabilities and their families require that professional practices include the direct, ongoing involvement of significant resources from the students' home communities and public community agencies.

Collaborations are built upon a commitment to the process of mutual problem solving and decision making focused on the student, an understanding of one's skills and abilities, and a desire to create an educationally meaningful plan in the delivery of quality special education services for all youth with disabilities (Cramer, 1998). The adequate preparation of administrators and teachers for collaborative-based leadership and planning must become a priority. Institutions of higher education have awesome roles to play in preparing all school personnel to engage in collaborative-based programming. At the same time, current administrators, teachers, and other significant school personnel must be provided with the knowledge, skills, and dispositions to facilitate productive collaboration with each other, parents, and community representatives. Ultimately, principals can make a critical difference by (a) recognizing the common barriers to collaboration and (b) facilitating constructive proactive and intervention strategies to plan for success.

## REFERENCES

Allington, R.L., McGill-Franzen, A., & Schick, R. (1997). How administrators understand learning difficulties. *Remedial and Special Education, 18*(4), 223–232.

Artiles, A., & Trent, S. (1994). Over-representation of minority students in special education: A continuing debate. *The Journal of Special Education, 27,* 410–437.

Banks, C.A.M. (1997). Parents and teachers: Partners in school reform. In J.A. Banks & C.A.M. Banks (Eds.), *Multicultural education: Issues and perspectives* (pp. 408–424). Boston, MA: Allyn & Bacon.

Bodine, R., Crawford, D., & Schrumpf, R. (1994). *Creating the peaceable school: A comprehensive program for teaching conflict resolution.* Champaign, IL: Research Press.

Bradshaw, J.K. (2000). The changing role of principals in school partnerships. *National Association of Secondary School Principals, 84*(616), 86–96.

Cambone, J. (1995). Time for teachers in school restructuring. *Teachers College Record, 96*(3), 512–543.

Carnegie Forum on Education and the Economy. (1986). *A nation prepared: Teachers for the 21st century.* Washington, DC: Author.

Clark, S.G. (2000a). The IEP process as a tool for collaboration. *Teaching Exceptional Children, 33*(2), 56–66.

Clark, S.G. (2000b). Including special education: A study of school board/teacher association master agreements. *Education Law Reporter, 144,* 451–472.

Comer, J.P. (1989). The school development program: A psychosocial model of school intervention. In G.L. Berry & J.K. Asaman (Eds.), *Black students: Psychosocial issues and academic achievement* (pp. 264–285). Newbury Park, CA: Corwin Press.

Cook, L., Weintraub, F., & Morse, W. (1995). Ethical dilemmas in the restructuring of special education. In J. Paul, H. Rosselli, & D. Evans (Eds.), *Integrating school restructuring and special education reform* (pp. 119–139). Fort Worth, TX: Harcourt.

Cramer, S.F. (1998). *Collaboration: A success strategy for special educators.* Boston: Allyn & Bacon.

Cummins, J. (1986). Empowering minority students: A framework for intervention. *Harvard Educational Review, 56*(1), 18–35.

Darling-Hammond, L. (2000). *Transforming urban public schools: The role of standards and accountability* (ERIC Document Reproduction Service No. ED459290).

Dorsch, N.G. (1998). *Community, collaboration, and collegiality in school reform: An odyssey toward connections.* Albany, NY: SUNY Press.

Fisher, R., Ury, W., & Patton, B. (1991). *Getting to yes: Negotiating agreement without giving in* (2nd ed.). New York: Penguin Books.

Foley, R.M., & Lewis, J.A. (1999). Self-perceived competence of secondary school principals to serve as school leaders in collaborative-based educational delivery systems. *Remedial and Special Education, 20*(4), 233–243.

Ford, B.A. (1998). Productive school and community partnerships: Essentials to improve educational outcomes for ethnic minority students. In A. Freeman, H. Bessent-Byrd, & C. Morris (Eds.), *Enfranchising urban learners for the twenty-first century* (pp. 91–113). Kearney, NE: Morris.

Ford, B. A., & Bessent-Byrd, H. (2000). Reconceptualization of the learning disabilities paradigm: Multicultural imperatives. In L. Denti (Ed.), *New ways of looking at learning disabilities* (pp. 19–40). Denver, CO: Love.

Ford, B. A., & Reynolds, C. (2001). Connecting with community resources: Optimizing the potential of multicultural students with mild disabilities. In F. E. Obiakor & C. A. Utley (Eds.), *Special education, multicultural education, and school reform: Components of a quality education for students with mild disabilities* (pp. 208–227). Springfield, IL: Charles C. Thomas Publishing Co.

Ford Foundation & John D. & C. T. MacArthur Foundation. (1989). *Visions of a better way: A black appraisal of public schooling.* Washington, DC: Joint Center for Political Studies. (ERIC Document Reproduction Service No. ED 312320).

Friend, L. C., & Cook, M. (1996). *Interactions: Collaboration skills for school professionals.* New York: Longman.

Friend, M. (1984). Consultation skills for resource teachers. *Learning Disability Quarterly, 7*(3), 246–250.

*Goals 2000: Educate America Act.* (1994/2001, March). P.L. No. 103–227. Available: www.ed.gov/legislation/GOALS2000/TheAct

Goor, M. B. (1995). *Leadership for special education administration: A case-based approach.* Fort Worth, TX: Harcourt.

Grossman, H. (1998). *Ending discrimination in special education.* Springfield, IL: Charles C. Thomas.

Harry, B. (1994). *The disproportionate representation of minority students in special education: Theories and recommendations.* Alexandria, VA: National Association of State Directors of Special Education.

Hatch, T. (1998). How community contributes to achievement. *Educational Leadership, 55*(8), 16–19.

Hocutt, A. M. (1997). Effectiveness of special education: Is placement the critical factor? *The Future of Children, 6*(1), 77–102.

Holmes Group. (1986). *Tomorrow's teachers: A report of the Holmes Group.* East Lansing, MI: Author.

Huefner, D. S. (1991). Judicial review of the special educational program requirements under the Education for all Handicapped Children Act: Where have we been and where should we be going? *Harvard Journal of Law and Public Policy, 14,* 483–516.

Hurley, O. L. (1995). Interview with Helen Bessent Byrd, author of *Issues regarding the education of african american exceptional learners. Multiple Voices for Ethnically Diverse Exceptional Learners, 1*(1), 38–46.

Individuals with Disabilities Education Act. (1997). 20 U.S.C. § 1400 *et seq.*

Kirby, P. C., & Blase, J. J. (1991). Teachers' perceptions of principals affect collaborative efforts. *NASSP Bulletin, 75*(538), 111–115.

Leverett, L. (1999). Connecting the disconnected. *School Administrator, 56*(8), 18–22.

Mostert, M. (1998). *Interprofessional collaboration in schools.* Boston: Allyn & Bacon.

Murphy, J. (1988). Methodological measurement, and conceptual problems in the study of instructional leadership. *Educational Evaluation and Policy Analysis, 10,* 117–139.

O'Brien, J., & O'Brien, C.L. (1994). Inclusion as a force for school renewal. In S. Stainback & W. Stainback (Eds.), *Inclusion: A guide for educators* (pp. 29–48). Baltimore: Paul H. Brookes.

Sage, D. D., & Burrello, L. D. (1994). *Leadership in educational reform.* Baltimore: Paul H. Brookes.

Sarason, S. (1990). *The predictable failure of school reform.* San Francisco: Jossey-Bass.

Schulte, A. L., Osborne, S. S., & McKinney, J. D. (1990). Academic outcomes for students with learning disabilities in consultation and resource programs. *Exceptional Children, 57*(2), 162–172.

Tanner, C. K., Vaughn Linscott, D. J., & Galis, S. A. (1996). Inclusive education in the United States: Beliefs and practices among middle school principals and teachers. *Education Policy Analysis Archives, 4*(19), 1–30.

U.S. Department of Education. (1994). *Strong families, strong schools: Building community partnerships for learning.* Washington, DC: Author.

U.S. Department of Education. (1996). *To assure the free appropriate public education of all children with disabilities: 18th annual report to Congress on the implementation of Individuals with Disabilities Education Act.* Washington, DC: Author.

Wald, J. L. (1996). *Culturally and linguistically diverse professionals in special education: A demographic analysis.* Reston, VA: National Clearinghouse for Professions in Special Education.

Welch, M. (2000). Collaboration as a tool for inclusion. In S. E. Wade (Ed.), *Inclusive Education: A Casebook and readings for prospective and practicing teachers* (pp. 71–96). Mahwah, NJ: Lawrence Erlbaum Assoc., Inc.

Wilderson, F. (1995). Interview with Helen Bessent Byrd, author of *Issues regarding the education of African American exceptional learners. Multiple Voices for Ethnically Diverse Exceptional Learners, 1*(1), 38–46.

Wolfram, W., Adger, C. T., & Christian, D. (1999). *Dialects in schools and communities* [computer file]. Mahwah, NJ: Lawrence Erlbaum Associates.

# Chapter 9

# A Parental Perspective on Teaming

*Margaret Burley*

In 1975, when the Education for All Handicapped Children Act (P.L. 94-142) was passed, the concept of having parents as equal partners in the education decision-making team seemed like a revolutionary idea and not one that all educators welcomed. Many educators thought that parents would not understand what school people were talking about. Many parents believed that schools would not value their ideas about their child. Today, times have changed but not enough. Teaming is a crucial part of Individuals with Disabilities Education Act of 1997 (IDEA '97) (P.L. 105-17). Parents and schools need to be on the same team, but many families relate that school meetings are still very uncomfortable.

It is important for a school leader to understand the background and experiences of his or her team members, especially those of the parents. Many times parents have deep-seated scars from their own childhood experiences. Some of these families have said that:

- They did not do well in school and got poor grades.
- They feel afraid to talk to "educated people" because they did not go to college.
- They are cautious about talking directly to the school regarding concerns because the school may "take it out" on their child.
- If their child is having trouble, they think the school will say they are bad parents.
- School meetings are too depressing because teachers and principals tell them all the things their child does wrong.
- As a child themselves, they did not fit in and were not accepted by their peers.

- They see school staff as authority figures and do not trust anyone in this capacity (e.g., police, children's services workers, teachers, and administrators).

While it has always been the goal for school personnel and parents to work cooperatively, today it seems more imperative than ever before. Funding for public schools is inadequate for either special or general education. These limitations, along with growing demands for lower class size, better test scores, and more specialized services for students with special needs, open the door for more potential conflicts between general education and special education over limited resources and between the school system and the students and parents it serves.

When the special education rules and regulations were written, they included options for addressing conflicts between the school district and parents over issues of identification, programs and services, and placement. These options are vital to our system but rarely need to be used if parents and school personnel make a concerted effort to establish a trusting relationship so vital to cooperation and collaborative planning. While surely there are other items, the following list is essential to establishing a good working relationship between the parent and the school district.

- *Acceptance that the IEP process is truly a joint responsibility.* In most cases both parents and the district staff recognize this. However, in some situations the staff takes the attitude that it knows best what the student needs and will only go through a perfunctory acceptance of the parents' suggestions and ideas. In other situations, the parent believes "that is my child" and knows best what he or she needs and what the district should provide. If any of these situations exist, trouble will surface, there will likely always be a contentious relationship between the parents and the district, and a dispute resolution process to resolve the differences will be employed.

- *Respect for what each has to offer.* Both parents and district staff must avoid developing an attitude that one or the other doesn't know what's best for the student. It is true that at any given time either the parent or school personnel may be wrong in what they are advocating. But each party must respect the other's opinion and continue to listen and try to understand why the other person believes as he or she does.

- *Remaining open to new ideas and suggestions.* There is usually more than one way to do most things. This is true in providing programs and services to special education students as well. Although you have something in mind that you believe is appropriate, always be willing to consider ideas and suggestions about alternative ways to meet the needs of the student.

- *If a problem exists, talk to the people involved, not others.* The last thing either a parent or district staff want to experience is having to find out that there is a problem from someone else—rather than the party involved. If you think the district representative or the parent is doing something that is not right, talk with that person. Give the person that is responsible the opportunity to correct the situation or solve the problem.

- *If you say you will do something—do it!* Nothing destroys trust more than a promise not carried out. At times either a parent or a district staff person will comment, "you can't trust that person to do what they say they will do." If, either as a parent or a district staff person, your word is not good, then planning together is going to be very difficult. No one wants to be viewed as untrustworthy, and few of us intentionally fail to carry out what we say we will do. However, circumstances beyond our control do arise that make what we promised impossible. Likewise, parents may promise to provide a doctor's report or provide some other information that is no longer available to them. The district then may see this as being uncooperative or failing to do what was promised. In any such situation, get back to the other person immediately and explain why your promise is now impossible and make alternative plans.

- *Don't make changes without involving the other party.* A mistake that districts sometimes make is to adjust a student's program or services that they perceive as minor but fail to involve the parent. Although the parents may not see this as a significant change in the student's IEP, they see it as a violation of the trust on the part of the district. Without consulting or informing the district, a parent may have a student's medication changed or cease a treatment program that is taking place outside the school but nonetheless very significant to his or her special education program. The district will likely view this action as being inconsistent with cooperative and collaborative planning.

- *Find someone with whom you can communicate—and then communicate!* Communication is not always easy, but it is the *key* to establishing and maintaining a good relationship between the parent and the district. Parents need to have someone in the district they trust and with whom they feel comfortable talking about their concerns. This will usually be the classroom teacher or other service provider. However, if that is not possible, seek out someone else such as the building principal or district administrator of special education—and then stay in frequent communication so that issues can be resolved as they come up rather than remain silent and allow them to become major problems. Districts sometimes need to encourage parents to involve an advocate when communication between the parent and district is a problem. If communication is a problem or potential problem, it is a good idea to discuss it at the IEP meeting and determine what will be the best way to communicate and who are the most appropriate persons to be involved.

- *Advocacy and planning is not a once a year happening. Stay in touch.* Both the district and parent should contact one another when things are going "right," not just when things are going "wrong." Nothing serves a building principal or district special education administrator better than picking up the phone and calling a parent just to ask "how are things going—is your son or daughter having a good year?" Likewise, a call from a parent to the district staff just to say "Thanks, my son or daughter is having a great year" is a wonderful thing to hear and goes a long way toward keeping relationships on a positive note.

Special education is a system of relationships that depend on cooperation and collaboration between parent and child, teacher and parent, child and teacher, parent and school district, general education and special education, as well as others—all of which takes careful nurturing and handling. And who assumes the responsibility for the nurturing and handling? We *all* do—it cannot be any other way!

When parents receive a letter inviting them to an Individual Education Program (IEP) meeting or an evaluation team meeting at school, many respond with anxiety. Most parents do not look forward to attending any school meetings about their child. They feel anxious, confused, and inadequate when talking to school officials about their child. Sometimes parents do not know what role they have in these meetings. What should they say? What can they offer? Because most parents are not educators, they do not understand what helpful information they can provide. Parents are the experts on their child.

Every day, every week, every year, parents are spending many valuable hours with their child, observing their child in hundreds of different settings and situations. Parents are emotionally connected to their child. They notice small but important changes in their child's behavior and emotions that the teachers and others may not notice. This is what makes the parents' role in the IEP meeting so unique. It also explains why, many times, the parents' opinions and observations of their child are very different from the views of educators, who usually only observe the child in a school setting.

Many children who have special educational needs also have underlying and related medical needs. Parents of these children have many experiences with health care providers before their children reach school age. In most instances, the health care profession views parents as a critical component of the treatment team.

When children are ill and taken to the family physician for medical treatment parents provide the medical staff with critical information about their child's illness and general health. Why does the doctor ask the parents for their observations? It is because the parents, more than anyone else, are most familiar with the child. It is the identical situation when parents discuss the educational needs of a child with special needs. The parents have spent many months, even years, observing their child at play, in various social environments, at church, in daycare situations, watching for indicators of learning styles, learning how to reinforce their child's successes. Observations of the child are an important source of information for school personnel. Parents can provide you with a wealth of knowledge about their young learner. School administrators need to establish a trust relationship with the family much in the same way the health professionals have learned to do.

Parents can contribute meaningfully to the development of their child's IEP in much the same way as parents contribute to their child's medical treatment plan. Does a parent have to be medically trained in order to do this? No. Then obviously a parent does not have to be an educator to contribute to the IEP. However, the value of the information obtained from families will depend on how skillful educators are in setting up a trusting and valued relationship and ensuring family members that their information is vital. The first step, of course, is getting the parents to come to school to meet with the team. Today, many families have two wage earners working outside the home, so meetings during work hours are difficult for parents. Sometimes schedules can be flexed, but parents are often required to be on the job during the usual school day. Consider meetings after school, evenings, or at the work place for hard to reach parents. Official-looking subpoena-like letters demanding attendance will not increase participation. A student-made invitation usually is welcomed and acted upon. Parents will come to school believing that you care about their child as an individual. It is usually helpful to ask the family if they would like to have their student in attendance. Children can also provide many insights to what is working for them and what is not. Often, students have suggestions about their individual schedule that are extremely helpful. One young person, whose IEP team was offering him tutoring the last period of the school day said, "No, I am too exhausted by then and I cannot concentrate." At the student's urging, a reading specialist provided tutoring at the beginning of the day, when he was alert and could attend to the individual instruction. His first period class was exchanged with a study center time slot, since this school had several sections of each subject. "Listen to the children" might be a good motto for all of us.

This brings us to communication. Accurate communication is an interdependent process. Interpersonal understanding is important to accurate communication and occurs when we recognize and understand another person's attitudes and values.

Some factors that help communication are:

1. Communicating with few people at one time.
2. Having prior experience with a person, which can give us a basis for understanding him or her.
3. Recognizing and being sensitive to other people's behavior.
4. Being motivated to interact with others and see their point of view.

Sometimes parents are invited to meetings where professionals outnumber them. Very often, individuals have had little or no chance to interact with each other. This is particularly true for parents who may only know their child's teacher. As parents and professionals work on the business at hand (reviewing information from tests, discussing program options, etc.) it is very easy to forget that the issues being discussed may have powerful effective responses. (For example, the parents are worried about their child's future; the principal is wondering how a service will be provided when he or she knows the program is already full.) School personnel, as well as parents, may have competing concerns for their immediate attention. There are many common problems that might decrease a person's motivation in the communication process, such as having a sick child at home, negotiation with the teachers' union that evening, a family member is out of work, year-end reports are due, and school budget costs.

There are several types of communication that can impact effective interaction. A type that may be used is one-way communication where one person speaks and the rest listen, but do not respond. Another form of communication, directive communication, appears to be two-way communication, but is not. Listeners merely reassure the speaker that they have understood what is being said. Finally, reciprocal communication occurs when each conference member talks or sends messages and each attempts to understand the others. All members practice the roles of the speaker, listener, and respondent.

Key communication skills need to be learned by all members of the team. Attending is the most basic communication skill. When you attend to the person who is speaking, you demonstrate interest and show the speaker you value input. Listening involves concentration on what is being said for content and major points, the speaker's feelings (worried, unsure, or confident), the message the speaker is sending, and the meaning of what is being said. Responding will usually fall into three categories: acknowledge what is said (nod or briefly comment), ask for clarification (could you explain), and express your opinion by paraphrasing, perception checking, sending "I" messages, and giving feedback.

Paraphrasing is a way to show the speaker that you understand what has been said. In order to paraphrase, the listener must state the speaker's ideas in his or her own words, withhold approving or disapproving statements, and give the speaker an opportunity to clarify what he or she said. Essential skills for effective paraphrasing include having the ability to make generalizations, identify examples, and use opposites. For example:

*Principal:* "I'm not sure that Michael can get speech therapy on Mondays, Wednesdays and Fridays."

*Teacher:* "Don't we have other kids who get speech three times a week?"

*Principal:* "Yes, but what I was thinking about was the schedule. The therapist comes only on Mondays, Tuesdays, and Fridays."

It is really the *quality* of the paraphrase and person's ability to know how *frequently* to use it that determines how effective this technique can be. Paraphrasing is *not* simply parroting back what the other person said.

Perception checking describes how you perceive the speaker's feelings. It allows a person to question whether his or her perception of the speaker's feelings is accurate. It does not allow approval or disapproval of feelings expressed nor does perception checking allow interpretation of the cause of feelings. In order to do this, the listener must change expression of feelings into descriptions and convey that he or she knows that inferences are being made.

Skills for effective perception checking are the ability to notice non-verbal clues (body language), the ability to draw tentative inferences about the feelings conveyed, and the ability to describe your understanding of the other person's feelings. Example:

*Parent:*    "Donna hasn't been in a regular class before."

*Teacher:*    "I get the impression that you might feel nervous about trying it. Do you think someone might make fun of her?"

*Beth:*    "I can't wait to start college this fall."

*Parent:*    "Are you feeling excited about the course work?"

Without perception checking, the listener may not receive enough information to understand the speaker's intent.

"I" messages allow the speaker to take responsibility for his or her ideas and feelings by stating them specifically and clearly. The speaker must be able to recognize and describe his or her feelings by name, action, or figure of speech and try to be specific rather than general. In describing someone else's behavior, use only what is specific and observable. Skills for effectively sending "I" messages are the ability to "own" one's feelings and thoughts by using pronouns such as "I" and "my" and the ability to make verbal and non-verbal messages convey the same thing. Examples: "I feel hurt when you only bring up the objectives we haven't reached," "I am concerned that my child needs this service to succeed in school, but you are indicating that it is not available in this district." When people make no attempt to communicate their feelings, they often feel hurt, neglected, resentful, or angry. Sending "I" messages also reduces the possibility that the listener will feel that he or she is being blamed for whatever is or is not occurring.

Giving feedback provides the speaker with information concerning the intended message. Ideally, feedback is a reciprocal interaction and can affect future communication. Skills for effective feedback are having a true concern for the other person and being willing to see how feedback can apply to self. Example: "I didn't realize Dan gets practice in gross motor activities at the Y. Maybe we should concentrate on other activities." When feedback is not used, the individual who contributed to an activity may feel that it was overlooked or not valued.

Good communication involves continually showing your respect for others by giving them the courtesy of your undivided attention, responding to their comments by sharing your perspective on what is being said, and presenting information you have to share in a succinct manner. It is inevitable that parents and school officials will sometimes disagree with each other on educational issues. Each side brings to an encounter its own views on school capabilities, parental roles, and educational goals. Parents and educators also have their own set of personal attitudes and feelings about themselves and persons who have disabilities.

As equal partners in the educational decision making process, parents and educators set down in a defined and organized way what is to be done with and for a particular child. They negotiate and arrive at a meeting of the minds regarding those activities and goals. Although parents, teachers, and administrators share a common goal (an appropriate education for each child), there may be a disagreement over the most appropriate method of reaching this goal.

Conflict is inevitable because of the strong feelings parents experience associated with a disability. Some parents may develop negative feelings toward "the system." Parents need to feel that they are doing all they can to help their child. Teachers and other educators must also feel they are doing their best to help the child. And, of course, there are limits to what a school system can do. When conflict occurs we need to look at it for what it is. Historically, people believed that conflict was a situation to be avoided and that those who caused conflict were troublemakers. More recently, people feel conflict is inevitable. It is more likely in times of change. Consider P.L. 94-142, now known as IDEA '97. Since its inception there has been a lot of change in the field of special education—especially in how we perceive the role of the parents and educators. Conflict can lead to constructive or destructive results. A moderate amount of conflict can have constructive results. It forces creativity by producing a need to search for alternative solutions. It requires clarification of points of view (to defend one's position). It can produce better ideas. However, conflict can be destructive when it causes bad feelings between people. Bad feelings cause distance to grow between people and trust is lost. Unresolved conflict tends to be additive. Future conflict is more likely because communication is hindered. We can't walk away from each other. We are in the same school system for years and must work together. Working together in the future becomes difficult or impossible, and relationships are damaged.

Assuming, then, that we would want to resolve a conflict (conflict resolution), rather than let a situation escalate and harm a relationship, we need to examine ways to reach resolution (problem solving). Above all, the attitude and behavior of parents and educators in a conflict situation can facilitate or block the resolution of a problem. Both parties must *want* to agree. They each need to be able to understand the position of the other party. Being closed-minded will not lead to problem resolution. Many times conflicts that occur between families and schools are over concerns that are just too important to be compromised. There are good points that should be considered by all parties. A collaborative problem solving approach incorporates the concerns of both. Using a collaborative problem solving approach is crucial to arriving at the best solution. There are four basic steps to this approach. First, identify and define the problem. This is the most important and often the most neglected step. The parties involved must agree to what the problem is before they can agree to the solution. Parents and educators need to share their information about the problem. Everyone needs to agree on the goals for the child and must become involved to ensure future participation. Second, as many solutions as possible should be generated through a brainstorming session. Make the alternative solutions as specific as possible. Then select solutions. The agreed-upon goals could serve as criteria (consensus is more likely if there are agreed-upon goals). Consensus involves ensuring that all group members have a chance to give their opinion on issues. Those who disagree or doubt the decision must still be willing to give it a provisional try without sabotaging it. Finally, evaluate the solution. The solution is incorporated into the ongoing IEP process. It becomes part of the IEP and evaluation occurs in the annual review. Hopefully, because everyone has contributed to the generation of the solution, they all feel committed to its success and will work together to that end. The eventual winner in this situation: the child!

## HOW TO MAKE THE MOST OUT OF A CONFERENCE OR MEETING

1. Be positive and friendly. Try to make the parents as comfortable as possible. Offer coffee (if available), and arrange seating so that conference participants can easily see and talk to each other.

2. In an effort to avoid making parents feel overwhelmed and outnumbered

   (a) encourage them to bring a friend or professional as a support person, and

   (b) limit the number of persons included in the meeting.

3. Maintain a relationship that is warm, yet objective.

4. Work to keep the information focused on material that directly affects the well-being of the child. Avoid playing the role of therapist.

5. Treat the parents as equal partners in designing an appropriate educational plan for their child. Avoid addressing the parents as you would their child.

6. Make arrangements for the parents to visit prospective classrooms before being asked to make a decision on the placement of their child.

7. Be sure the parents understand that there is no such thing as a one-shot, final, and unchanging diagnosis. Make sure the parents understand that if a label must be given it is merely a shorthand device for communication purposes. Caution the parents about using that label to "explain" the child's condition to other people.

8. Write your reports in clear, jargon-free language. Professional terminology is a useful shortcut for your own use, but it may only confuse the parents. If jargon is used, make sure to explain the terms.

9. Give copies of the reports to parents, who will need them for the slow diges-
tion and understanding of the information in them, for sharing the information with people close to the child who could not be present at the diagnostic
interview, or for use with other professionals.

10. Try to send home your ideas about IEP goals and objectives *before* the IEP
meeting, so that parents can be ready to discuss them and offer suggestions for
goals and objectives of their own.

11. When suggestions are given to parents, offer more than one so that they can
choose alternatives and make their own decision. However, try to avoid giving
too many suggestions.

12. Encourage parents to offer their own suggestions.

13. Work for "our" decision, not "my" decision.

14. Do your part to follow through with decisions that are reached.

15. Encourage parents to think about long-term goals and career plans for the
child before high school.

16. Receive criticism openly. Listen and ask questions to clarify parents' concern
so that you fully understand the issue. Avoid arguments.

17. Ask leading questions that will give the parents the opportunity to express
their feelings about their child. Examples of such questions are: "How would
you describe your child to others?", "What does he or she like to do at home?",
"What do you want him or her to learn at school?"

18. When the conference is over, stress to the parents that this is not the end of
their involvement. Invite them to come to the school anytime!

19. When the conference is over, evaluate the session. Use some form of record
keeping to note important information and impressions. Record this as soon as
the conference is over.

20. Assess your role in the conference. What were the strengths and weaknesses?
How did you communicate? Were you prepared? Ask the parents to evaluate
the conference.

The IEP has many purposes and functions. The immediate use is to provide a communication vehicle between parents and school personnel. As
we have just reviewed, communication is the key. Parents expect to be
viewed as equal participants with equal decision-making power and to
jointly decide what the child's needs are, what services will be provided to
meet those needs, and what the anticipated outcomes will be. The changes
brought about in P.L. 105-17, IDEA '97, which require access to and
progress in the general curriculum for students with special education
needs raises the expectations of parents. They will expect that their child
will be reading, writing, spelling, and doing math like their non-disabled
peers. The IEP then, becomes the educational tool whereby we plan for the
progress, measure the progress, and report the progress to the family.

The IEP team meeting provides an opportunity for resolving any differences between parents and the agency concerning the child's special edu-

cation needs resulting in a negotiated plan to build the student's competence in ways that matter to them and to their families. The document itself is also a written commitment of time and resources necessary to enable the child to receive special education and related services in order to participate in the general education curriculum and to achieve to high standards. This document is a management tool that is used to ensure that each child with special needs is provided all of the services appropriate to the child's special learning needs. It also provides a compliance-monitoring document, which may be used by authorized monitoring personnel from each government level to determine whether the child with disabilities is actually receiving the free appropriate public education agreed to by the parents and the school. Finally, the IEP serves as an evaluation device for use in determining the extent of the student's progress toward meeting the projected educational outcomes.

## WHAT ARE THE COMPONENTS OF THE IEP?

1. Statement of the Student's Present Level of Educational Performance includes: (1) how the child's disability affects the child's involvement and progress in the general curriculum; or (2) for preschool children, as appropriate, how the disability affects the child's participation in appropriate activities. Information may be gathered from:

A. Parents—provide a history of their child; include child's likes and dislikes, preferred methods of communication, strategies that work and those that do not, child's strengths and abilities

B. Previous and Current Educators (include classroom teacher(s), related service personnel, principals, counselors, and psychologists)—indicate skills mastered both in and out of class; academic assessment

C. Multi Factored Evaluation (MFE) and Multi Factored Evaluation team report—the information in these reports should be used as guidelines for developing the IEP; the reports should indicate what the student's abilities and needs are (present levels of performance)

D. Student (as appropriate and whenever possible); questions to ask:
1. What are some things I'm really good at?
2. What are three things I have trouble with?
3. What are some ways that I can provide help to others?
4. What are some things I need help with, and what help would I like?

E. Informal observation—both behavioral and academic

2. Statement of Measurable Annual Goals that Describe the Education Performance to be Achieved in One Year—IDEA '97 states:

"(ii) a statement of measurable annual goals, including benchmarks or short-term objectives, related to—(I) meeting the child's needs that result from the child's disability to enable the child to be involved in and progress in the general curriculum, and (II) meeting each of the child's other educational needs that result from the child's disability;

"(iii) a statement of the special education and related services and supplementary aids and services to be provided to the child, or on behalf of the child, and a statement of program modifications or supports for school personnel that will be provided for the child—(1) to advance appropriately toward attaining the annual goals; (H) to be involved and progress in the general curriculum in accordance with the clause in #1 (1) (Statement of the Student's Present Level of Educational Performance) above and to participate in extracurricular and other nonacademic activities; and (III) to be educated and participate with other children with disabilities and non-disabled children in the activities described in this paragraph;

"(iv) an explanation of the extent, if any, to which the child will not participate with non-disabled children in the regular class and in the activities described in (iii) above;

"(v) (1) a statement of any individual modifications in the administration of State or district wide assessments of student achievement that are needed in order for the child to participate in such assessment; and (II) if the IEP Team determines that the child will not participate in a particular State or district wide assessment of student achievement (or part of such an assessment), a statement of—(aa) why that assessment is not appropriate for the child; and (bb) how the child will be assessed;

"(vi) the projected date for the beginning of the services and modifications described in (iii) above, and the anticipated frequency, location, and duration of those services and modifications;

"(vii) (I) beginning at age 14, and updated annually, a statement of the transition service needs of the child under the applicable components of the child's IEP that focuses on the child's courses of study (such as participation in advanced-placement of courses or a vocational education program); (II) beginning at age 16 (or younger, if determined appropriate by the IEP team), a statement of needed transition services for the child, including, when appropriate, a statement of the interagency responsibilities or any needed linkages; and (III) beginning at least one year before the child reaches the age of majority under State law, a statement that the child has been informed of his or her rights under this tide, if any, that will transfer to the child on reaching the age of majority under section 615(m); and

"(viii) a statement of (I) how the child's progress toward the annual goals described in (ii) will be measured and (II) how the child's parents will be regularly informed (by such means as periodic report cards), at least as often as parents are informed of their non-disabled children's progress, of (aa) their child's progress toward the annual goals described in (ii); and (bb) the extent to which that progress is sufficient to enable the child to achieve the goals by the end of the year. [section 614(d)(I )(A)(I) through (viii)]

3. Development of the IEP—The new law adds specific factors that the IEP team must consider when developing a child's IEP, including most notably, behavior issues and the specific communication needs of the child, if he or she is blind or visually impaired, of limited English proficiency, or deaf or hard of hearing.

(A) In General—In developing each child's IEP, the IEP Team, subject to sub-paragraph (C), shall consider—(i) the strengths of the child and the concerns of the parents for enhancing the education of their child; and (ii) the results of the initial evaluation or most recent evaluation of the child.

(B) Consideration of Special Factors—The IEP Team shall—

"(i) in the case of a child whose behavior impedes his or her learning or that of others, consider, when appropriate, strategies, including positive behavioral interventions, strategies, and supports to address that behavior;

"(ii) in the case of a child with limited English proficiency, consider the language needs of the child as such needs relate to the child's IEP;

"(iii) in the case of a child who is blind or visually impaired, provide for instruction in Braille and the use of Braille unless the IEP Team determines, after an evaluation of the child's reading and writing skills, needs, and appropriate reading and writing media (including an evaluation of the child's future needs for instruction in Braille or the use of Braille), that instruction in Braille or the use of Braille is not appropriate for the child;

"(iv) consider the communication needs of the child, and in the case of a child who is deaf or hard of hearing, consider the child's language and communication needs, opportunities for direct communications with peers and professional personnel in the child's language and communication mode, academic level, and full range of needs, including opportunities for direct instruction in the child's language and communication mode; and

"(v) consider whether the child requires assistive devices and services.

(C) Requirement with Respect to Regular Education Teacher—The regular education teacher of the child, as a member of the IEP Team, shall, to the extent appropriate, participate in the development of the IEP of the child, including the determination of appropriate positive behavioral interventions and strategies and the determination of supplementary aids and services, program modifications, and support for school personnel consistent with paragraph (1)(A)(iii)." [Section 614(d)(3)]

4. Review and Revision of the IEP—The new law maintains prior requirements and adds new language emphasizing revision of the IEP, as appropriate.

(A) In General—The local educational agency shall ensure that, subject to subparagraph (B) [see page 23, "Consideration of Special Factors"], the IEP Team—

"(i) reviews the child's IEP periodically, but not less than annually to determine whether the annual goals for the child are being achieved; and

"(ii) revises the IEP as appropriate to address—(I) any lack of expected progress toward the annual goals and in the general curriculum, where appropriate; (II) the results of any reevaluation conducted under this section; (III) information about the child provided to, or by, the parents, as described in subsection (C)(1)(B) [see page 25, "Additional requirements for evaluation and reevaluations"]; (IV) the child's anticipated needs; or (V) other matters.

(B) Requirement with Respect to Regular Education Teacher—The regular education teacher of the child, as a member of the IEP Team, shall, to the extent appropriate, participate in the review and revision of the IEP of the child." [Section 614(d)(4)]

5. IEP Team—the new law maintains prior requirements regarding IEP Team membership and adds members to the team, including the regular education teacher. The IEP Team, then, is a group composed of.

"(I) the parents of a child with a disability;

"(ii) at least one regular education teacher of such child (if the child is, or may be, participating in the regular education environment);

"(iii) at least one special education teacher, or where appropriate, at least one special education provider of such child;

"(iv) a representative of the local educational agency who—(I) is qualified to provide, or supervise the provision of, specially designed instruction to meet the unique needs of children with disabilities; (II) is knowledgeable about the general curriculum; and (III) is knowledgeable about the availability of resources of the local education agency;

"(v) an individual who can interpret the instructional implications of evaluation results, who may be a member of the team described in clauses (ii) through (vi);

"(vi) at the discretion of the parent or the agency, other individuals who have knowledge or special expertise regarding the child, including related services personnel as appropriate; and

"(vii) whenever appropriate, the child with a disability." [Section 614(d)(1)(B)]
6. Parent Participation in Placement—The new law explicitly states parents' right to be involved in all placement decisions regarding their child. Unlike IEP changes, this change takes effect immediately.

"(f) Educational Placements—each local educational agency or State educational agency shall ensure that the parents of each child with a disability are members of any group that makes decisions on the educational placement of their child." [Section 614(f)]
7. Reevaluation of Students—Under IDEA '97, reevaluating the student at least every 3 years is still required. Now, however, the IEP Team is required to review existing evaluation data on the student and identify if additional information is needed to determine if the student continues to have a disability and what his or her present levels of performance and educational needs are. If sufficient information exists, the child does not need to be reevaluated. (However, if parents request the reevaluation for the purpose of determining continued eligibility, then the school must conduct it.) If data are needed in a particular area, then the child is reevaluated in that area. Parents must give their consent before any reevaluation can be conducted.

"(c) Additional Requirements for Evaluations and Reevaluations—

"(1) Review of Existing Evaluation Data—As part of...any reevaluation under this section, the IEP Team...and other qualified professionals, as appropriate, shall—

(A) review existing evaluation data on the child, including evaluations on information provided by the parents of the child, current classroom-based assessment and observations, and teacher and related services providers observation; and

(B) on the basis of that review, and input from the child's parents, identify what additional data, if any, are needed to determine—

"(i) ...in the case of a reevaluation of a child, whether the child continues to have such a disability; (ii) the present levels of performance and educational needs of the child; (iii) whether the child continues to need special education and related services; (iv) whether any additions or modifications to the social education and related services are needed to enable the child to meet the measurable annual goals set out in the individualized education program of the child and to participate, as appropriate, in the general curriculum.

"(2) Source of Data—The local educational agency shall administer such tests and other evaluation materials as may be needed to produce the data identified by the IEP Team under paragraph (1)(B).

"(3) Parental Consent—Each local educational agency shall obtain informed parental consent...prior to conducting any reevaluation of a child with a disability, except that such informed parent consent need not be obtained if the local educational agency can demonstrate that it had taken reasonable measures to obtain such consent and the child's parent has failed to respond.

"(4) Requirements If Additional Data Are Not Needed—If the IEP Team and other qualified professionals, as appropriate, determine that no additional data are needed to determine whether a child continues to be a child with a disability, the local educational agency "(A) shall notify the child's parents of—(i) that determination and the reasons for it; and (ii) the right of such parents to request an assessment to determine whether the child continues to be a child with a disability; and "(B) shall not be required to conduct such an assessment unless requested to by the child's parents.

"(5) Evaluations Before Change In Eligibility— A local educational agency shall evaluate a child with a disability in accordance with this section before determining that the child is no longer a child with a disability." [Section 614(c)]

8. The IEP must specify all of the special education services necessary to meet the student's special education and related needs, not only those that are available. The IEP is an agreement for services. The services specified in the IEP must be provided at no cost to the parent.

## RIGHTS: IDEA '97—PART C: EARLY INTERVENTION SERVICES IN NATURAL ENVIRONMENTS

In creating the Part C legislation, Congress recognized the urgent need to ensure that all infants and toddlers with disabilities and their families receive early intervention services according to their individual needs. Three of the principles on which Part C was enacted include (1) enhancing the child's developmental potential, (2) enhancing the capacity of families to meet the needs of their infant or toddler with disabilities, and (3) improving and expanding existing early intervention services being provided to children with disabilities and their families. To assist families in this process, Congress also requires that each family be provided with a service coordinator to act as a single point of contact for the family. The service coordinator's responsibilities include assisting families in understanding and exercising their rights under Part C, arranging for assessments and Individualized Family Service Plan (IFSP) meetings, and facilitating the provision of needed services. The service coordinator arranges the provision of required early intervention services, as well as medical and other services the child and the child's family may need. With a single point of contact, families are relieved of the burden of searching for essential services, negotiating with multiple agencies, and trying to coordinate their own service needs.

Part C requires the development and implementation of an IFSP for each eligible child. The evaluation, assessment, and IFSP process is designed to ensure that appropriate evaluation and assessments of the unique needs of the child and of the family, related to enhancing the development of their child, are conducted in a timely manner. Parents are active members of the IFSP multidisciplinary team. The team must take into consideration all the information gleaned from the evaluation and child and family assessments in determining the appropriate services to meet the child's needs.

The IFSP must also include a statement of the natural environments in which early intervention services will be provided for the child. Children with disabilities should receive services in community settings and places where typically developing children would be found, so that they will not be denied opportunities that all children have to be included in all aspects of our society. Since 1991, IDEA has required that infants and toddlers with disabilities receive early intervention services in natural environments. This requirement was further reinforced by the addition of a new requirement in 1997 that early intervention can occur in a setting other than a natural environment only when early intervention cannot be achieved satisfactorily for the infant or toddler in a natural environment. In the event that early intervention cannot be satisfactorily achieved in a natural environment, the IFSP must include a justification of the extent, if any, to which the services will not be provided in a natural environment.

Section 303.340(b) requires that the IFSP must be developed in accordance with §§303.342 and 303.343 and must be based on the evaluation and assessments described in §303.322 and include the matters specified in §303.344. According to 34 CFR §303.344(d), the IFSP must include a statement of the appropriate early intervention services and supports that address the unique needs of eligible infants and toddlers and their families and the natural environments in which these services will be provided.

Parents and service providers must be clear that services offered to families are based solely on the identified needs of the child and its family. Otherwise, some infants and toddlers will not receive physical or speech therapy services that they need in order to make developmental progress. Waiting lists for early intervention services are clearly illegal and would make a state ineligible for early intervention dollars. Parents cannot be made responsible for the payment of therapy services. Also, transportation services must be provided. Other services which are many times overlooked, but which must be provided when needed are respite care services to help young families cope with extreme stress and 24-hour care, assistive technology to begin language development early, and year-round services, since early intervention must be intensive and continuous to help the toddler reach his or her full potential.

## REFERENCES

Individuals with Disabilities Act. 20 U.S.C. §§ 1400–1485 (1997).
Ohio Coalition for the Education of Children with Disabilities. (2001a). *How to write an IEP.* Marion, OH: Author.

Ohio Coalition for the Education of Children with Disabilities. (2001b). *Students with disabilities and the general education curriculum.* Marion, OH: Author.

Parent Training Collaborative Consortium. (1983). *Parent to parent training manual.* Boulder, CO: Author.

Pasanella, A. L. (1979). *Trainer's manual for module four: Effective parent-teacher interaction.* Los Angeles, CA: California Regional Resource Center.

*Reducing adversarial relationships between parents and schools: Successful practices.* (1981, July). Proceedings of the TRIAD System for Technical Assistance and Resources (TRISTAR) Conference, McAllen, TX.

# Index

Feelings, 178–79, 180
Financial aid, federal, 26
Financial responsibility, 125
Flexibility, of educators, 109
4/4 schedules, 110
Free and appropriate public education
  (FAPE): administrator knowledge
  about, 4–5; and appropriate placement, 28–29; and assistive technology, 33; and compensatory services,
  35; and discipline, 36, 39; and
  extended school year services
  (ESY), 137; and punitive damages,
  35; and remedies, 34; and transportation, 136, 148; and tuition
  reimbursement, 35
Functional behavioral assessment
  (FBA), 38, 42, 55

General educators, 108–9
Generality, 97
Goals, 181, 183, 184
Graduation, 33, 97–98
Grievances, 155
Guidelines, 16

Handicapped Children's Protection
  Act (HCPA), 36
Health impairments, 66–68
Hearing assessment, 61
Hearing impairments (HI), 64–66, 185
Heterogeneous schooling, assump-
  tions of, 22–23
Home-based instruction, 67, 144
Homelessness, 73
*Honig v. Doe*, 37
Hope, providing, 41

IDEA Local Implementation by Local
  Administrators Partnership
  (ILIAD), 16
*Implementing IDEA: A Guide for Princi-
  pals*, 16
Inclusion, 90–91; and change, 18; and
  collaboration, 17; on continuum of
  services, 144; and least restrictive
  environment (LRE), 30; and principal involvement, 17–18; school

culture of, 13; and space shortages,
  154; standard, 91–92; teacher concerns, 111, 112, 155
Independence, 68
Individuality, 73
Individualized education programs
  (IEPs), 50, 84, 107, 120–24; administrator participation in, 100; and
  assistive technology, 32–33, 185;
  and behavior, 184; and communication, 184–85; as communication
  tool, 182–83; components of,
  183–87; and curriculum, 94–95; and
  extended school year services
  (ESY), 137–39; and hearing impairments, 185; and the Individuals
  with Disabilities Education Act
  (IDEA), 83; as joint responsibility,
  174; and language needs, 185; and
  level of service, 125; and minimum
  competency tests (MCTs), 34; modifications in, 184; and multifactored
  evaluation (MFE), 117; parental
  involvement in, 41, 176–77; purposes of, 182–83; and reevaluation
  of students, 186; revision of, 185;
  team membership, 185; and transportation, 132–34; and visual
  impairments, 185
Individualized Family Service Plan
  (IFSP), 100, 187–88
Individualized 504 Plans, 123
Individual small group instructors,
  143
Individuals with Disabilities Education Act (IDEA), 25, 28–39;
  administrator compliance with,
  100–101; appropriate placement,
  28–29; assistive technology, 31–33;
  attorney fees, 36; and behavioral
  interventions, 64; case study,
  118–19; categories, 66; compensatory services, 35–36; and co-
  teaching, 142–43; coverage, 42, 43;
  damages, punitive, 35; definition of
  disability, 89; disabilities covered
  under, 51, 90; discipline, 36–39; due
  process rights, 107; early interven-

Private school transportation, 136
Procedural safeguards, principals'
    knowledge of, 7
Procedures, 117
Professional association barriers to
    collaboration, 167
Professional development, 8, 76, 77,
    78, 79, 101
Proficiency tests. *See* Minimum com-
    petency tests (MCTs)
Promises, keeping, 175
Proportions, natural, 108, 157
Psychological services, 125

Quality of life, 67

*Rachel v. Board of Education Sacramento
    City*, 91–92
Racial discrimination, 147–48
Rate, 97
Reading skills, 114–15
Reasonability, 136, 137, 141
Records, 40, 113, 114, 138
Recreational therapy, 125
Regression of skills, 30–31, 138, 146
Regulations, 129
Rehabilitation Act of 1973, Section
    504. *See* Section 504 (Rehabilitation
    Act of 1973)
Reimbursement, 35, 137, 146
Related services, 31, 124–26, 131,
    141–42, 147, 188
Relevance, 97
Remedies, 34
Representation, disproportionate, 108,
    157
Research, methodological integrity of,
    93
Residential school placements, 30
Resolution (problem solving), 180–81
Resource rooms, 143, 144
Resources, 75, 77, 78–79, 113, 129–49.
    *See also* Community resources
Respect, 174, 179
Responding, 178
Responsiveness, 96
Risk of injury, 27
Risks, educational, 163, 168

Role models, 158
*Roncker v. Walter*, 91–92
Room assignments, 154

Schedules: bus, 145; individual,
    110–11
Scheduling, 107, 108–12, 124, 126, 154,
    177
School health services versus medical
    services, 31
School resources, 74
School Study Council of Ohio (SSCO),
    3, 5
Schoolwide assistance teams (SWATs).
    *See* Intervention assistance teams
    (IATs)
Secondary level, considerations for,
    110
Section 504 (Rehabilitation Act of
    1973), 25, 26–28, 42–43, 50–51, 108;
    and accommodations, 42; on
    ADHD, 69; disability qualifications,
    90; and punitive damages, 35; and
    transportation, 130, 134–35
Section 504 plans, 122–23
Segregation, 28
Self-esteem, 53
Sensory impairments, 64–66
Service coordinators, 187
Service delivery, 12
Service, level of, 129
Services, continuum of, 96, 142–44
Severe disabilities, 57–60, 66
Site-based managed schools, 156
Social validity, 93
Special education, defined, 84–85, 163
Special education law, 5–6
Special Education Regional Resource
    Centers (SERRCs), 121
Special needs, 50–51
Specific learning disabilities and
    developmental handicaps
    (SLD/DH), 154
Specific learning disabilities (SLD),
    51–53
Speech disorders, 60–61
Speech pathology, 125
Staff, training of, 41, 42

# About the Editors
# and Contributors

KEVIN L. BRIGHT has been the superintendent of Mason City Schools, a growing suburban district north of Cincinnati since 1998. He earned his bachelor's from the Ohio State University and master's and doctorate degrees from Bowling Green State University. He has been an assistant superintendent in Mason and Findlay City Schools and has worked as a principal, assistant principal, teacher, and coach.

MARGARET BURLEY has been an instrumental force as an advocate for persons with mental retardation and other developmental disabilities and their families since 1971. She launched her career in that year with a letter to President Richard Nixon outlining how she believed her son's rights had been violated. In 1974, she became a founding member of the Ohio Coalition for the Education of Children with Disabilities and was instrumental in writing H.S. 455, Ohio's legislative response to the federal enactment of Public Law 94-142, the Education of All Children with Handicaps.

SUSAN G. CLARK is an Assistant Professor in Educational Administration at the University of Akron. Previously, she has worked as a special educator, work-study coordinator, early interventionist, and school administrator. Dr. Clark's interests are in professional leadership development and education law; she has published numerous articles and book chapters on the topics of special education, the principalship, and individual rights.

BRIDGIE A. FORD is a Professor of Special Education within the Department of Curricular and Instructional Studies at the University of Akron, Akron, Ohio. Her writings and research focus on effective service delivery for youth from culturally diverse backgrounds and their families and effective school/community partnerships. Currently, she is the editor of *Multiple Voices for Ethnically Diverse Exceptional Learners*, the refereed publication of the Division for Culturally and Linguistically Diverse Exceptional Learners (DDEL). She also co-edited and authored a chapter in *Effective Education of African American Exceptional Learners: New Perspectives*.

YVONNE L. GODDARD is an Assistant Professor in Special Education, with an emphasis in mild to moderate disabilities, at the University of Toledo. Her research interests include effective teaching strategies for learners with special needs, literacy, and teacher collaboration. Dr. Goddard has experience as a teacher of K-12 students with a variety of disabilities and as a special education administrator in a suburban school district.

TIMOTHY E. HERON is a Professor at the Ohio State University. Dr. Heron is a former special education teacher, consultant, and supervisor. His teaching and research interests include learning disabilities, instructional programming, consultation, and behavior analysis.

CAROLYN TALBERT JOHNSON is an Associate Professor in the School of Education and Allied Professions at the University of Dayton. Her research interests include equity initiatives, inclusive education, urban teacher education, and school reform.

ELLIS A. JOSEPH served as Dean of the School of Education at the University of Dayton for 23 years. Currently, he is Dean Emeritus and Distinguished Service Professor. He has authored over 75 publications, including two books: *Jacques Maritain on Humanism and Education* and *The Predecisional Process in Educational Administration: A Philosophical Analysis*. He chairs the Ohio State Superintendent's Task Force for the Preparation of Personnel for the Handicapped.

MARY F. LANDERS is the Director of Accreditation at the University of Dayton in the School of Education and Allied Professions. She taught at the elementary level in both the general education and special education fields prior to becoming a university professor in special education. For the past ten years she had headed grant activities, spoken, and written on the inclusion of all students in our schools based on the gifts each has to offer.

JON J. NIEBERDING is Assistant Research Professor at the University of Dayton and Assistant Director of the School Study Council of Ohio.

ALLAN G. OSBORNE, JR., Principal, Snug Harbor Community School and former Visiting Associate Professor, Bridgewater State College, writes extensively on the law relating to special education.

STEPHEN B. RICHARDS is an Associate Professor and Coordinator of the Intervention Specialist Program at the University of Dayton. He has 25 years of teaching experience in public schools and higher education. His interests are in pre-service teacher education, inclusive education, behavioral interventions, and working with students with moderate/intensive disabilities.

STEVEN C. RUSSELL is Dean of the College of Education and Human Services at Central Michigan University. As a Professor of Special Education, Dr. Russell served on the faculty of Bowling Green State University prior to arriving at CMU. Dr. Russell is currently the Chair of the National Joint Committee on Learning Disabilities, past Chair of the Professional Advisory Board for the Learning Disabilities Association of America, and Vice President for Members and Executive Director of the International Academy of Research in Learning Disabilities. His most recent work has resulted in two book chapters in *Child and Adolescent Psychiatric Clinics of North America: Academic Difficulties, Vol. 6* (1977), a book co-authored with L. Sternberg and R. Taylor (1996) entitled *Negotiating the Disability Maze: Critical Knowledge for Parents, Professionals, and Other Caring Persons*, and a co-edited book with F. Kline and L. Silver (2001) entitled *The Educator's Guide to Medical Issues in the Classroom.*

CHARLES J. RUSSO, the Panzer Chair in Education in the School of Education and Allied Professions and an Adjunct Professor in the School of Law at the University of Dayton, writes extensively on an array of topics in education law.

THOMAS M. STEPHENS is Professor Emeritus, College of Education, the Ohio State University and Executive Director of the School Study Council of Ohio. He is the author of 10 textbooks and over 100 other professional publications.

BEVERLY A. TILLMAN is an Associate Professor of Education at the University of Dayton where she teaches courses in general and special education. Her research interests include inclusive education, professional development, school renewal, and diversity initiatives.

MATTHEW J. TINCANI is a doctoral candidate in Special Education and Applied Behavior analysis at the Ohio State University. Prior to enrolling Ohio State, Mr. Tincani was a teacher and consultant to children and adults with moderate and severe disabilities. He has conducted research in the area of effective instruction and consulted with teachers on a variety of classroom management and instructional issues.

H. ROBERTA WEAVER is an Assistant Dean in the School of Education and Allied Professions at the University of Dayton. She is a career urban educator and special educator. Her experiences include teaching at the secondary level prior to coming to the university, service on a number of local, state, and national boards, numerous presentations and publications. She is a recognized leader in teacher education and in the area of special education.